EXCERPTS FROM MORE THAN READERS

Your observations about history and people are so true and inspiring. Thanks. **Dutchie**

I find your article, YUBA CITY: A CITADEL OF *PUNJABIYAT* IN USA very inspiring, to say the least. I would like to know a bit a more about you, the only thing I know from this article is that you are a Professor of Mathematics, but if you did not reveal it, my guess would have been that you had a solid background in social sciences, that you do. It seems to be based on experience, not just on books. I am also guessing that you are deeply committed for the betterment of India. **Ram Chaudhari. Emeritus Physics Professor**

Life is truly a Komagata Maru. Rest is BS. Dr. **Subhash Sood**

Your article 'Alexander..' deserves abundant accolade for its skill of neat compiling of historical facts, subtle analysis, inferences and selective vocabulary. **Col Ravi P. Bhatnagar**

This is one of the best pieces of your reflection. I will definitely save it. My only **curiosity** is about Babur's will. **Subhash Saxena, Distinguished Math Professor**

Your last reflection was a moving one. It brought tears. I felt how ignorant I am about my own country's past history! We are in far south untouched by any of these human butcheries. We study in history a little about it. Your global presentation with facts & figures could not but move anybody's heart. …Your presentation of Indian holocaust scenario is a good remainder for Hindus like us. We never harmed anybody in the name of war, but we were wiped off like insects. Thank you for this thought provoking, balanced, educative & human value presentation. **Sooriamurthy** Retired Physics Professor

It is interesting to note that Franklin did have slaves, as house servants, I think. This is commented on by Walter Isaacson, author of a recent and excellent biography of Franklin. **Dave Emerson, Emeritus Chemistry Professor**

VECTORS IN HISTORY:

MAIN FOCI—INDIA AND USA Volume I

Satish C. Bhatnagar

Books by the same Author

Scattered Matherticles Mathematical Reflections, Volume I (2010)

Order this book online at www.trafford.com
or email orders@trafford.com

Most Trafford titles are also available at major online book retailers.

Printed in the United States of America.

ISBN: 978-1-4669-0484-2 (sc)
ISBN: 978-1-4669-0485-9 (e)

Trafford rev. 01/17/2012

 www.trafford.com

North America & International
toll-free: 1 888 232 4444 (USA & Canada)
phone: 250 383 6864 ◆ fax: 812 355 4082

DEDICATED TO

SUBHASH C. SOOD
(1933-2007)

CONTENTS

A KIND OF HISTORICAL PREFACE! xi

I. HISTORY IN GENERAL

1. THE GRASSROOTS OF INDIA'S SECULARISM 1
2. HAITI: A LAND OF PERPETUAL STRIFE AND PASSION 4
3. VINOBA DARSHAN 13
4. WHY TO WRITE A HISTORY? 16
5. GADAR MEMORIAL CENTER, SAN FRANCISCO 18
6. A GLIMPSE OF INDIAN DIASPORA 20
7. TELLING STORIES OF YOUR LIFE 23
8. ON TRIVIALIZATION OF HISTORY 25
9. A KIND OF INTELLECTUAL HOLOCAUST 27
10. TUBERCULOSIS AND INDIA 30
11. WHEN HISTORY AND LITERATURE BLEND 32
12. HISTORY IN THE BACKYARD 34
13. MISS AND MAKE OF BHAGAT SINGH 36
14. MY PERCEPTION OF HISTORY 38
15. RAMIFICATIONS OF THE DERA SACHA SAUDA 41
16. FROM THE BY-LANES OF HISTORY 45
17. MUSINGS OF MANDU MONUMENTS 47
18. HISTORIC SITES CRY OUT! 49
19. THE SHADOWS OF SERIAL BOMBINGS 53
20. PERILS TO INDEPENDENCE 57
21. IS IT A MELTDOWN OF ......? 59
22. HISTORY, ANTIQUES AND HEIRLOOMS 62
23. HISTORY, MATHEMATICS & HERITAGE 64

II. CONTEMPORARY HISTORIC EVENTS

24. GREENING OF THE DEMOCRACIES.................................. 66
25. THE QUAKES IN PUNJAB 69
26. INDIRA GANDHI MORTEM 73
27. A LESSON FOR OPPOSITION 75
28. RESERVATION POLICY & ITS AFTERMATH..................... 77
29. POLITICIZATION OF ELITE SERVICES 79
30. THE MUKTSAR MASSACRE....................................... 81
31. PEOPLE AND POLITICS OF PRAYAG 83
32. RECENT ELECTIONS IN INDIA AND ISRAEL.................... 85
33. THE ADVENT OF CHRISTIANITY IN INDIA.................... 87
34. THE MAN OF THE MILLENNIUM CONTEST.................... 89
35. POLITICS AND NATIONAL AWARDS............................ 91
36. ON DENYING THE US AT WAR 92
37. A PERSPECTIVE ON HOMELAND SECURITY................... 95
38. CONGRESS PARTY HAS LOST!.................................. 98
39. THE GROWING POWER OF A RELIGION 100
40. VAJPAYEE MUST STEP DOWN 102
41. TALES OF MONARCHY 104
42. TIME TO REACH OUT TO ISRAEL 107
43. WASTED CHIVALRY 109
44. JODHAA AND JALAAL 111
45. OBAMA ONTO OMAN... 113
46. MUSCAT MUSEUM & MORE 115
47. GURDWARA VS. HINDU TEMPLE 118
48. SUBBARAO & NOBEL PEACE PRIZES 101 120

III. GLIMPSES INTO A HISTORY OF OVERSEAS INDIANS

49. SETTLING OF INDIANS IN THE US: AN OVERVIEW 123
50. THE GADAR MEMORIAL CENTER: A PERISCOPE........... 129
51. YUBA CITY: A CITADEL OF PUNJABIYAT IN USA............. 141
52. SOME LESSONS OF GADAR MOVEMENT 151
53. MY SECOND VISIT TO THE GADAR CENTER................. 153
54. KOMAGATA MARU: THE FIRST MARITIME REVOLT...... 159

55. FIRST INDIAN PIONEER IN LAS VEGAS 167
56. INDIAN COMMUNITY AT CROSSROADS 169
57. THE MOVING SPIRIT OF THE GADAR 171
58. KNOW THY BLOOD 177
59. KHALSAS IN THE USA 179

IV. REVISITING THE ANCIENTS

60. DANIEL DEFOE AND ROBINSON CRUSOE 181
61. PETS, FOREST AND BUDDHA 185
62. A LESSON FROM AJANTA AND ELLORA 187
63. ALEXANDER THE GREAT: A PERISCOPE 189
64. WHEN A SOCIETY SOFTENS UP 197
65. THE HOLOCAUSTS IN INDIA 200
66. GHALIB PERISCOPE AT SIXTY-SEVEN 204
67. BENJAMIN FRANKLIN PERISCOPE (I) 208
68. BENJAMIN FRANKLIN PERISCOPE (II) 210
69. BENJAMIN FRANKLIN PERISCOPE (III) 214
70. BABUR'S WILL, BABRI MASJID & 9/11 217
71. A DEAR HISTORIC TRILOGY 224
72. OUR FORGOTTEN HOLOCAUSTS 228
73. PERU (INCA CIVILIZATION): A PERISCOPE 230
74. SEXY SERMONS IN STONES 236
75. THE HOLIEST, BATHINDA 239
76. MAHARANA PRATAP: A PERISCOPE 241
77. FRACTALS IN STONES 247
78. AN HISTORIC IF 'N BUT 250
79. RE-DISCOVERING CHIVALRY IN ARYA SAMAJ 253
COMMENTATORS AND ANALYSTS EXTRAORDINAIRE 256

A KIND OF HISTORICAL PREFACE!

Background: A couple of months after seeing my first book finally published in November, 2010, I started feeling different at age 70+. It was as if a new dimension was added to my persona. At least, now I am a published author of a book, *Scattered Matherticles: Mathematical Reflections*, **Volume I**. When it came to rolling out the next book, it was not for another mathematical one - though its material was ready. The choice fell on a history book - to be written in the most unconventional format.

What is my Claim on History? This question has really possessed my mind for a long time. I needed an internal assurance and manifestation of confidence in my history writings. My wife questioned it - based on her knowledge of history textbooks that she had seen or heard of during high school and college days in India. Otherwise, she has no interest in anything historical - from that of a family to a nation. Over years of observation, I dare to conjecture that there is a male gender and history correlation.

My early days with History: In high school, I hated history the way it was taught during my days of the 1950s in Bathinda, India. The main reason was its emphasis on sheer memorization of the dates of the wars, coronations, grandiose construction projects, and births/deaths of foreign rulers of the Hindus in their own homeland, called Hindustan in Arabic form, and India (derived from Hindu or Hindi) in Germanic form. The exams were solely based on one's ability to essentially spit out hundreds of pages. By the age of 15, I had realized that history, as a profession, was not going to get me any bread and butter.

Besides, I took exceptions to terrible distortions of history of ancient India. This dormant seed of discontent and dissatisfaction gradually started sprouting after the age of 50 - like chickenpox virus, when not expelled out of the body, going dormant in vertebrae # 4-5, and bursting out in a painful fury of shingles - in later years of life, when the immune system is weak. That is how my hatred for history, during teen years, transformed into a passion for history- in its every aspect. History is turning into another window of life. As an offshoot, I regularly teach a course in History of Mathematics by taking a holistic approach.

Trajectory of my interest in History: During four years of college, I remained light-years away from history for curricular reasons of that era. However, literature became a distant second pursuit to mathematics. After I started college teaching in 1961, interest in history started kicking in. Initially, it branched out of my curiosity about the lives of great personalities - Indians as well as non-Indians. I enjoyed reading biographies and autobiographies. Subsequently, I read Winston Churchill's volumes on WW II and books on Sikh History by Ganda Singh and HR Gupta. However, the books on Aurangzeb and Shivaji by historian, R. C. Majumdar had disappointed me. In general, whether reading any piece of literature or watching movies, I still prefer stories based on historical legends and folklores.

Intellectual exorcism is a very long process, as I have gone through one. The system of education I grew up in India, the raw scores in the final exams were interpreted as the index of overall intelligence – intellectual, emotional and spiritual – all combined! Being good at any artistic or physical activity or sports was considered wasteful. In such a culture, its extensions are that people either don't develop any new intellectual pursuits beyond their high school or college education, or, if rarely developed, then no one gives any credence to it. You are literally branded by your raw scores for the rest of your life.

It reminds me of a childhood friend, Virender Kapur. He went on to a medical college, served as a physician in the Indian army with distinction, and after retirement, became a well known urologist in Chandigarh. Now here is the punch: three years ago, while introducing me to his wife for the first time, he said, "Satish is very intelligent, he scored 612 points in high school, while mine was 609." Even at this age and stage of life, he is not able to let it go - holding on to it since 1955.

My history hang-up is also connected with some friends and relatives in India, who for a number of reasons, would go for a master's in history after their bachelor's. It was done as a 'private candidate' without ever going to a regular college. The system of master's exam was simple: pass 3-4 exams at the end of each of the two years. I have known people getting MA's in history by 'mugging up' a dozen questions from various 'guess papers', openly sold in the market. By Indian standards, it was still considered laudable, but by the US academic standards, such master's degrees are jokes. There is no development of any sense of history of events, leaders, movements and ideas. They could never connect the dots and interpret events. But they earned all professional perks and benefits of master's degrees.

THE LAND OF HISTORIES: In the US, over the years, the works like that of Will and Ariel Durant have deeply influenced me, as I enjoyed writing articles and letters for daily newspapers and weeklies. The real breakout came when I started listening to radio talk show hosts – while driving back and forth to work. I was stunned by their knowledge of history, connections with the current issues, power of communication, and a following of 5-25 million people, per week, across the great lands of the USA. The current 3–hour format of radio talk shows is only 20 years old - very young as compared with 30-60 minutes of TV shows. On examining their academic credentials, I was flabbergasted. For instance, Rush Limbaugh, the marquee radio host has attended only one year of college. Sean Hannity has done every menial job, you name it, and hardly went to college. Glen Beck, a flamboyant history buff, did not attend college either.

I do not mean to imply that schools and colleges do not contribute in the making of careers, nor is it implied, that all media personalities are college drop outs. In the US, there are so many avenues and fields where men and women can cultivate any expertise far beyond the confines of schools and colleges. There are my favorite radio hosts who have solid college degrees too, but they don't draw professionally from them. Laura Ingraham, Neal Boortz and Mark Levin are law graduates. Laura Schlessinger has PhD from Columbia.

Michael Savage, my most favorite radio host, has a PhD from UC Berkeley, but not in history or political science, but rather in nutritional science. He has authored over twenty books in nutrition areas and on the life of politics, history and sociology combined. He speaks out with courage and conviction, and often goes out on a limb to discus any tropic under the sun.

I too like to write my *Reflections* with passion on any subject. While stretching my intellectual limits, I challenge those of my readers as well. To the best of my knowledge, Radio and TV host, Bill O' Reilly may be the only media personality drawing or extending bits of values from his three college degrees - including one from Harvard. Collectively, they have made me feel intellectually 'liberated' at age 70 – better late than never! I thank the US life styles for letting men and women become what they want to be. The credit also goes to these individuals for following non-traditional career paths.

On a personal note, they cut Khushwant Singh, an Indian man of letters, to size for me; since for years, his two volumes on Sikh History had awed me. By his frank admissions, his academic background is so-so, but he is also a scion of a very wealthy and influential family of Delhi. Khushwant Singh, to his credit, literally took off with his down-to-earth wit and conviction in his penmanship – specifically in the realms of journalism and non-fiction writings. The bottom line is that I no longer wonder, as to how he wrote two volumes of Sikh History (nearly 1000 pages) in one year, 1963; at the age of 48. He is going strong at 96 - four more years to go for being a centenarian!

About the Title of the Book
The word 'Vector', in the title of the book, *VECTORS IN HISTORY*, is borrowed from mathematics, where vectors are not restricted to only two or three dimensions, as used in physics and geometry. Vectors represent quantities that need both magnitude and direction. Popularly, vectors are shown by directed arrows 'freely flying around'.

Each *Reflection* is, indeed, like a vector. Its magnitude is subjective, if measured by its impact factor - but tangible, if it is measured by the number of words in it, varying from 600 to 6000. Its theme provides a direction; however, it may change its course during its flight. In other words, a particular *Reflection* may have more than one attractor points. In mathematics, a zero vector has zero magnitude, but no unique direction. Naturally, it does not correspond to any ***Reflection***!

As far as the variety in the directions of a vector is concerned, they are doubly infinite in 2-dimensions and triply infinite in 3-dimensions! These ***Reflections*** do bring out a similar flavor, when it comes to the number of sub-topics that are touched upon. They are not bounded above - be that in the context of a country, person, religion, or region etc.

These ***Reflections*** are truly like free vectors having any arbitrary initial and terminal points. They can fly off from anywhere and land anywhere. In the world of mathematics, two vectors are defined equal, when their magnitudes and directions are the same. This is never a case in my ***Reflections***, as any two would differ both in words and themes! Who will read equal ***Reflections***, anyway?

In mathematics and physics, two position vectors/forces can be added. In ***Reflections***, there is generally no connection between the ending of one ***Reflection*** with the beginning of the next. Consequently, one can read any ***Reflection*** from anywhere without missing a beat from the previous one! That is a kind of beauty and uniqueness of this book.

Where is the Heart? That is spread out in ***Reflections***! Quite a few of them are modified from articles and letters written to friends and various publications. The range of topics is very wide and long. Often there is more than one strand, and my style remains compact. Nonetheless, these ***Reflections*** are snappy and penetrating - like arrows - vectors!

For convenience of the readers, the ***Reflections*** are divided into four sections – General, Contemporary, Indian Diaspora and Ancients, but they are not strictly mutually exclusive. A general structure of a ***Reflection*** is that it spins off from a specific incident - whether in India or the USA. I basically dive into a vortex with it, or look out through it as a window to the universe - far and beyond. In the process, it is wrapped with other stories and concepts which are often cross-cultural and inter-disciplinary.

Why should one read it? Each of the 79 ***Reflections*** contains at least one nugget, though it may not glitter equally for everyone. For the last six months, while sorting, compiling, and editing them, I would get so absorbed in them, that they gave me moments of new thrill and gratification. Each ***Reflection*** is dated. Reason: while reading other's works, I am increasingly curious to know at what age or stage a particular writing took place, or a mathematical theorem proved. It may have some connections with contemporary political, social and economic conditions. The second date on a ***Reflection*** means some significant changes were done since its first writing.

Lately, my mind is becoming a single track that I can't work on two *Reflections* side by side. Once, a new *Reflection* is started off, the previous one is literally expelled out. The book has something for everyone – including students, laypersons and professionals. It may be used as a supplementary book for any course on history of India from a global perspective. Above all, its purpose is to ignite interest in general history. For a couple of reasons, *Reflections* written after the year 2009 are not included in this volume.

Traditional Features: The book is lean and free from traditional fat of footnotes, notes at the end of chapters and bibliography at the end of a book; containing references to books, papers and links. Lately, the two inks of the book are approaching equal. It is inflating a book - like some professors do by inflating the grades of the students.

A long bibliography is interpreted as a sign of scholarship in humanities and social studies. Recently, I confronted a person about this when some works were never even looked at. In my experience, over the years, bibliographies - like intellectual mafia, may be perpetuating myths or stretching facts of a particular school of thought. For instance, the British colonial historians systematically created numerous myths about India - from the contents of the Vedas to Aryan origins and invasions. They have been thoroughly debunked. But it is an ongoing battle - between the scholars with little resources and establishment of centuries.

A bibliography makes sense only in the world of mathematics, as it historically began! It makes sense that proofs of proven results be referred in a bibliography rather than reproducing them again. In general, any discipline that has theories, excessive modeling and simulation, any bibliography at the end should be given scant attention.

Unique Features: Over the last ten years, these *Reflections* have been shared with friends and relatives, and their friends and relatives, and so on – making a list of nearly 500 e-readers. I seldom posted them on a website or blogged them. Reason – high-tech arthritis! Naturally, quite a few readers would react or comment now and then. At times, I would individually respond, and thus ensuing a dialog that enhances and brings clarity on the issues. This volume contains only sparkling comments and analyses at the end of some *Reflections*. Early on, I did not save any comments. However, all the commentators are acknowledged with their thumb nail introductions.

Also, at the end of each *Reflection*, there is a variable space for readers' **NOTES AND COMMENTS**. It is useful, as it provides a record of individual thought process. Personally, I like to scribble and add my remarks, as I read on a book.

Thank-You: Ever since I started writing for public consumption, English language is mastered every day. Being a rebel for decades, I have often said that

I was re-learning English. A few persons who helped me, in this process, were acknowledged in the first book. But I must single out Francis Andrew, a Scotsman, I met in Nizwa, Oman. He is a professor of English, and we hit it off well after a chance meeting in the lobby of Al Dayar Hotel. We taught in different institutions in Nizwa. Since 2009, Francis has suggested improvements in every *Reflection* written since then. I have yet to write an error free *Reflection*! Francis can catch an infinitesimally small weak spot! I am linguistically grateful to him.

Dedication: The book is dedicated to the Late Subhash C. Sood, a friend of 25 years, an avid reader and critic of all my *Reflections*. Often, he urged me to put some *Reflections* in a book. In life, he did not pursue what he was trained for years, but followed a mysterious drummer within his heart – basically lived off his eccentricities!

Satish C. Bhatnagar
Nov 11, 2011

THE GRASSROOTS OF INDIA'S SECULARISM

A Muslim friend, known for six years, expressed his jubilation at the fall of the BJP Govt. He strongly believes that BJP is a party of Hindu fundamentalists and Congress stands for secularism in India. My friend, also a professor, comes from a well-connected family in Bangladesh. I explained that BJP's negative image is a media creation - both inside India and abroad fueled by power hungry Congress Party. Intellectuals are not easily swayed by arguments. However, it became a personal challenge to be clear on India's secularism vis-a-vis Hindu fundamentalism.

Secularism in the Constitution of India: It may be worth recalling that members of the Constitution Draft Committee and the Constituent Assembly which approved and adopted the Constitution represented all political parties. The concept of secularism was not much of a moot point. Once the country was divided and the Muslim League got Pakistan as a haven for the Muslims, the remaining India was renamed Bharat. Bharat or the divided India was to be a place for everyone who did not believe in the two-nation theory of the Muslim League. To the best of knowledge, there were no walkouts, boycotts on the inclusion of secularism in the Constitution. Nor, there was a debate on a brand of ideological secularism – like that of Congress, Communist, or Hindu Mahasabha etc.

It must be pointed out that for a long time Gandhi wished that after independence the Congress Party should be dissolved, as it was much more than a political party under his stewardship - it symbolized a national movement. He was never a primary member of the Congress. But the top brass of the Congress - Nehru, Patel and Azad, did not like his idea. They knew that dissolving the Congress would spell out different polarizations, and they may not get the public mandate, as they had it then. They were impatient to get into the seats of power.

Secularism not Congress Hegemony: Secularism in India, supposed for religious tolerance in public life, has lead to communal vote banks during the Congress regime. It is astonishing to note that much bigger and more communal riots have taken place during the Congress regime than during the entire British rule of India! The entire blame may not be attributed on the Congress, as the new national leaders did not have any experience of governing a vast and diverse population. Some communal problems may not have been absent with any party in power, as Pakistan always fanned it. Thus on the record, either Congress has failed, or the current practice of secularism is not working. The time for a fundamental change is overdue.

The Fountainhead of Secularism: Secularism as envisioned by the founding fathers, and for which Gandhi gave his life, is embedded in the ancient heritage of India. If we briefly look at the early leaders of freedom movement from the end of the 19th century to the beginning of the 20th, then one encounters men like Vidyasagar, Gokhley, Tilak in political arena and high souls like Swami Vivekananda and Ram Tirath. They were all Hindus, and they believed in the Hinduism of ancient *RISHIS* - embracing all people, all creeds, all thoughts.

Gandhi was a devout Hindu. His autobiography reveals that his heroes were from Hindu folk tales and he derived inspiration from the Hindu scriptures. Gandhi's maxim, that **Truth is God** is the epitome of the *SATYANARAIN KATHA* (that God is Truth Personified) recited in every Hindu home! It is the essence of secularism in India, called *Hindutava* that defines the secularism of India. After all, terminologically speaking, how one is to capture all what India has stood over the centuries in assimilation of believers of all foreign religions - including the Jews, Parasis, Muslims and Christians. *Hindutava* is the spirit behind tolerance. Today, the BJP is the only national party that is not ambivalent about it. During the freedom movement, there were Congress leaders like Acharya Narindra Dev and Dr Bhagwan Das who stood for *Hindutava*.

Hinduism and Democratic Traditions: Let us have a look at Indian secularism from a new perspective by examining the political evolution of countries of South Asia. Afghanistan, a Muslim country; Nepal, a Hindu country and Thailand, a Buddhist country, were never colonized by any European power. They survived the colonial onslaughts by their national character, a beautiful piece of history. In Pakistan, the democratic model envisioned by its founding leaders, hardly survived a few months before the army took it over. The story of Bangladesh is similar - the democratic government of Mujabber Rahman was thrown by the army after a couple of years, and the unrest continues. In the Buddhist countries of Sri Lanka and Myanmar (Burma), the democratic rules have been touch and go. In India alone, a democratic model has survived constitutional crises, civil unrest and wars, and without an army takeover!

The Indian political system is resilient and getting stronger. It is a pertinent question as to why and how in a vast country like India, democracy and the cliché of unity in diversity continue to be vibrant. It is the *Hindutava* that pervades all walks of life. The **Hindutava transcends all organized religions of India.** The Communists, while in power in Kerala and Bengal, did not create re-education camps for their political opponents. Jyoti Basu did not put a ban on the Bengalis from worshipping the goddess *KALI*. Temples were not shut down, as the churches were shuttered down in the Soviet Union. The spirit of Hindu religion is too powerful and pervasive. In ultimate analysis, real secularism lies in Hinduism and is embedded in *Hindutava*.

(June 22, 1996/Sept, 2011)

NOTES AND COMMENTS

HAITI: A LAND OF PERPETUAL STRIFE AND PASSION

[**Note**: This piece is extracted out of 25-page article written after visiting Haiti. It had a unique format - collection of letters, journal and travelogue.]

I spent 15 unforgettable days (May 22 - June 6, 1997) in Haiti. The trip was prompted by my first cousin, Sushil, who came from India to Haiti on a UN assignment - setting up of the Police Department in Haiti, chaotic since 1993-94. Haiti has a long bloody history, despite being a free country, in the sense of colonial occupation, since 1804. Historically, Haiti was the first country in the 'new world' where the African slaves, with support from the natives, had militarily thrown the French colonials out. **Perhaps, it gave a lesson to the European colonizers, that they never lost their grip on any colony for the next 150 years.**

During my stay, and particularly, at times of arrival and departure, it reminded me of India, where it is neither easy to get into the country, nor easy to get out. Without any connection or greasing the palms, you are not going to move an inch in a waiting line. Luckily, during the flight, a passenger sitting next to me was a Haitian lady, who turned out very helpful. She was returning from Boston after attending the graduation ceremony of her son.

All the letters below are reproduced in entirety except the mundane and non-historical material.

(Sushil's letter of April 7, 1997 from Ft Liberte, Haiti reaching Las Vegas on April 13)

"I arrived here on 3/20/97, after a long official ping-pong going on since June, '96. It draws lot of tourists to its beaches by shipfulls. The people here are 95% blacks of African origin, but French/Creol speaking. The rest 5 % of population is millotts (browns) & whites. American, Canadian and Pak army is here under the UN control. The UN provides its peace cap with its insignia. It also provides 4 WD Nissan vehicles, left hand drive. At the moment this mission is to last up to July, '97. Why not make some program and enjoy the Haitience Hospitality. You will not get such opportunity again. Here the mail system is very poor. Six hours of electricity is in the evening only - no tap water, lots of mosquitoes."

On the receipt of this letter, my initial interest was quickly turned on, and I started looking into Haiti for a short overseas excursion. Netscape did not have any touristy information on Haiti. So, I wrote him back asking for more travel tips and guidelines to entice me to visit Haiti.

(Sushil's second letter of May 5, 1997)

"I am much thankful to you for the prompt letter. It was the first ever letter in Haiti for me. It is a very colorful letter depicting your ever youthful, adventurous and happy mind. I feel I am lacking this zest now. Anyway, I am eagerly awaiting your arrival here. I am having leave from 25-30 May, so that we can meet each other conveniently. Yours was the first phone also to be received by me. Incidentally, I picked that phone on that day. It was really delightful to have heard you on phone that day. Merci beaucoup."

The UN staff do not use the Haitian postal service between Port Au Prince (PaP) and Ft Liberte, instead, they rely on some colleague going to, or coming from PaP for mail drops and pickups from the UN P.O. Box. There is no regular mailbag between FL and PaP. The UN office in FL is housed in a mobile trailer parked right in front of the FL police station. Incidentally, it was inaugurated on the day I landed Cap Haitian (CH). It was due to the Haitian dignitaries invited at this inauguration that Sushil got delayed in reaching CH for picking me up at the airport. There are no public phones in Ft Liberte, and the ones in the capital PaP are not reliable.

The fellow Haitian passenger called Ft Liberte or Northwest of Haiti as a bush country. She gave me the impression that even Haitians seldom visit that part of the country. It reminded me how we Indians, having not seen most of India due to lack of comfortable modes of communication, carry misconceptions about other parts of India. Nearby FL is a village of 20,000 inhabitants with no power at all! Ft. Liberte population is 30, 000 and is a seat of department headquarters.

Before leaving Las Vegas for Washington, DC, I expected to hear from Sushil. There is no railroad track in Haiti. Some overcrowded bus service is visible, but no one seems to know its schedule. During my entire stay, I saw only two buses plying on a national highway connecting PaP to CH, another coastal city and department headquarters. I have come to a conclusion, *that being too informed could be as crippling as ill informed, at times.*

In Washington, I called several travel agents to get information on air travel from PaP to CH. Each one gave the same story line that the computer does not have any information. Suddenly, I thought of Haitian Embassy. Twice, I called them and was put on hold to get disconnected! I was beginning to get a little edgy now. Next day on Wednesday, a day before departure, I personally decided to go to the Haitian Embassy in the morning. It was a disappointing experience. A couple of girls, I spoke to, had not lived in Haiti! After nearly an hour of waiting and talking, I got the impression that there is no service of any kind, and then it started concerning me.

In the evening, I visited the travel section of the Border bookstore. **It had travel books on all countries except on Haiti.** Even the ones on Caribbean islands excluded Haiti only! When I pointed out this situation to a Border employee, he expressed disbelief. It added to my growing anxiety for the first time before an overseas trip. I am usually very confident, rather uppity about any travels. The only thing to balance it out at that moment was to dine in Vietnamese restaurant and withdraw some extra $$ from an ATM. I packed my bags till midnight, still got up at 4 AM for the 6 AM flight from Washington to Miami.

(Letter to my wife: dated 5/23/97 received in LV on 6/9/97)

"The first thing I told Sushil after arrival at his dwelling, that had Prabha traveled to Haiti, then she would have become a basket case by now. I said why the hell did you ask her (even as a formality) on the phone to come here? **It is a land, particularly his habitat----unthinkable in terms of lack of basic conveniences, one would call normal** in USA.

Backing up to my flight, during one-hour stopover in Miami, I called Sushil and told him of my arrival in PaP. He informed me that two Indians - Tilak and Tulsi by names, would meet me at the PaP airport, and assist me for the next flight or overnight stay in PaP, if needed. I felt good. During travels, one encounters both angels and crooks. Anyway, the flight took under two hours. 300 passengers, from American Airline plane, filled a small immigration room. It was chaotic - no lines, or clear directions. While I was trying to find a line in a mass of humanity, that lady came over and asked me to follow her.

Since I did not have any luggage checked in – she asked me to go out and look for my friends. Instead, I requested her to help me find a restroom! She spoke to some worker, who showed me a place which I would have never figured it out from outside - forget its state from inside. Anyway, it was a big relief to empty out the bladder. For a couple of minutes that I was in the toilet, the lady went out, spotted Tulsi and Tilak (only Indians) and told me about them. I profusely thanked her. All this took no more than 15 minutes, which may have taken two hours. Without her assistance, I would have missed my connecting flight to CP.

So here, in a tiny plane, I was buckled up in the seat right behind the pilot. David, an American entrepreneur, has been running these flights for the last 2 years, and raking money in one of the poorest country in the world. A few Haitians are very wealthy due to their diligence or at the 'exploitation' of millions poor - a basic human urge not found in other creatures! Here was a flying experience, where I could touch both wings & wheels of the plane out from the windows.
There were some drops and jolts during its passage through the clouds. I wished I had a beer and binoculars in my hands!!

The flight from PaP and CH took an hour, but the rugged Nissan van took an hour to cover 30 miles. The poverty on the roadside was stark. Still, in contrast with poor in India, the Haitians don't beg. Religion is Catholic, or native African

Voodism. During an election, President Bush popularized Voodoo in labeling his opponent's ideas on economy, as Voodoo economics."

(Letter to son/Monday, May 26, 1997)

"I am counting days in some sense, and yet like to remain disconnected from the US life routines for a while. Imagine my not reading a local newspaper for four days in a row, no TV, or even radio! Sushil's housemates are also UN officers from Mali - a former French colony in Africa. On a short wave band radio, they are always turned to the broadcasts in French.

FL, being on coast, has been explored since early Spanish days of 16th century. There is a dilapidated coastal fort, a big 100+ year old cathedral, a huge house for its bishop (perhaps the biggest in the town). Like in early days, the poor who walk to work in wealthy houses, or small farms etc., live on the outskirts and the wealthy ones in the heart of the town. The automobiles have turned the living styles around - now the rich live in suburbs and poor around downtowns.

A new place enhances my capacity to observe and reflect. We drove to the border town of Dajaban in Dominican Republic (DR), a Spanish speaking country occupying the remaining 2/3 of the Hispinola Island. It is relatively far more developed than Haiti. It would surprise anyone to see, across the border, better houses, road conditions, vehicles, fast food restaurants, public cleanliness and utilities etc. In Haiti, almost everything is from the US and priced more than in the US - from breakfast cereals to Scotch. In DR, most things except computers were locals. Dajaban, being away from the coast, is relatively warm. In FL, a cool breeze is always blowing.

Yesterday, we drove 60 KM away to a nearby beach resort there, called Labadee - a white enclave far away from the locals. The locals only serve as waiters, porters, gatekeepers etc. and their young girls for the sexual escapades of the tourists. It appears in this society threshold of morality is lower or higher depending upon one's point of view. What is this morality any way - at individual or collective level - for a time or all the time - for one place or everywhere? I personally find my own norms and measures shifting that Shakespeare's famous lines ring in my ears – nothing is good and nothing is bad, but thinking makes it so.

However, a thought did flash my mind on while lying on a beach chair - how to measure two societies in term of superiority? The answer that flashed my mind is: **In general, if the women of society A are attracted to the men of society B for their wealth, power, or looks, then society B is superior to A!** Well, that is quiet a food for thought."

(Letter to my younger daughter written on 05/30/97 and received on 6/23/97)

"Haiti is some place on this earth, yet not easily visited. It has been exactly 8 days since I arrived here. After a couple of days, a thought of returning to LV took hold of my mind. But I told myself to "tough this stay out, as the going gets tough." In life, it happens all the time, whenever we encounter a new situation. Either the situation gives it in, or we give in to it! Life is a sequence of high and low experiences - sometimes they may go out of control.

"It is the leadership in a nation which makes the difference in the lives of its people - never the natural resources, as some economists expound. The US runs like a symphony of Wagner at one time, that of Bach, or Beethoven at other! In the US, the leaders come and go, but, the systems are left stronger. In many developing nations, the leaders literally bankrupt their own countries.

"There are two other Indians in the UN mission in Haiti who are friendly to me just being Indians. That shows strength of Indian culture and ethnic bonding. In a true sense, Haiti has no museum, or art gallery. A living art is when you see some 30 people sitting in a small Toyota pick-up! In Haiti, I have encountered all conceivable modes of transportation of goods and persons. You may only see similar sights in Calcutta (India) or Dacca (Bangladesh)!

'Haiti is really run by the US directly or indirectly through the UN. All big US oil companies and banks are here. They have their own power generators and security systems. During an evening outing, armored vans were protecting ESSO service stations! And right there, bunches of students were studying under the lights of the service stations.

'The importance of education in poverty reminded me of India of my days. Education is the exit door out of poverty. In the mornings, students are seen studying outside their homes at the crack of dawn! They memorize questions/answers of history, biology, and sociology etc. - the way done in India. In a rote system, educators think that understanding grows out of the memorized material vs. the US system based on: things fully understand are not forgotten.

'Seafood items like lobsters, crabs and fish are called here as the fruits of the sea! I have not tasted any one yet, the reason being that my hosts are vegetarians. The general health of Haitians is relatively strong partly due to the African stock slaved here, and also due to high proteins in their diet from various meats and seafoods - available in plenty.

"A question often posed is why one would leave a country like USA to come to a place like Haiti? It is not different from - why one would go to the top of Mt. Everest, or cross Sahara Desert, or run a mile under 4 minutes etc.? If there is an immediate public recognition or financial reward, then one normally rationalizes such a course. Otherwise, it is all internal urges and self-motivation. Eventually, such adventures strengthen the infrastructure of a personality.

"In PaP, we spent couple of hours in a hotel casino, El Rancho - the biggest in the city. There are a few smaller ones with recycled LV slot machines. The casinos close at 2 AM. A lot of time was spent in the mission of the UN in Haiti. The USA knows how to make a lasting impression on people coming from, Canada, India, Pakistan, Algiers, France and Mali. A huge TV screen gives continuous CNN news coverage and other popular US shows. The UN hospital facilities reminded me of MASH shows! The nurses and doctors are seen pacing around in their fatigues.

"At a certain age or perhaps with greater 'understanding', one begins to accept all life styles. All 'isms' and systems become delusions in one deep moment of reflection. Any one telling the other of how to be happy in life etc. seems so out of line. How can one know the mind of the other, when one barely knows one's own? This letter is being finished in the verandah of Bayah Hotel facing the ocean. It is owned by a Haitian married with a classy white French lady."

(Letter written to older daughter on 06/02/87 - received by her on 6/24/97)

"Overall, Haiti is very different from India. India has far superior defense forces, university and transportation systems. On the other hand, in India, you see men, women and children going out public for toilet calls. It is not seen even in Haiti. In urban India, piles of garbage are all around. The streets in Haiti are rarely paved, but they are not dumping places for the garbage.

Outside every home here in FL, I have noticed at least one *NEEM* tree. They may have forgotten its use except perhaps air purifying property. Sushil and I daily break a twig for brushing our teeth, *DATUN*. Actually, I also eat 6-7 tiniest pink leaves as my first morning food intake. It supposedly wards off tropical health problems and repels insects. It is a fact that *NEEM* purifies blood. Even common people in India are so much aware of its herbal properties.

The Haitians go to their churches in fine clothes. Church seems central in their lives. There are typical white sisters and nuns working in remote villages. Some of them have been there for 5-6 years! It is this kind of dedication that missionary spirit became a proverbial phrase, and has been the spear tip of the colonial power of the West since the 18th century. The money for such international missionary expense comes from individual church collections and funds from the US corporations. The rest of the Haitians believe in Voodism - some form of tribal Hinduism.

If one asks a typical touristy question- what do you do all day in Haiti? Then the answer may have nothing to satisfy the questioner. However, it is the total change in air, water and surrounding that makes a lasting difference. Air is truly unpolluted at all hours of the day and night. The doors and windows are left open. It is one thing to spend a weekend, or even a week in a hotel room where one is warded off from the local life around. But I think myself fortunate that I got this opportunity of living with a relative for two solid weeks

Such experiences bring one's perspectives in life on firmer foundations. Returning home and going back to work in the US becomes more meaningful. Human nature can't take monotonocity of any kind, no matter how good it is. The outlets could be different with different persons.

"OK. I close this letter and mail it out as my last letter from Haiti. Let us see how long it takes to reach you, after I do. It is more than fun to get a letter in mail. **One may not have time, or even zest to write letters, but everyone looks forward to receiving one**."

During this trip, it struck me how persons grow out very differently as the life moves on. There was another point which incidentally made me think a lot. Sushil and his colleague are paid $3000 PM on the top of their salaries and benefits fully paid in India. This dollar amount is the same for officers of every nationality. Yet, they were planning to petition the Government of India for more money. After listening to their strategies, I told them that Indians and Pakistanis are paid at least ten times of their salaries in India, where as officials from the USA may be getting less than their home salaries. They come to Haiti for sheer different experiences in life. Indians and Pakistanis come to save money by penny pinching. At times, I would get shocked at the quality of their life styles in Haiti. The British differentiated it while ruling India. Many countries in Middle East still do it when it comes to hiring an American and an Indian

Once, Sushil mildly protested on my non-vegetarian meal. Hindus, as a race, are very phony about food habits. Their poverty of centuries has pushed false values in their collective psyche. They would rather eat at others' place and expense, and equate frugality with their brand of vegetarianism. They claim to see meat coming from life, but think vegetables have no life!

The same attitude goes on when it comes to moderate drinking. In a social gathering, they would drink with protestation, when offered, but never paying it from their own pockets. I often agree with a French maxim, **that poverty is a disease**, and its damages are pervasive. It may take years for a healthy recovery, or perhaps generations.

Travel is not just experiencing new sights and sounds of places, things etc., but also leaving your imprints of ideas on some persons and vice versa. I won't forget when Sushil's very next-door neighbor told me one day that I was the only one in this house, lived by UN personnel, who had spoken to them. And what of speaking, just simple greetings in my broken French delighted him and he responded in his broken English. His wife came out watching me speak to her husband, and stayed there amused; quite an unforgettable sight. Living boils down to a sum total of little connections one is able to make every day.

(RP Sharma's letter of July 5 received on July 17, 1997)

"It was very nice time to spend about two weeks with you during your visit to Haiti. I was amazed with your quality of adaptability, as you had adjusted yourself with such an ease with the hardship of day-to-day life in FL coming straight from a totally contrasting living conditions of US. Plus, watching your way of perceiving and viewing the life, was also a novel experience for me. I had a lot of interaction with you on varied topics and I am really impressed of the depth of your analysis and uniqueness in viewing the things. In fact, your arrival here broke the hitherto monotony of our life. Unfortunately, I could not give you sufficient company due to my restricted movements owing to the backache. Anyway, I know that your visit was not fully satisfying to you, as many things which you thought of, could not be accomplished due to some reason or other. Still, I believe that you could see much of the socio-cultural, religious and economic life of Haitian people in PaP as well as remote. I spent ten days at PaP undergoing medical treatment and rest from 10th to 20th June. I am much better now. Literally, on the first occasion, you dragged me to the hospital! Thanks a lot."

Sex, sensuality and AIDS in Haiti are often reported in the US media. Yes, women are easily procured for sex. In the US sex is easy because of sexual freedom. For instance, the other half of the FL house was shared by two Malian officers. Both had women visiting them openly. One woman even had a small daughter come with her. She would spend a night or part of the day as his schedule allowed. The women did not have any inhibition when seeing us around. In the adjoining house, there were two other girls. One was not more than twenty and often she was gone out with a UN officer, and once gone for a few days.

One day, it occurred to me what these girls must be thinking of we Indians. Don't Indians like women? Neither Sushil nor Sharma, and now I myself, ever tried to lure any one for female relationship. Is it something typically Indian, real or contrived morality of some sort? From the girls' point of view, we were depriving them of a living. We are phony too, as how lecherously Sushil and Sharma would talk with each other, and ogle at the girls! Indians, Hindu in particular, are sexually repressed people, but project themselves as ***BRAHAMCHARIS***, high moralists!

Big money of foreign tourists and UN officials does create a market of demand and supply. But then, what else most poor Haitian women would do? There are no jobs in stores, factories, farms etc. However, they see good things of life around them. May be, their men folks either push their women, or are least concerned, if their women are just picked up.

Such sexual scenarios do not turn me on, rather, de-sex me. Like in every other aspect of life, there is a sexual conditioning too. One of them is to be the first to have sex with a girl, who is to be your wife. Having sex with a bitch is degrading one self. I don't proclaim them to be norms for any one at every age and period of a life. If one is sexually starved for months, then it may be a sensible thing to have an honest relationship. Islam permits its adherents to keep a sexual partner (called *MUTAH*), if one is away from one's wife for more than six months.

In Haiti, significant number people visit Voodoo medicine men practicing a native healing system. The house of a medicine man is identified by a flagpole outside. I remained curious to meet someone, or watch him treat a patient. At the same time, I knew my watching could be misconstrued. Without any local intermediary it was not possible. Sushil and his colleagues had no local contacts. Hence this desire remained unfulfilled. In fact, that is how I like to leave off a tourist place - clearly telling myself that those are going to be the reasons for coming again!

(July 17, 1997/Sep, 2011)

NOTES AND COMMENTS

VINOBA *DARSHAN*

VINOBA *DARSHAN* means Vinoba's practical philosophy. The ***India Post*** (IP) is not a forum for discussion on any philosophy. However, for the benefit of Indian Diaspora, this article presents a glimpse of Vinoba's mind during the turbulent time around the 1975-Emergency imposed in India. There is a wealth of information to be released in three special issues of the ***Ashram*** monthly, ***Maitri.*** Vinoba's ***Ashram*** is known as ***Brahama Vidya Mandir.***

Most Indians know Vinoba (1895-1982) as a disciple of Gandhi, who took Gandhi's practical philosophy of non-violence to newer and greater heights. For example, in the 1950s, the violent means, advocated in communism, were spreading like wild fire in China and Indo China. Indian communist leaders had more faith in Marx and Lenin as the saviors of the downtrodden than in Indian saints – like Nanak, Kabir, Raman Maharishi and Ramkrishna Paramhans.

It was the ***Bhoodan*** (Land Donation) movement of Vinoba that completely stemmed the tide of communism in India. Some scholars venture to say that in the next 10-20 years when communism will be erased from the world as a socio-political ideology, it may survive in some pockets of India as a relic. During 1951-64, Vinoba walked fifty thousands of miles - traversing entire India. He tried to keep India united. Eventually, his streams of ***Bhoo-dan, Gram-dan*** (village donation), and ***Shrma-dan*** (labor donation) merged into the Ganga of ***Sarvodaya*** movement (uplift of all) - ably lead by Jay Prakash Narain (JP), as Vinoba's field general.

After the 1960s, Vinoba stayed back in his ***Ashram***. And that is the beginning of the most exciting period in Indian history, and so is Vinoba's role in it. It tested the will of the people of India, its Constitution, states and central governments to their limits. The Congress Party was vertically split for the first time. There was an exodus of over ten million Muslim refugees from East Pakistan that later on became Bangladesh. It strained India's poor economy, and it gave rise to institutional corruption in India for the first time.

Some scholars are of the opinion that it was China's Cultural Revolution (1966-76) in India. However, in China, it turned things upside down, at the expense of millions of Chinese lives! In India, a loose students' organization ***Yuva Sangharsh Vahini*** (Youth Fighting Band), with JP at the helms, essentially toppled the state governments of Gujarat and Bihar. Then, the President of India, on the recommendations of PM Indira Gandhi, imposed Emergency. I think that is point to stop here, as the focus is Vinoba - and not any analysis of Emergency.

Over the last forty years, a Hindi monthly, ***Maitri*** (means friendship) has been published from Vinoba's ***Ashram***. It is a small, 30-page publication, containing no ads, but words of practical wisdom. At least for three years, 1974-76, the *Ashram* has kept assiduous records of all what Vinoba had uttered. **These records have never been published before**. Vinoba went into *Maha Samadhi* (a voluntary meditative state for the last breath of life) in 1982. Since then, some scholars and politicians have harbored mistaken views on Vinoba's role during Emergency. Hopefully, to dispel misinformation and misgivings, the *Ashram* decided to release complete transcripts of each of the year 1974, 75, and 76 in three special issues of the *Maitri*.

I have gone through two of these special issues; the third one is not yet published. Primary reason is the lack of funds! Now here comes the question: what is so big about their contents? Well, Ken Starr's congressional tapes on Clinton have already started gathering dust in six months. Reason: they do not contain any material that affected the lives of American people on a day-to-day basis. The story in the special issues of *Maitri* simply reads incredible even after 25 years. It is no exaggeration to say that during Emergency, the real nerve center of India was not Delhi, but Pavnar village, where Vinoba's *ashram* is situated!

Vinoba had a continuous stream of Indian and foreign visitors coming from every walk and shade of life. He had the uncanny wisdom to find a common working platform with any person or party. No one was given any extra special treatment. During 1974 and 75, PM Gandhi personally visited Vinoba thrice. Her special emissaries were coming more frequently as were the leaders of every political party. The *Sarvodaya* leaders were naturally confused about the roles of JP and Vinoba during Emergency.

A particular scenario stands out in my mind. In Dec 1974, Vinoba went on a silence fast for one year. Emergency was in full swing. JP came to Vinoba for a few days in Nov 75 to discuss some burning issues. The dialogues, as reported in the second special issue of the *Maitri*, would take anyone to great heights of ethics, morality and spirituality – all in politics. So much so, that Vinoba broke his silence for two minutes to say the most profound words to JP! The bond between Vinoba and JP was like that of between Gandhi and Nehru.

Most importantly, these issues bring out a national character and psyche of India. It is so closely connected with India's Vedic heritage. After living in the US for nearly 30 years, I do wonder if a person like Vinoba can ever command such a stature without holding any office. We know how saint Guru Ramdas counseled Chatrapati Shivaji. Chandraswami may have proved a crook, but a prime minister or president of India, putting faith in a guru or gurumai, comes from ancient heritage of India - to the eons of Ramayana and Mahabharata. It beholds spiritual aspiration and achievements of greater value in the service of mankind.

I take this opportunity to in asking the general IP readers, Publisher Dr. Japra, and corporate American India to come out in support of Vinoba's work lying unpublished for lack of funds. His ideas bring a glory to India, and deserve a place on the shelves of libraries and hands of the public all over the world. The ASHRAM address is the following: *MAITRI*, Brahama Vidya Mandir, Pavnar (Vardha) 442 111. Tele: (7152) 43518.

(Feb 5, 1999)

PS – Sept, 2011: communist parties have lost power in every state of India.

NOTES AND COMMENTS

WHY TO WRITE A HISTORY?

Thoughts of writing a history of Indians (from India) in Las Vegas have been on my mind for the last five years. It first struck a cord when a Chinese history professor, at UNLV, wrote a book on the Chinese Immigrants in Northern Nevada. By then, I had lived in Las Vegas (LV) for 25 years. Also, I consider myself a history buff. Three years ago, Lam Kundargi, a 1970-resident of LV inquired about this project. I felt embarrassed telling that it had not even gotten off the ground. One reason being that I was not clear on its format - be that a book or a monograph. A friend of mine, a retired Indiana University professor sent his pamphlet about Indian immigrants in Indiana State. With the backdrop of **9/11 Attack on America**, I am convinced of the need for a history of Indian community in every major city the US.

Frankly, not having ever written a book was a mental hindrance too. One needs to have some vision of a book from its beginning to an end. I did not have it. My forte is to weave stories around small observations. After having written more than 100 *Reflections* during the last one year, I seem to have discovered my strength. It is, in fact, a transformation of my letter-writing prowess into varied reflections and articles. Impetus for this project also came from my son-in-law. Recently, he decided to launch a community website, and approached me for a regular column on the history of Indians. I readily agreed. It fits into another write-up series.

For the last one month, I tired to find out about Indian pioneers or settlers who came to Las Vegas before 1960. The reason for choosing 1960 is simple. It was during the Kennedy Administration that the **US** Immigration Act allowed professionals from India to immigrate to the US. Prior to 1960, Indian immigrants in the US have individual stories. My search of Indians living in LV before 1960 turned out to be an empty set.

Las Vegas population jumped after the completion of Hoover Dam in 1936. In 1950, Nevada Test Site was designated for nuclear tests, yet its 1960 population was only 64,400. Incidentally, that was the population of my hometown Bathinda (India) around 1950s! With no agriculture and no major educational institutions, besides a few casinos, professional Indians had little interest in moving to LV. Also, by and large, generations of Indians before mine were relatively less adventurous.

There is always a question on the undertaking such a project. History is an ongoing progress report of a community. It is meaningful in the US, as the second and third generations of Indians have started their lives here. No matter whether they are born and educated in the US, for all intents and purposes, they shall always be identified as Indians first. Having some knowledge of achievements and challenges faced by early immigrants is always inspirational and educational. I hope it makes a few connections. If in this series, any point needs to be corrected, then please feel free to provide me feedback. It is a project for the Indian community by one who has seen it grow exponentially.

(March 28, 2004)

NOTES AND COMMENTS

Excellent project. You will do it well. **Inder Singh**

GADAR MEMORIAL CENTER, SAN FRANCISCO

As soon as my plans of visiting Davis, California were finalized, I e-mailed the Indian Consulate Office in San Francisco (SF) about visiting the Center for my ongoing research on the Gadar Movement. After a week came a reply that the Consulate Library had no material on the Gadar, but a UC Berkeley library has it. Writing back, I explained about a small holding of original documents in the Center, and also of my previous visit in 2002. Finally, an arrangement was worked out that someone from the Consulate office will open the Center which is half a mile from the Consulate. Having gone through a harrowing experience previously, I accepted the arrangement.

The Consulate lunch time, for all, being from 1 to 2 PM, it was suggested that I be at the Consulate on time. Before leaving Las Vegas, I called up to confirm my program. The drive from Davis to the Consulate Office, situated in a congested SF area on Friday morning, was time consuming. At 12: 45 PM, I called the concerned person of my running on time, as I did not want to waste any time.

It was my first visit to the Consulate. Its atmosphere reminded me of a typical government office in India. One 'gatekeeper' on the 'reception' desk kept telling me to pull a ticket number and take a seat. He won't understand my purpose. A teller on the other side of a service window was receptive and called the lady that I had been communicating with. She quickly came over, but told me to wait till she works out the logistics of opening the Center! Finally, one person drove me and a security man with a key of the Center. My son followed the Consulate staff to the Center.

It was a July 4 long weekend, and my son had other plans too. As soon as the man opened the Center door I went to work on the material displayed in one of the four open bookshelves. The security man asked for my identification card. I don't know what he did with it, but returned it after an hour. He stayed in a room that probably was some lodging. Around 4 PM, he came over to tell me politely of his evening engagement at the Consulate. Essentially, he was requesting me to finish the work. I came out at 4 PM, and waited my son to pick me up.

Being keen on signing the visitors' register, I noted that the last visitor was there two months ago! It is unfortunate that when every few years a national memorial is opened in the US, the Gadar Memorial belonging to all Indians is being closed down. **Those who make history know alone how to write, read and preserve history**.

If the Center management is handed over to an enterprising American, it would be bustling with a gift shop and visitors of all kinds. The Consulate has to be out of its present operation. A group of concerned local Indians need to come together for the promotion of the Center. In the meanwhile, the Government of India, through its SF Consulate, should keep the Center open for at least one day a week.

(July 02, 2004)

NOTES AND COMMENTS

A GLIMPSE OF INDIAN DIASPORA

While working on the history of Indians (from India) in Las Vegas my thoughts took me away from it. What about a history of Indians, in general, outside of India, I wondered? It has to be understood that the history of Indians, by and large, is the history of the Hindus. The Muslim and Christian populations were mathematically zero in India at different points just in the last millennium.

A related question is: **What would have attracted Indians before independence to leave India?** Gandhi's autobiography effectively captures a popular perception of the Hindus of never going overseas for fear of social ostracization. It prevailed in the present coastal regions of Gujarat and Maharashtra. Once the British were entrenched in India after quelling the 1857 Mutiny, they imposed heavy measures on the masses - including McCauley system of education and Indian Penal Code. An oppressive and punitive taxation broke the backbone of Indians for any future rebellion against the British.

The late 19th century was a golden period in the British Empire, ruling over half of the world, but it was the darkest period for Indians. The African slavery, abolished in UK (1834) and USA (1864), the British devised a new concept of slave labor from India. It was called indentured labor. Essentially, Indians were slaves for a period of five years and then set free. The British badly needed manpower for various plantations, factories and mines in their colonies - over 60 in number, and spread in every continent.

The sturdy Punjabis, Sikhs in particular, were shipped to the cold Canadian regions of Alberta and Vancouver for working in agro industries. In African colonies, men from Tamilnad, Gujarat and Kerala were brought in. In Latin American and Pacific Island colonies, men from eastern UP and Bihar were sent out. The present states of Rajasthan and Maharashtra seem to have supplied scant indentured labor. Women and children could only join their men after five years.

I don't have the exact records at hand, but close to 1.5 million men may have left India under this scheme. To the best of my knowledge, not even a single Christian went as an indentured labor from India. A few Muslims from Gujarat, sent to Africa, received preferential treatment over the Hindus. The dark Tamilians, being classified as Dravidian, were nearly equated with Africans, called Negroes then. But as an ethnic stock, the Muslims were considered as Caucasians, as defined by Europeans, but not by Indians.

It must be pointed out that most indentured labor came from the princely states of India. The Indian officers of princely rulers used coercion, deceit and lies in rounding up their own people. The British officers were seldom at the scene of 'rounding up'! It was the same approach that worked in Africa for slave trading, except for the fact that the Hindus were not chained in the ships sailing to British colonies.

I always wondered at the absence of people from present Bengal, Orissa and Southern Bihar. Well, an insight came in due course. **People of this region were physically emaciated due to systematic starvation caused by decades of famines due to the British punitive measures**. The agriculture was destroyed and so was the cottage industry including the famed muslin of Dacca that villagers thrived on. **According to the official British Gazetteer more than 6.7 million Indians died of famines and diseases during 1896 and 1912**. For the next one hundred years, hunger in India has been proverbially associated with Bengalis. Naturally, there was no question of recruiting unfit men for any physical labor.

Once the indentured labor was outlawed in 1920, there was little migration of Indians till the freedom movement gained momentum. However, it must be noted that 'unlegislated' export of indentured labor from India to some countries like Trinidad was going on as early as 1843! Also, some Indian leaders went abroad in exile. or sought political support against the British.

After India's independence in 1947, the British allowed citizens of the British Commonwealth countries (collective name of the former British colonies) to emigrate to UK under an employment voucher system. Under this scheme, thousands of Indians went to UK. This scheme was drastically curtailed around 1965.

With the 1960 amendment in the US Immigration Act, professionals from India started coming to USA, as the first wave of Indian settlers. **It is a historical event in the sense that for the first time, Indians who went abroad were not only free, but respected professionals**. The history continues.

(Feb 15, 2005)

NOTES AND COMMENTS

TELLING STORIES OF YOUR LIFE

"I need more volunteers for motivating the kids. We have only 29 speakers for 45 classes having 1700 children." said Joyce Woodhouse, the Director of the **PAYBAC** (acronym for **P**rofessionals **A**nd **Y**outh **B**uilding **A** **C**ommitment). It is a fully funded community partnership program of CCSD (Clark County School District). However, the speakers are volunteers, and not paid anything.

My participation goes back to four years when I joined it primarily to hone my public speaking skills, in addition to membership in the TNT Toastmasters Club. It did not take me long to realize its usefulness. In subtle ways, I was making a difference in the lives of some children. How do I know it? After each lecture, the students fill out a comprehensive evaluation. Moreover, the staff tells instances of how it has touched students' lives over the years.

Well, here is an opportunity for the Indians to tell the community that they make a difference where they live. Whereas, volunteerism defines the US society - however, this concept is foreign to Indians living in India or in the US. By and large, Indians look up for the government for everything.

There are no qualifications to join PAYBAC, except a passion for what you have done, or doing presently. The program is limited to junior/middle schools (grades 6-8) and a few high schools (grades 9-12). One needs only two things - a reasonable command of English and not being shy of speaking with the kids. One gets over both after a few visits.

This morning, group of speakers came from metro police, air force, fire dept, and companies like Radio Shack, retirees, banks, engineering firms, and individual entrepreneurs. A university regent and owner of an accounting firm, Mark Alden, took time for it, at 8 AM! In the past, I have seen Nevada state senators and assembly persons. Some of them are seen every time I go. Some volunteer 15-20 times a year, but I do it 3-4 times. So far, I have yet not run into any other Indian in this program, though Indian kids are noticed in every school. Education always has been a high priority for Indians.

Through this program, Indians can change the stereotype image of India prevalent in the US. The kids know little about India. Today, I was identified from 15 countries besides India! Irrespective of the subject taught during that hour, it is up to the speaker to inspire the students for staying in school. That is the only mission of PAYBAC.

What an infrequent guest speaker tells in a class sticks the mind deeper than routine class lessons. A motivational speaker puts seeds of ideas in the fertile minds during the formative years. Some are bound to sprout. Call Joyce/Victor/

Cindy at 799-6560 for more information about this program. It is worth a try. Speakers from every background are needed, particularly from medicine that Indians dominate in Las Vegas.

(Feb 10, 2005)

NOTES AND COMMENTS

Great idea! **Cyriac**

ON TRIVIALIZATION OF HISTORY

Four days ago, during my stay in a Florida hotel, I read an e-mail from a Delhi University professor that the police brutality on Honda Auto Factory workers in Gurgaon was worse than the Amritsar Jalianwala Bagh. I was literally shocked and immediately Googled to read the details. To my surprise, there was no headline! Finally, I read a posting, and then Parliament news. A leader of a political party also compared it with Jalianwala Bagh massacre! But there was not even a single death reported at that time. In today's internet news from India, there was no mention of this event - after five days! Perhaps, it is drowned in the Mumbai floods.

It is a social tragedy to be ignorant of basic historical facts affecting the nation. But it is a height of travesty to trivialize historical events of national importance. In the Parliament, there were walkouts over this incident. That is street politics. Unfortunately, it has entered inside the Indian Parliament. Its members are known to spend more time outside the House than making constructive impact inside it.

In the Jalianwala Bagh massacre on Vaisakhi Day of April 13, 1919, nearly 500 Punjabis were killed and 2500 wounded by the barrage of bullets fired by the Hindu Gurkhas under the express orders of the British officers. The objective was to teach Indians a harsh lesson for protesting against the British policies of repression as symbolized by the Rowlett Act. Prior to the Jalianwala Bagh massacre, the British, amongst many methods of torturing, used to force the defiant Punjabis to crawl the lengths of the narrow streets of Amritsar on their bellies while being hit by batons from above. Is there any comparison between Gurgaon police action and Jalianwala Bagh? Indian media, in reporting such a comparison, has displayed utter ignorance.

In the Gurgaon melee, scores of police officers were injured. **Rarely, during the British rule, a policeman was ever attacked, as he was absolutely feared**. His loyalty was totally with the British Raj. Gandhi was stopped from visiting Amritsar and arrested for disobeying the orders. In the Gurgaon incident, a high-level inquiry report has been ordered in 15 days.

India is free, as far as the protests are concerned - whether they are raised in the hallowed halls of the Parliament, or on the streets. Nevertheless, let the history be not trivialized to meet short political ends. Indians, by and large, need to upgrade their historical perspectives. That is an index of a free mind.

(July 27, 2005/Apr, 2011)

NOTES AND COMMENTS

Objects at a distance look small. Objects close by look big. **Ved Sharma**

A KIND OF INTELLECTUAL HOLOCAUST

What a powerful day was it today! It coincided with *Vaisakhi,* the beginning of a new Hindu Year. A half of it was for a lecture scheduled in the evening to commemorate the birth centenary of Kurt Gödel (1906-1978) who in 1931 proved one of the most famous theorems in entire mathematics. Ivor Grattan-Guinness, British Professor of History of Mathematics and Logic (Middlesex University) spoke on *The Reception of Gödel's Incompeletability Theorems by Logicians and Mathematicians, 1931-1960.*

Guinness detailed how this landmark theorem was not recognized by generations of mathematicians till the 1950s. The world of mathematics was dominated by German mathematician, David Hilbert (1862-1943). Guinness described Hilbert's influence on mathematics as that of a Field Marshal! Hilbert witnessed the purge of Jewish mathematicians, and never stood up for them. Though Gödel's Jewish hereditary is uncertain, but he escaped to the USA in 1940 via Russia and Japan.

However, I walked into the other half unknowingly. After a couple of hours working on the office PC, I just walk out to straighten my neck and back. The UNLV's Museum of Natural History is a place to check out the new exhibits. Today, on display were 85 black and white photographs. It did not take me more than 6-7 frames and a few minutes to recognize that they were of the Nazis concentration camps, though there was not even a single human face in any one of them! Nevertheless, my mind provided the missing images of the millions who were systematically exterminated.

The pictures from various angles of the camps are relatively recent and taken by the photo artist, Michael Kenna during 1988-2000. The collection is called, *Impossible to Forget.* The photographs and one-hour documentary, *Memory of the Camps* (Frontline PBS, 1985) are timed with the April 1945 surrender of Nazi Germany in WW II.

The documentary has April 1945 photos and sound tracks taken within two weeks of the Allied Forces' takeover of more than 300 concentration camps in Germany and in its occupied countries. **For reasons that are unclear, it took 40 years to turn the material into a documentary**. I thought I had read and seen everything that went inside these camps. But here the scenes are unworldly enough to shake one's faith in humanity.

A paradox is presented there. The people living only a couple of miles away from the concentration camps either had no idea what went on inside or were brainwashed by the Nazi propaganda. Or, they were so desensitized by the knowledge that they casually went about their daily business. Human nature could be so revolting!

At the end of the lecture when most in the audience had raised some remarks and questions, I said. "There is a similarity between what I saw in the museum this afternoon and what I have just heard about the neglect of the celebrated theorem by mathematicians from Germany and other countries." Guinness, in his British 'muffled' accent, described how the Theorem, published in 1931 in an Austrian journal of repute, was not mentioned in the works of distinguished logicians, Hahn (1933), Quine (1934), and MacLane (1934) - to name a few! Curiously enough, Hahn was Gödel's PhD thesis supervisor in 1929 and had accepted his epochal paper for publication in 1931!

Famous European mathematicians - like Dieudonne, Hardy, and Bell, did not include the Theorem in their books/monographs. The US mathematics was not on the radar yet. It went on through the 1960s. It reminds me of the New York Times in 1945 not publishing the Holocaust pictures and news coming out of the concentration camps!

As the top logicians deliberately chose to ignore Gödel's Theorem, the lesser ones followed suit. The scientific and mathematical traditions in the west (different from the Eastern traditions) build upon the past references. Few top researchers have the time to understand others' researches. Often, lies and inaccuracies perpetuate in textbooks and research papers. At times, collaborative research is no different from mafia operations.

The Nazi Germany, or for that matter, every authoritarian regime tries to revise history. The Nazis did not stop at the extermination of the Jews and their dissidents, but undermined, minimized and distorted their intellectual achievements. There are hundreds of instances. The German Ministry of Education had the fullest control over their intellectuals, professional organizations, conferences - their foreign visits and invitees.

A lesson of history is that once a dictator wins over the intellectuals, then the masses are easily converted, or conversely. **There is only a small window of opportunity when individuals can speak up against an historical wrong before it is too late.** If that opportunity is missed, then the voices of discord are snuffed and muzzled out ruthlessly. The price of freedom - like in the US today, is paid by constant vigilance, willingness to fight, and readiness to go at war.

The denial of recognition to Gödel's Theorem, or the holocaust of six million Jews is the ultimate price a society pays for not participating in its national politics. This is not the first holocaust in history. During the last one hundred years alone, the countries - like Russia (under Stalin), China (Mao), Cambodia (Pol Pot) and India (British 1895-1905) have suffered from genocides far worse in magnitudes and brutality. Ninety minutes in the museum exhibits and ninety minutes in the lecture have opened my eyes again to the past, present and future of mankind. **It tells what a single man can do, and what a man can undo!**

(April 13, 2006/Oct, 2011)

NOTES AND COMMENTS

TUBERCULOSIS AND INDIA

Sometimes, joining enough dots do not help in the making of a composite picture. It needs a lightning bolt from within to make a final connection. That is how I felt last month while pouring over the material in the Gadar Memorial Center, San Francisco.

Tuberculosis (TB) and plague in India are of European origin. Once ravaging plague in England forced the closure of Cambridge University for two years (1665-66). Isaac Newton then a student escaped into countryside. Due to industrialization in the 18th century, poor working and living conditions in damp climate, TB raged in England, Europe and even the US. Many persons of name and fame are known to have died of TB at young ages. The great Indian mathematician Ramanujan also contracted TB in Cambridge and died in India within weeks of his return from UK in 1920. He was 32.

During 1962-65, while living in Shimla (at 7000' elevation), the summer capital of British India till 1947, we learnt that TB was very common amongst the natives. It really surprised me. Instead of rosy cheeks and glowing faces, people of this hilly region were pale, light built and short. I couldn't connect the dots then.

The mass vaccine for the TB treatment has only been available since the 1960s. However, by the middle of the 19th century, it was demonstrated that the isolation of the patients in the open environment of pine and fir trees at an altitude of 3000'-5000' coupled with good diet cured them from TB. Thus as early as 1850s, the hill stations in India were peppered with sanatoriums, where the TB patients from Britain came for treatment.

Attending the British patients would be battalions of Indian servants. **Here is the connection**! While the British would eventually get well and go back to their normal lives; but their servants, over the years, caught the TB en mass – it being highly infectious and contagious disease. The life style being close knit and less mobile, over a span of a few decades, the TB spread in all the hill states of India.

A common legend in Shimla was that the apples orchards were first transplanted in this region by an Englishman, Mr. Stoke who settled there after marrying an Indian woman of royalty. While living in Shimla YMCA, a resident told me how tea gardens in India were first cultivated by the English. But the TB was also carried to India by the English!

A few years ago, Italian researchers showed that the cow dung and urine have germicidal property to kill TB bacillus. The cows, being sacred to the Hindus, have been a part of the households of the rich and poor. Cow urine is still used for medicinal and ceremonial purposes. The dung is used for fuel and plastering the floors and walls of thatched dwellings. The point is that TB bacteria may be dormant in every human system, but it never erupted in India before the British took control of it after the 1757 Battle of Plassey.

(June 05, 2006)

NOTES AND COMMENTS

1. The British did not just spread TB in the world but are also directly responsible for more than half of the political turmoil's and suffering in the world. Partition of India, Kashmir issue, Iraq, Israel, Northern Ireland just to name a few.

2. Many diseases were imported into India by the British. I largely agree to what has been written. There is a disease in Ayurvedic texts called *Yakshma*. Symptoms are very similar to those mentioned for Tuberculosis. Tuberculosis is found in people living in poor physical, mental, and nutritional state. I worked with Tuberculosis patients on two occasions in England and one occasion in India. **Subhash**

WHEN HISTORY AND LITERATURE BLEND

This is my third annual trek to the Shakespeare Festival in Cedar City, 180 miles north of Las Vegas. Out of the four Shakespearean plays running during the summer season, it was *Antony and Cleopatra* that pulled me in. The historic theme, passionate romance, the hey days of Roman Empire were the right mix for my mood. The current wars in the Middle East with historical claims and counterclaims had some bearing on it.

While prepping up for the play, suddenly it struck me that while Shakespeare was a poet and playwright par excellence, but he was not a historian by any stretch of definition of his era, or today. With shrewd business sense, he fully enjoyed his life with the name and fame that came after each play - smartly spaced one year apart.

Due to the royal patronage, Shakespeare (1564-1616) wrote ten plays with historical themes. The greatness of his plays is measured by the fact that they are, perhaps, enacted everyday in some part of the world! The public perception of 2000-year old Roman period is what Shakespeare has projected through *Antony and Cleopatra*. It is a perfect example of a literary work becoming a source of history for the masses.

The Hindu notion of life and time being cyclic, history did not take intellectual eminence amongst the Hindus. Generally, little is known of the official records of the Hindu kings – whether big or small time. The Hindi word *Itihaas* means old story - a chronicle of certain age. The Muslim emperors, however, are known to have their individual *Shahnamas* (records of kings) maintained by the court officials.

In literature - poems, stories, novels and plays are known to have historical themes. But they are not considered sources of historical facts, as poets and writers have a license to stretch facts and imagine their own world. One makes a distinction between literature and history. However, when one talks of an era that is hundreds of years old and reliability of records lost, the literary works - like that of Shakespeare, become sources of history too.

In the lobby of the theater, there were exhibits of dresses worn by Shakespearean characters. It was very educational to learn about the research undertaken in bringing historical authenticity while keeping modern stitching technology invisible. Shakespeare does not describe details of design and color combinations in his plays. Shakespearean costumes, continually changing with times, truly make a multimillion-dollar industry.

It also reminds me of the impact on Indians of the play, *Shakuntala* by Kalidas, called Shakespeare of India. Kalidas lived around the 4th century AD (exact dates not known). The era he portrayed in this play goes back to more than 5000 years! Forget any kind of records or monuments of that age. Yet, a vivid public perception of that era has been created by this immortal work. Digging out of historical facts through archaeological work is cost prohibitive for the individuals or nations - only a few nations can afford it.

(Aug 20, 2006)

NOTES AND COMMENTS

Dear Dr. Bhatnagar, I have been greatly benefited by your writings so well researched, informative and interesting. It will be a rare honour to meet such a hugely wise and articulate person. Kind regards, **S.R. Wadhwa**

HISTORY IN THE BACKYARD

Just like - milk turns into yogurt, sugary syrup into vinegar and alcohol, under right temperatures - all personal documents gain some historical significance after 30-40 years. This realization dawned on me recently, when I was browsing the letters of my younger brother written to me during 1965-1978; before his moving to the US. This number, being more than 100, speaks of some history of communication between two brothers.

In democratic states, the classified documents are periodically released to the researchers after 25 to 50 years. In some individual cases, it may take longer. For example, the records of the trial of Gandhi's murder in 1948 were released after 55 years. They now portray the assassin, Nathu Ram Godse, differently from what he was projected before.

Historical merits lie in every of human endeavor - cultural, artistic, intellectual, sports and entertainment. During my high school days in India of the 1950s, history meant only the lives of the kings, their wars and ego building monuments. Since history exams stressed upon the right dates and places, I lost interest in history for a long time.

The purpose of history varies with age. In high schools, the objective may be to provide continuity with the present, and instill pride in national values and institutions. At sixty, the objective may be in the movement of ideas and ideologies. History provides benchmarks for the individuals and society to measure life and avoid some pitfalls.

It was fascinating to read about my 21-year old brother rescuing a girl from a burning house bombed in Bathinda during the 1971 Indo-Pak War and liberation of Bangladesh. It is a matter of pride how our families in India and USA raised funds for 11 million Muslim refugees who escaped into India. Most of them never went back to Bangladesh.

Of course, there were several family anecdotes. I was emotional again to read the details of the days before and after the demise of our father on New Year Day. He never woke up from the siesta taken after his favorite lunch. Individual and the society determine what is of historic significance. **The world forgets what we let the world forget it**.

Lots of changes take place in individuals and communities during 25-40 years. It was amusing to note the postal rates - 6 p (paisa) for a postcard, 15 p for an inland introduced in the 1960s and 85 p for international aerogramme. The US dollar was for Rs 7.50 against Rs 45 today. Some salaries rising to 10 times indicate India's growing economy.

The evolution of human personality remains enigmatic. Some individuals turn their lives around, as the environment challenges them and others stay on a pre-determined course. What makes one to challenge the present and the others to accept or ignore it remains complex. I have started to 'declassify' my thousands of letters that are carefully piled in several boxes. It is fun, refreshing and educational. What else matters in life?

(Sep 24, 2006)

NOTES AND COMMENTS

1. Dear Satish, Thanks for your articles, which have widened my outlook. **VED BHUSHAN**

2. I agree it is just fascinating to go through old letters, both written by me and those written by others to me. You have scored full marks on this. **Subhash**

3. Dear Satish, You observations about history and people are so true and inspiring. Thanks. Love, **Dutchie**

4. Satish: Your note is another example how you have become a storyteller. I loved the beginning. **Alok Kumar**

5. Dear Satish, I am reading all your e-mails. Very thought provoking. Thanks. **Matt.**

MISS AND MAKE OF BHAGAT SINGH

The legend of Bhagat Singh is far bigger than his age. He was hardly 22-year old when he courted his arrest for throwing a bomb (not for killing anyone!) on April 08, 1929 in the hall of Delhi Central Assembly. At the end of a 2-year secret trial, he was sentenced to be hanged on March 21, 1931. He was not even 24, as he was born on Sept 27, 1907.

I am 67; still the name of Bhagat Singh stirs fervor in my entire being. Since his martyrdom, all men, named Bhagat Singh, must have lived exemplary lives because of him. **A name is also sanctified by supreme sacrifices.** He left the comforts of his home, quit college, and refused to marry, though engaged. He was only 18 years old then!

At one time, I used to say that had I been born in that era, I would have joined a revolutionary party. This attitude is a cop out and escapist. **The challenges of every kind are around all the time.** One needs to have a passion and insight to recognize and pick a cause and fight for it. A focus in life is gone when life is on a drift, or on a cruise control.

Before joining the National Revolutionary Party led by Chandra Shekhar (Sharma) Azad, Bhagat Singh and his friends were actively engaged in anti-British plots in Lahore. My father-in-law (1913-1990), belonging to Lahore, told me only once - how the British police (made of Indians!) spied and persecuted the youthful revolutionaries. The youths used to escape into the labyrinth of narrow alleys of his neighborhood. He recalled once letting one inside the home during a wintry night. Father-in-law was stocky, courageous, and man of temper. His not joining the freedom fighters must have gnawed him in life.

The pedigree and environment make a big difference in the making of personality. My father-in-law's mother married at age 18 was widowed before 26 with two sons. He, being the older, she kept a close watch on his activities. Inwardly, he may have envied the revolutionaries, but he never joined them. Thus he missed the posthumous awards and accolades reserved for the freedom fighters and martyrs. My wife thinks it otherwise!

Bhagat Singh came from a peasantry family. His father and uncle were also freedom fighters. My father-in-law came from an urbanite family. The older brother of his father, Besant Lal Bhatnagar was the first Indian to be appointed as Income Tax Commissioner. During teen years, father-in-law must have struggled between the opportunities in British service and the life of a revolutionary. In my estimation, he missed the best of the two!

Reports, articles, videos and functions have started to commemorate the birth centenary of Bhagat Singh. In Punjab, the plan is to celebrate it for one full year. Every 20 years, a movie is made on his life. Bhagat Singh and Chandra Shekhar had charismatic looks and magnetic personalities. Unfortunately, both were betrayed by their own acquaintances. **Life is all about making a cut, or missing it**.

(Oct 21, 2006)

NOTES AND COMMENTS

MY PERCEPTION OF HISTORY

History, at any level of depth, does not belong to only the historians in the academe. At any given time and place, there are history makers, history readers, and history keepers. **In a limiting case, each individual knowingly and unknowingly combines all the three facets of history at different points in life.**

While undertaking to teach a graduate course on *History of Mathematics* (MAT 714), I questioned my credentials. Being in the business of mathematics teaching and research, my mathematics background does stand on solid footing. For justifying history credentials, besides having taught an undergraduate course on history of mathematics, I love to interject historical anecdotes in every mathematics course that I teach.

The Hindi equivalent of 'history' is *ITIHAAS* that literally means story of the olden times. The word history, having roots in Latin and Greek, comes from *historia* - meaning inquiry, to know etc. In a common parlance, history is a chronological record of **significant** events. (Mathematically speaking, like - every nice non-linear function at a point can be 'locally' linearized.) However, the word 'significant' is very subjective.

History does not occupy the same prominent place in every culture. The Hindus having faith in reincarnation and the **Law of Karma** have a cyclic view of life and death. Hence chorological linearity is absent in the Hindu way of life. History is not discerned in any ancient treatises of India. Even the big time Hindu kings never chronicled their reigns, as compared with the Muslim rulers who commissioned artists and court chroniclers for their *SHAHNAMAS* meaning royal chronology in paintings and words.

In contrast with the Hindus, the Sikhs have taken their 500-year old short history to new heights. Prominent gurdwaras (Sikh temples) have permanent exhibits only on the martial side of the Sikh history. During the *ARDAAS* (concluding Sikh prayer), homage to the men and women who sacrificed their lives for Sikh religion, is an integral part of invocation. The first series of history books, *The High Road of Sikh History* - prescribed in junior high schools, were written soon after India's independence in 1947. By the 1960s, H. R. Gupta and Ganda Singh had established themselves as well-known Sikh historians.

Bu and large, history in Asian countries continues to be all about events affecting the kings, presidents and prime ministers. On the other extreme, the American culture - transplanted from the European cultures want lineage and continuity of ideas and persons in newly discovered lands. They are obsessed with 'history making' - from putting the historical markers on the roadsides, hiking trails to the world's largest museums of natural history etc. Anthropology and archeology (space, land and marine) are corollaries of this mind set, as these disciplines have no roots in any other cultures; past or modern.

Until recently, the history of India existed mostly in the form of diaries written by the British officers posted in India and by Indian scholars under the British influence. They have perpetuated the distorted facts on India. It even challenged me, while I was still in junior high. Because of the curricular restrictions, history and mathematics could not be studied together in college. However, I have continued to explore history on my own for the rest of my life.

During the last ten years, several articles and **Reflections** on different aspects of history have been written up. The preciseness in thought, due to my mathematical background, gives a unique dimension to my discovering and analysis of historical facts - their interpretation and relevant connections with the present.

Now at my age, nearing 70, I understand why history is considered for the wise, and how history makes one wiser. On Day Number One, in a diagnostic history quiz, I challenged my graduate students to bring any piece of record on their great grandparents. I don't know even the name of my great grandparents! But the family record keepers, in Hindu holy cities, have been maintaining the ancestral records of the pilgrims for centuries. My father once told me that a full-fledged genealogical tree of our family exists; it and goes back to 1560. But I have not seen it.

Last week, one student brought excerpts of his great grandmother's life written 80 years ago. It was a joy to go through them. Another student brought meticulous genealogical notebooks that her great grandmother researched and traced back to the 16th century. She sought assistance from the genealogical archives of the Mormon Church headquarters in Salt Lake City, Utah.

I really want my students to have an unforgettable hands-on experience on an aspect history of the last 50 years. A span of 50 years, in the life of an institution, is a speck in the time line as compared with 'recorded' history going back to 2500 years. Students are only used Google searches, or running to a library. **To be able to find a source of information is only searching, but not doing basic research!**

UNLV was founded in 1957. Its one-year long celebrations will begin in fall semester. To make an 'historic' contribution, I decided to discover construct the history of our Mathematical Sciences Department from every conceivable aspect - faculty, students, programs, curriculum etc. The project has been divided into ten smaller projects and assigned to the ten students registered in the course according to their interest and background.

History and mathematics have one thing in common. It is easy to pose a good question, but very difficult to find an answer. The contrast is, whereas, there is little disagreement amongst mathematicians over a proof of a theorem, but if two historians agree on a theory, then one is faking it, or taking a free ride. **Incidentally, discoveries and inventions define the homosapiens from the rest of species**.

(Feb 04, 2007)

NOTES AND COMMENTS

1. Satish, I really enjoyed your take on history. Perhaps a tendency to want to record events for future generations is one thing that differentiates (to use a mathematical term) humans from animals. Of course animals, in a sense, record history in their genes. My son, Eric asked me to send you his greetings. **Dave Emerson**

RAMIFICATIONS OF THE *DERA SACHA SAUDA*

Whether one examines the history of Punjab 60 years after India's independence or 60 years before it, the social and political turmoils are perpetual. My US Indian friends, coming from the states of Tamilnad, Karnataka and Kerala, often have no clues about Punjab since the southern states stayed relatively calm. For the last ten days, the most recent crisis of Punjab has spilled outside, wherever the followers of the sect, *Dera Sacha Sauda* (means **House of True Deal**) have their centers. Its headquarters are located in Sirsa (Haryana) bordering with Punjab.

The *Dera Sacha Sauda*, founded 60 years ago, is a spin-off another sect, *Radha Swami* (Beas, Punjab). Yes, there is at least one more parallel sect, called *Radha Swami* (Dayalbagh, UP). Theoretically, it can go to minus infinity in time! A few years ago, I researched into the history of these sects in the region covering parts of western India and eastern Pakistan. It is traceable to the time of the first Sikh Guru, Nanak Dev. He had two sons and a devout devotee, Baba Buddah. But none was spiritually qualified enough to succeed him. He chose a newer devotee, Lahina and re-named him Angad (limb of the body/Nanak) as the second Guru. It may be added that the term *Sacha Sauda,* as a religious phrase, was first popularized by Guru Nanak. This name was probably given to the first gurdwara. Initially, the Sikh gathering places were called *dhramshalas*!

The leadership succession in any organization - whether political, business, social, or spiritual, is always contentious, as it means yielding 'power' over the people and controlling resources. **The lust for power distinguishes human beings from other creatures.** Guru Nanak's two sons did not protest against his intension as long as he was alive. But the diehard followers of his sons continued to fan their human weakness for power and the first offshoot was known as *Udaasi*.

After all, the close associates of the leaders, in any walk of life, also stand to gain power and prestige. It is an organizational theory too. That is how the new branches of any growing organization are born - like in a tree. However, every growing 'organism' has a limit. It is fair to conjecture that throughout the Sikh history; at least 20 splinter groups have come out of the mainstream of Sikhism.

The power behind an organization comes from its adherents. Larger the number, better is the its business. Temptation and coercion for conversion are common in major religions like - Islam and Christianity. All the offshoots of Sikhism proclaim the love of God through *NAAM*, meditation and service to the poor - the billboard slogans of every sect and religion. However, the Sikhism is unique. Its strength rests on great personal sacrifices of the Gurus, the battles they fought for the new faith, and Sikh masses butchered in *GHALUGHARA,* the Sikh Holocaust (1716-38). Greater the sacrifice, greater is the purification and unity amongst the survivors.

The temporal authority of the SGPC (Shiromini Gurdwara Prabhandhak Committee) comes from the readiness of the Sikhs to die for their religion. The other offshoots have little history of sacrifices! The Jews provide a recent example of collective suffering and annihilation during WWII. It ultimately led to unity in Jewish Diaspora, and Israel was created for the Jews in 1948. History of sacrifices always inspires the masses. Collectively as well as individually, **if you are not willing to die for a cause, then you are not living for any purpose either**.

One may question the centralized authority of the SGPC. Again, the power behind the edits- whether of the Sikh *Hukamnamas* or Muslim *Fatwas* comes from fierce unity of the believers. On the other hand, the resolutions passed by the Hindu organizations - like Shankaracharya *MATHAS* (4) or 'Arya Pratinidhi Sabha (2 or 3!) are not even noticed by the media. They carry no executable religious authority over the Hindus. Hinduism encourages ultimate freedom of thought and practice, and hence for this dis-unity, the Hindus would continue to pay heavy price for their collective freedom. Unity demands sacrifices; not talks and talks.

There is a global dimension to this conflict between the Sikhs and followers of *Dera Sacha Sauda*. It may appear like Shia and Sunni clashes amongst the Muslims. After the 9/11, the worldwide resurgence of Islam, particularly in Kashmir and Bangladesh, has been creating communal tension in the border states of India. For 20 years (1975-95), Pakistan fully exploited the Khalistan movement in Punjab. Eventually, the diehard Hindus and Sikhs realized that the future of Punjab is better secured and served under the combine of Akali Dal (Badal) and BJP. If they can rule the state for a generation, then the Greater Punjab of Maharaja Ranjit Singh can be envisioned!

Most human conflicts arise from various proprietary rights. The conflicts also stem from the '**Spiritual Rights**' of faiths. People understand and honor the publishing **Copyrights**. However, after 100 years, any print material comes in a public domain for free reproduction. During the last 25 years, the western nations have imposed **Intellectual Rights** to protect the fruits of their fundamental researches. Developing countries are big time losers. For example, India has lost the rights over the use of some chemical compounds found in their common *NEEM* trees and (turmeric) *HALDI* plants. It is amusing to recall that a US based religious organization tried to patent the word *Yoga*, but the request was denied.

The **Dera Sacha Sauda** is embroiled with the Sikhs over the use of some '**Spiritual Rights**'. Huzoor Maharaj Sant Gurmeet Ram Rahim Singh Ji (born, 1967) is the present sectarian leader of the **Dera Sacha Sauda** (since 1990). He is pulling lot of gullible followers with his name alone. Typically, Gurmeet and Singh are Sikh names; Ram, Hindu; and Rahim, Muslim. It is not clear from the available sources, if this was his birth name or connivingly adopted after his succession. He has been 'charged' by the Sikh clergy for blasphemy by dressing and performing ceremonies like the 10th Guru Gobind Singh performed. In India, where emotions run high, it takes small fake incendiary act of sacrilege to inflame the masses.

Having grown up in Bathinda, the heartland of Punjab, I remember stories behind communal disturbances. One would hear a dead pig thrown in a mosque compound, cow's head in a Hindu temple, and pack of cigarettes and damaged pages of Guru Grant Sahib in a gurdwara. Immediately, the communal clashes were reported. I am sure once Gurmeet Ram Rahim Singh explains his stand before the Akal Takhat, the public fury will quickly subside and peace restored in Punjab, but for a while.

(May 22, 2007/Oct, 2011)

NOTES AND COMMENTS

1. I think some of your research in this article is flawed. *Naam* did not originate with Guru Nanak nor did religious sects start with Guru Nanak. Sacha Sauda did not originate as name of Gurdwara and Gurdwara was not a name coined by Sikh although it was popularized. Radha Swami mat did not originate in Beas.
    Sikhs and Muslims have one thing in common and that is both are fanatics and when it comes to so called religion they are immune to reasoning. Both religions offer no freedom; both are totally intolerant. SGPC and Congress are also using these gullible followers (Sikhs) for their political gains. **Rahul**

2. Bhai Shri Satish Ji, Sasneh Namaste! You have certainly taken a great pains to write the under noted facts of history & the causes of past & present crisis & unrest in Punjab; **you deserve 100's & 1000's of Congratulations for such a wonderful detailed account of the facts. Regards, sincerely yours, S.C. Gupta.**

3. Excellent analysis. **B S Yadav**

4. Thank u...informative piece...religions have always divided people, they have never united them..."We have enough religions to hate man, hardly any religions to love man" **Abraham**
    I wrote: Religion that unites more, also divides more of them. While united people accomplish a lot, but their damage is also wider.

5. My dear Bhatnagar Sahib, Namaskar, The said reflection was more of information than actual reflection of/on Sacha or otherwise sauda. I am a liberal Sikh but even than I felt that this man had insulted the Sikhs by his 'acting as the tenth Guru' and saints do not have to be so adamant as to refuse

to simply apologise for the sacrilege. If a simple word 'sorry' could have saved the state of Punjab from so much of anxiety and apprehension why he could not utter this simple word. There also seems to be very strong political angle as being a non-congress govt. in Punjab has always invited trouble from the Cong govt at centre. First it was Nirankaris then it was Bhinderwala and now this. However in your reflection your mention Guru Nanak as only Nanak Dev and the sauda man as Hazoor et al. and ending with a Ji. This is an immediate reaction after reading your reflection just once I shall re-read it later. **Jagjeet Singh**

I wrote: That full name was taken from a website. It becomes a parody when he is referred again at the end! This came about after reading the online **Tribune** a couple of times. My thrust is on the growing concept of *"Spiritual Rights"* in intersecting domains of sects. Just like the powerful US had the "*Intellectual Rights*" approved through the UN and now enforced over the world, likewise the united militant religions whether Sikhism or Islam will always prevail in such disputes. Good or bad, is for the people to understand. Being in the eye of the storm at the moment, I hope you do re-read and think it over.

6. I am impressed with your knowledge of the history on the subject. **Inder Singh**

FROM THE BY-LANES OF HISTORY

"Who was King Ashok?" Its answer, before the year 1750, may have drawn blanks from the masses! Yes, today's, the so-called great Indian Emperor was totally forgotten from the public psyche and pages of history. It was the ravage of time since 250 BC, and more due to the political and cultural subjugation of the Hindus over the last 1000 years.

However, it should be understood that the legends of the epics - Ramayana and Mahabharata, have been victorious over the mighty Time. That speaks of their transcendent divine nature. In fact, recent political controversy over a Ramayana episode (over Raam's Bridge), smacks puerile and is totally irrelevant.

A few days ago, I caught sight of a booklet on the edicts of Emperor Ashok. It turned out to be a well-researched publication (2006) of the Vipashyanaa Research Foundation. The Foundation is a part of a global organization started by Satyanarain Goenka in 1975 to spread *Vipashyanaa*, a meditation technique. It is like Transcendental Meditation (TM) of the 1960s - popularized by Maharishi Mahesh Yogi, and such other meditation techniques that periodically sprout out of India.

Like the archaeological ruins of Mohenjo-Daro and Harappa civilization, the caves of Ajanta and Ellora in India, and Cambodian Angkor Wat, the largest complex of Hindu temples in the world, and many more, were discovered and preserved in the museums by their European colonizers. Now I feel intellectually indebted to them! At times, life is topsy-turvy. The present generations of European colonizers feel remorse for the exploitation and acts of cruelty committed by their forefathers in the colonies. Last month, there was a big political furor when a group of 20 British landed in India to visit some sites in Lucknow associated with Indian uprising in 1857. The British called it a Mutiny, but Indians call it as India's First War of Independence.

Amongst a few fascinating facts that emerge is of an English priest, Tiffenthaller credited for the discovery of the first stone pillar edict in Delhi region, in 1750. I was really impressed at the amazing curiosity of the European mind set. Here is a man assigned in India to spread the Gospel of Christ. Mind it, that East India Company had no political hold on any part of India until 1757. It was perhaps the first 'public' trading company in the world; Adam/Eve of today's Microsoft, IBM and Reliance.

It took many more years to decipher the language on this rock. The credit for it goes to an English scholar, James Princep, in 1837. Out of Ashok's 84,000 various edicts in stones, only 42 are known to survive! Eventually, Indian scholars followed the British in the gigantic project of discovering these chiseled writings and deciphering them. The colonial scholars are like vultures that run to the carcass after the kill by the lions. Intellectual mindset in India has a long way to break into the stratosphere of Nobel Prize caliber. Great institutions, public and private, are alone the nurseries of great ideas.

(Oct 13, 2007/India)

NOTES AND COMMENTS

MUSINGS OF MANDU MONUMENTS

December 11 falling on Tuesday, my mind was looking for new angles in Mandu history. Tuesdays, being days of total fasting, are helpful in bringing points in focus. For solid six hours, I walked up and down the ancient monuments. At times, I wondered and questioned my purpose of such close examinations. Nevertheless, new places generate newer ideas. Though it is only 100 KM from Indore, yet a private taxi took 2.5 hours. There is no other convenient transportation to, perhaps, the largest fort city of India!

The city had several huge security gates during its heydays, but a few now standing are in dilapidated conditions. The topography of rolling hills, deep gorges carved by Narmada River, lakes, valleys and plateaus are all compressed in a perimeter of 45 KM. It is beautiful! Mandu traces its history to 500 AD. The Archeological Survey of India (ASI) has a small museum of excavated artifacts. The legendary Hindu Raja Bhoj was one of its rulers. The Parmar Dynasty reigned over the region through the end of the 13th century.

Seeking independence from Delhi Sultanates was common feature of Muslim governors of the provinces. As soon as political instability was observed at in Delhi or Agra, the local chiefs revolted. Since the 18th century, the French, English and Portuguese also took advantage of unstable Mughal rulers. No Hindu king ever tried to re-claim their own country! King Hem Chandra (Hemu) is the only exception - reigning over the present regions of Haryana, UP and Rajasthan surrounding Delhi. He challenged Akbar and lost his head in the second battle of Panipat, in 1556.

A popular Mandu legend is of Rani Rupmati - made famous by a movie shot at her palace here. Her romantic associations with Baz Bahadur, Akbar and Jahangir speak of a sense of history of Indian public! My curiosity was to know if a Hindu prince who ever went after her. **The empire builders go after the most beautiful women, and conversely**.

The monuments have undergone changes under different rulers - the Hindus, Muslims, and Europeans. The lotus motifs on the exterior walls indicate the influence of Hindu architecture. **My mind was possessed with the continued glorification of Afghani and Mughal rulers of Mandu**. What would the present Afghanis think of the Hindus after visiting Mandu? It reminded me of a Hollywood movie, set in a small US town, where a young man raped a girl. To add insult to this ghastly act, he often strutted in front of her house. One day, the girl picked up her father's gun and blasted him away!

During this spectacle of monuments, I wondered at the mission of the ASI. It is stupid to preserve the monuments that rub salt over the wounds of the Hindus.

Though only one of the seven storeys is left of the tower symbolizing the victory of Mahmud Khilji over Rana Kumbha, but what is a point of its edification? Now, I see some merits in the implosion of the 2000-year Buddha statues by Talibans, the new rulers of Afghanistan in March, 2001. A new national identity arises only over the ashes of the old eyesores.

(Dec 13, 2007/India)

NOTES AND COMMENTS

It is simply elevating and inspiring. I am now saving these treasures. **Sham**

HISTORIC SITES CRY OUT!

Two weeks ago, I climbed up nearly 1000 steps - starting from an elevation of 13,000'. It was wrenching. By pausing to catch breath and taking one step at a time, I made it. The top was a flattened mountain - with ancients Spanish structures on three sides and a small restaurant facing an ocean size, Lake Titicaca (Bolivia) on the fourth. Everyone else went in for lunch. Taking out my candies and beer, I sat next to a native Aymara couple. The woman was spinning yarn on a hand-held spindle and man weaving a woolen cap. Their small stall of gift items was set up on a piece of pavement - an ageless scenario. The Spanish conquistadores have come and gone!

Suddenly, the open courtyard was filled with groups of tourists. Everyone was European with the exception of a couple of Japanese and Korean - a new class of rich nations in Asia. Bolivia, Peru and scores of South American countries were a part of a vast Spanish Empire through the middle of the 19th century, when gradually the colonies started winning freedom.

My thoughts were about the thinking going on in the minds of the young tourists from Spain, as they looked at the colonial buildings, architecture, and history. Some of them must be filled with pride at the adventurous and fighting spirits of their forefathers who risked their lives in crossing the Atlantic in the 15th century! It was heroism to the power n! Yes, a few of them may feel remorse for the cruelty inflicted upon the Incas and Aztecs. Overall, there is no question, that the young Europeans must feel inspired for undertaking unchartered courses in their present lives.

As a Hindu, originally from India, I tried to fathom my feelings. What am I looking here in Tequile, an island in Lake Titicaca? Where is my connection point? Suddenly, I felt out of place. I wished I could also take some cultural pride in a Hindu Empire. There is, and there is not!

In Oct, 2007, I took a sightseeing tour of Delhi, India's most famous political city for millennia. Though I have seen all the touristy places many a times since the age of 10, but you never see the same thing again in monuments filled with history. One of the stops was at the Qutab Minar, a 238' red-stone tower - started in the 12th century by Afghani Qutbuddin Aibak, to commemorate his victory over the Hindu rulers. At age 68, I could not stand its sight. I myself wanted to blast it away the way the Afghani Talibans blew away nearly 2000-year old Buddhist monuments in Baniyan, in March, 2001. In Dec, 2007, this anger had surged again in Maundu Fort (near Indore), where I witnessed an Afghani Khilji victory tower built after defeating the Rajputs. These historic monuments rub salt in the wounds of the Hindus that will/should never heal!

Whenever the Afghanis, Turkish, Arabs, or the Muslims from other countries visit such historical sites in India, their hearts must be filled with pride at the achievements of their forefathers. Have the conditions in India changed? No! The Hindus did not fight then, and now non-aggression is a government policy! In brochures after brochures, published by the state and central tourism departments, the foreign invaders and rulers are hailed. It is revolting sickness. **Free nation revise their histories. Only cowards glorify their enemies**. These eye sore historic structures should not be preserved by the Archaeological Survey of India.

(July 02, 2008/Oct, 2011)

NOTES AND COMMENTS

1. This is a good one. **Ved P. Sharma**

2. Hello Uncle, You are exactly right. We were in Qutab Minar this past December and a crew from Turkmenistan and Kazakhstan was there filming a documentary. They were very proud of the fact of the people who built this were of central Asian origins --- to a point of smugness. I find the ambivalent Hindu attitude towards this very disconcerting. It is almost that they are hiding themselves behind ideas like pluralism/secularism. **Bharat**

3. Satish Bhatnagar Sahib; All your reflections are excellent and never go unread by me. These are your practical experience/ interpretation of events and facts of life so well and simply presented that I felt guilty not writing you back my appreciation now which I felt like doing when I received your fist e-mail.; Thanks for writing and keep up with excellent work of enlightening your readers.; All the best to you and your family both of us.; **Mohan Khare**

4. On visiting Qutub Minar one can easily see statues and pictures of Jain social and religious symbols within the premises. Qutub Minar is on the Aravali Range of mountains and a number of old Jain temples are there is the surrounding areas because in old days Jain temples were built on dry hills. So, in all probability, Qutub Minar has also been built by demolishing an important Jain temple. Temples used to be the centre of social, cultural and religious life of people in India. So, by demolishing these temples the invaders achieved two objectives. First, they would destroy the Hindu cultural fabric and second, it gave them a ready-made ground for building their own Mosques. They would not demolish the temple completely but only so much as was necessary for converting it into Mosque. Thousands of important old temples were demolished by the Muslim invaders in India over centuries.

Slowly and systematically all these facts are being taken out of history books. The future generations may not be able to know about it at all.

As if it were not enough, Muslim rule is being glorified in a number of ways. Just to take an example, the most important roads of New Delhi converge at India Gate. Naturally, their names are--Akbar Road, Shahjahan Road, Humanyu Road, Aurangzeb Road, etc.

Government is not the only entity responsible for this. I think we people are like that. In Jodha Akbar, as you mentioned, Akbar is portrayed as a romantic hero who dots on Jodha. Taking various facts from History and mixing them with some fiction a movie has been made which a large number of Indians saw and formed their own opinions regarding Akbar and Muslim rule in India. But has the complete truth about Akbar's personality been shown? Akbar had a harem and people know it. But do people know that a separate Brigade of his army was kept just to move around the country and capture most good-looking women for their king? I feel, such things should also be shown in the movie to make the picture complete.

Cores of rupees are spent by the Government of India on Haj every year. But a few acres of land allotted to the Amarnath Yatra Board for creating facilities for the Hindu pilgrims proved too costly of the government and the country!

All this may be because of our tendency to resign to faith and say--whatever is being done is as per God's own will. We never take action ourselves. At most we are looking forward to some Avtaar to come and redress our grievances.
Raman Mittal

I wrote: "*At most we are looking forward to some Avtaar to come and redress our grievances*." That has been the bane and Hindus' greatest curse for a millennium; depending on others; natural or supernatural. We, the Hindus from the lowest common denominator, have to believe in ourselves as the Avtaars!

Have you ever pondered at the success of the US conceived countless support groups like Cancer support group, Stroke, and so on? Or, like the Weight watchers, Gamblers Anonymous, Toastmasters, Alcoholic Anonymous etc?

There is no leader in any group. Just like the concept of 'Guru in Granth Sahib', that works. Each member has to adhere to a simple principle of never criticizing any member during the meeting. Two, say at least one word of genuine encouragement and support. The rest is garnishing! With mutual support, the ordinary persons become extraordinary in every group! That is all, we, the Hindus have to start in our daily lives.

For practical purposes, go to a temple once a month or two, sit there for a while, give generous support, and discuss issues in the premises. Above all, celebrate all family functions in the temple premises. The elusive Hindu unity shall emerge sooner than later!

5. Great comments from arm chair militants. Most of the observations are distortions of the truth and then there is more to the truth then presented in the article. If someone really wants to service Hinduism then they should propagate the Greatness of Hinduism and its philosophy in their view. Spreading hate will not get to many followers. If you want to be proud of Hindu civilization then go to South East Asia and see Hindu influence. Angkor Vat is a prime example. **Rahul (MBBS)**

6. Dear Sir; I am in full agreement with your emotions. However it is not that Hindus did not fight then. We, generations after generations have been taught a falsified history. You will feel happy that the Qutub Minar was not constructed by Aibak but it dates back to Gupta period. Some books are there about this and nobody has challenged it either. It's high time that true version of history be taught to us. Since we don't know many things we feel as you very rightly felt. With warm regards. **Parag (Delhi Travel Agent)**

THE SHADOWS OF SERIAL BOMBINGS

The seismic waves of Islamic serial bombings in India sear through my entire being, despite sitting 12,000 miles away from it. Their frequency has been increasing over the last couple of years. Earlier, single bomb blasts used to be more powerful - requiring more careful logistics. As a matter of fact, the explosions in remote eastern states and border areas do not even get reported. The local Hindu print media, being so scared, that the news is never picked by national and foreign wire services, unless a powerful lobby backs it up.

Ahmedabad, the site of yesterday's 16 serial bombings, is the state capital of Gujarat having the fastest growing economy in India. A couple of days ago, an explosion shook Banglore, the capital of Karnataka and first cyber city of India. Last month, a blast bloodied Jaipur, the capital of Rajasthan, known as the Pink City of India. These cities draw visitors from all over the world. Consequently, the perpetrators get instant worldwide publicity. These explosions throw off the administration and weaken the morale of the Hindus – the main objectives of the perpetrators.

After all, who are behind these bombings? Why are they on rise in India? Is there an individual, organization, or an ideology behind them? **There is never a crisp answer in the world of Hindu politics and social unrest**. Predominantly, it is ideological. Paul Huntington's thesis, on the clash of civilizations, is meritorious. He looks at western civilization, based on Christian beliefs of Western Europe since the 17th century, when the Islamic empires began to decline.

Huntington divides the world into eight civilizations, but only three are majors. His 1993 research paper and subsequent 1996 book are the most widely quoted political works in recent times. Huntington analyzed and foresaw the clash of Islamic and Christian 'worlds'. It may be largely a 're-conquering' of Spain and parts of Europe lost to the Christians. The same mindset is taking place in India. Before the advent of the English in India, various Muslim tribes - Mughals, Arabs, Iranians, Turks and Afghans had carved out northern and central India.

For centuries, the Hindus, in India, have been pulverized by exemplary retribution for putting up even a token resistance. More Hindu holocausts have taken place in India than perhaps in the rest of the world combined. The net result is that since the 18th century, the Hindus have accepted foreign Muslim rulers as their own! In present history and literature textbooks, the Hindus 'laud' the Muslim rulers and preserve their monuments - including victory towers over the Hindus!

Despite Gandhi's efforts to keep India united at independence, one third went out in the creation of theocratic Pakistan. The English ruled for over 100 years, but they literally left India in 1947 – only leaving behind the converted Hindu

Christians. However, it is different in the case of the Muslims. The Islamic canons of Darrul Islam and Darrul Haram amount to the Islamization of the entire world. The Muslims in India make nearly 13% of the present Indian population vs. 3% Christians. **Behind the chaos of serial bombings lingers an Islamic vision of recovering and ruling the two thirds of India again**. How can these bombings take place without the support of some Islamic forces right in India? Any Hindu, saying it, is branded as fascist!

Unfortunately, the Hindu psyche about war has not changed over centuries. In fact, grossly misunderstood Gandhian non-violence has made the Hindu masses, army generals and intellectuals allergic to wars, as it happened after King Ashok. Many peace-loving Gandhians were extinguished during the Muslim rules. The martyrdoms of the Sikh Gurus, during the Mughals, are perfect examples. It has been debated that Gandhi's 'weapon of non-violence' would have failed against Hitler or Stalin.

Any isolated rise of Hindu militancy whether in 1992 (Barbari Masjid), 2000 (Bombay), or 2002 (Godhara/Gujarat) is met with 100 times by the world Islamic forces. The Islamic-Sino axis has made the eastern states of India very porous with Chinese occupying a million square miles after the 1962 war. In the northwest state of Jammu and Kashmir, the minority Hindu population has been totally ethnically cleansed. It has been percolating down along the border states. On the contrary, many cities of Punjab, with zero Muslim population in 1947, have now thousands of them. The Muslim population in my hometown Bathinda has gone up from zero to 30,000!

A side bar question is why India has always declined Israeli offers for establishing cultural, political, or scientific ties? Indian governments have remained under pressure for going against the Arabs. The Hindus have not come out of the Muslim fear psyche. The serial bombings are linked with two major policy shifts - India getting nuclearly closer to the US. Also, the US and India can tilt the balance of Sino-Islamic axis. It means a check on the Islamic influence.

The Bush II Administration will go down in history for taking upon the global challenge of Islamic terrorism into its breeding places. The Clinton Administration failed to foresee the 1993 bombing of the World Trade Center, 2000 attack on USS Cole in Yemen and 2001 **9/11 Attack on America**. In seven years, Bush has clamped on terrorist attacks on the US soil. Muslim terrorism has awakened the fundamental Christians credited for Bush's winning the 2nd term.

Furthermore, the US has tightened its internal security by new legislation and overhaul of intelligence agencies that India fails miserably. Bush rightly took this war in Afghanistan, but he failed to give Truman's nuclear punch to the mountain tunnels of Bora Bora. Consequently, the leaders of Al Qaeda and Taliban escaped into Pakistan's Northwest state adjoining Kashmir.

Had India joined the Bush's 2001 worldwide call against terrorism, "with USA or against USA", the Indian forces through Kashmir would have squeezed out these Islamic militants sheltered across the Pak border. The Vajpayee Government missed an historic opportunity of solving Kashmir and related problems. Presently, the Hindus Diaspora cannot protect themselves.

Gone are the days of open battlefields - like Kurukshetra and Panipat. Also, are gone the days of rural Gorilla warfares. Modern warfares are urban like sporadic bombings, ethnic cleansing, biological, and high tech from within and without. Unless 80% Hindus in India realize the need for collective consciousness, the history is not going to favor them. Currently, there is not even a single block of 10% Hindus of all strata that openly protects their heritage in their own land. The escalated serial bombings will eventually implode the Hindus from within. The Hindus, locally, must cultivate and nurture visionary leaders in religion and politics for galvanization. Otherwise, the political freedom, won in 1947, is likely to be lost again – long before realizing its fruits.

(July 27, 2008/Oct, 2011)

NOTES AND COMMENTS

1. Good reflection. Regards **Mohan Sharma**

2. Dear Shri Satish Chandra Ji, Many thanks for your excellent mail under the subject: **"The shadows of serial bombings"** received through one of the Yahoo Groups. Your analysis is impeccable; and calls for immediate follow-up action. I share your feelings about the dismal situation. I am sure that *Sanatan Dharma,* commonly known as Hinduism, will certainly survive and prevail because of the noble efforts of persons like you. I have no words to express my thanks and gratitude for your services to Hindu society.

    From your e-mail ID, it appears that you are based in the United States. How I wish that persons like you were in Bharat to lead and strengthen Hindu society! It will be a pleasure to remain in touch with you. More on hearing from you. With thanks and regards, **J.G. Arora**

PERILS TO INDEPENDENCE

"I wish I could join the Independence Day program on 15th," e-mailed S. N. Subba Rao, the undisputed social integrator of India. It stirred a pile of my thoughts. Here is a man, nearly 80 year old, and is so keen about India's Independence Day! For most Indians, it is another day that comes and goes. He is actually beyond having seen the struggles and sacrifices for freedom. In order to protect it, the new generations have to be aware of it.

However, my mind took a U-turn, and I said to myself that concern for India should not be a one-day political ritual. For a few, everyday reminds them of independence. This idea hit - like a sixer (a home run), in my heart. Today, being 15th August, by chance, I attended its celebration in two places. The first one was at 9 AM, on the campus of University of Nevada Las Vegas, organized by Indian Students Association. The second one at 8 PM, held in a city park, was organized by the Friends of India Club.

At the Campus celebration, I was invited to say a few words. Addressing nearly 50 graduate students, I recollected my first and unforgettable experience of US Independence Day of July 04, 1969, later followed by India's on Aug 15. From public enthusiasm, it appeared as if the US had won its freedom only a couple of years ago!

Freedom to the US came through the barrel of the gun with heavy sacrifices in blood. It toughened the Americans in their march for new territorial victories. Thirteen colonies of 1776 hardly covered 1/10 of what the US is today! Since the adoption of its constitution in 1789, it has become the greatest nation in the history of mankind.

On the contrary, India has been shrinking since 1947. It lost 1/3 of its territory in the creation of Pakistan, as a price of her freedom. Two weeks ago, China protested on Prime Minister Manmohan Singh's visit to Arunachal Pradesh, an eastern state of India! China claims on it on while occupying 100,000 square KM of Indian territory since 1962. Most Indian leaders and generals are not even bothered. Sadly, the textbooks do not mention it!

Under present protest rallies of Kashmiri Muslims for freedom and support of the militant Muslims organizations of the world, the PM does not dare visiting Srinagar. Hardly 1% of Indian lawmakers have visited Kashmir since 1989, when the urban warfare of Hindu ethnic cleansing started. Now Bangladesh has been pursuing Hindu ethnic cleansing.

Anything won can be lost, if one is not willing to die for it. Exhorting the students, I said, earning a master's or PhD alone should not be a goal of coming to the US. Indians have to learn from Americans how to fight and protect their heritage. However, the rise and fall great civilizations portend that all kinds of people entering into the US will soon make this great nation porous. It happened to India 1000 years ago. The golden sparrow, that India was known to the world, became a kick ball for the invaders and marauders from all over the world for a thousand year. That is what Aug 15, 2008 has meant to me.

(Aug 15, 2008)

NOTES AND COMMENTS

1. Dear Satish, A very powerful reflection today. Wow! I'm so impressed with the passion and the facts. Thanks, **Dutchie**

2. Satish, How true! **Bob** (Gilbert)

3. Nana, this is such a disheartening way to think of India and its independence! **Anjali**

IS IT A MELTDOWN OF ......?

Today, before covering **Synthetic Division** in a standard *College Algebra* course (MATH 124), I quizzed the students on a simple long division problem, namely, $x-2$) $2x^3-5x^2-2x+5$. For the fun of it, I also added a problem on division of integers, namely, 2 7 6) 1 9 3 7 6 9. The simple instruction was to find the quotients and remainders in each case without the use of a calculator. Being a bonus quiz, it had no negative effect on the grades. Out of 31 students, only one got the algebraic division right, and ten had no idea on the 5th Grade arithmetic division!

The prerequisites for this course are a remedial course, *Intermediate Algebra* (MATH 096) or **three years** of high school math at the level of algebra, or above. As a matter of fact, long division is covered in another remedial course, *Elementary Algebra* (MATH 095). These remedial courses, not existing in the US colleges 50 years ago, are now standard. At UNLV, they do not count towards graduation. Several sections of remedial courses are offered each session to meet the growing demands of all kinds of students. Besides servicing, it is a good business too.

Math instructors commonly share such stories to mutual amusement or disappointment. But this scenario struck a deeper cord in my mind. Is it a meltdown of mathematics corresponding to the meltdown of the US economy making headlines for the last couple of years? The housing industry is the engine of the US economy. The affordable housing was so much politicized that individuals and institutions got loans upon loans 100 times of what they were qualified for.

The closure of some name banks including 158-year old Lehman Brothers made me think of iconic universities - like Harvard and Stanford, closing their doors one day. For the last 20 years, college education has prominently entered into presidential elections. It must be affordable! That means giving out loans to undeserved students, softer admission standards, but expecting higher retention and graduation rates. It is a recipe for busting the great American higher education.

The writings on the wall have been for the last two decades. In 34 years at UNLV, I have noted falling standards due to students' greater commitment to their jobs, families, and social obligations over the courses. No matter how enthusiastic one is about teaching, but encountering such students semester after semester, is bound to lower one's mathematical abilities too.

Affordable housing, affordable college education, affordable medicine, affordable insurance etc, are buzz words of greed and extreme socialism. The American Dream was realized with hard work and honesty. It is becoming a social responsibility.

Uncle Sam must provide it. The last straw is the 'affordable' immigration and US citizenship. It is ironic that during this election campaign, no presidential candidate has uttered even a single word against the illegals in the US.

A lesson of history is that every great nation and civilization first collapses from within. We may be witnessing the beginning of meltdown of America. Despite inevitability of the fall of a great civilization, it can be slowed down by men and women of vision and self-sacrifice.

(Sep 30, 2008)

NOTES AND COMMENTS

1. The civilization collapses when its leaders do not have vision but on top of it are obstinate. There is a big difference between resolve and obstinacy. Current administration's policies on all fronts domestic or foreign have done irreparable damage to USA. History will look at Bush to be the President who led to rapid start of the end of American Empire. Even McCain and Palin in their debates try to run away from Bush record. They are becoming agents for change from what, Bush policies of course. How sad.

    Unbridled Capitalism and greed are also leading to collapse of this country. The subprime loans were not given because of socialistic idea but because of greed. There needs to be balance between capitalism and socialism. Both systems have pros and cons. When one lives in a community a society then socialism does play a role. People on right give all kinds of socialism a bad name to grind their axe. **Rahul**

2. Yikes....I have copied this to Ann McDonough**.... Neal Smatresk**

3. I'm so profoundly grateful we have the Academic Success Center!!! **Ann Macdonough**

4. Agreed. But I wonder if standards have dropped perceptively or our memories are imprecise. When I joined UNLV in 1971, Vietnam veterans were crowding back - and they were a bad lot; standards seemed abysmally low to me. Students' capabilities and performance seemed to rise slowly over the ensuing years. I wonder now if my standards had dropped at the time or if students got better. I suspect the latter. I started teaching upper division and graduate courses and continued over the years, then in my last year, I taught freshmen and sophomores and their lack of preparation and plain dumbness was a shock. It gave me a retrospective appreciation of the whole educational process. **Robert W Moore**

5. Beautifully written--I couldn't agree more! I've seen the same thing, but in less years! **Aaron Harris**

HISTORY, ANTIQUES AND HEIRLOOMS

The scars of poverty and scarcities are known to run deep in individual consciousness. By and large, in a deprived society, many customs and traditions are explainable in terms of paucities of life. It applies not just to objects, but in intellectual matters too. The study of history, its importance, and its awareness is a privilege of the rich and powerful. Ability to distinguish antiques from trinkets defines a culture. Antique collection makes no sense for the poor.

For the last one week, my wife has been sorting out articles for a charity organization. She pulled out her fur coat - saying that it has not been used for years. It was bought from a fur coat shop in the **Caesars Palace, Hotel and Casino**, thirty years ago. I was at an age, when men wrapped their women in furs, jewelries and perfumes. Is it worth keeping? Yes, by every count. My father bought a fur coat for my mother. After 60 years, she passed it over to my only sister. Apart from associated memories, it describes the fur quality, sewing art, and workmanship of a bygone era.

Heirlooms set the rich apart from the poor. They are passed on from the parents to children to grandchildren. In the USA, there are regular movies and shows depicting their importance. In life, the riches and poverty come and go in cycles. It is a human condition, and applies to nations and civilizations too. From the top of the world, they are hurled down into abyss of oblivion.

I always oppose the sale or exchange of a gold ornament – whether for buying a new one for its design or/and fashion. My wife's argument has been that why to keep it, if she was never going to wear it. This has been going on for the last 45 years of our marriage. Her thinking is grounded in a popular scenario depicting Indian life, still commonly seen. A poor woman bathes wearing her sari since that is all she has. How can she wear it again?

Last November, in Delhi, I saw an unforgettable exhibition on Nizam's (Hyderabad) jewelry. Some items go back to more than 200 years. Never ever, a piece was sold, as it meant stigma to the family name of the great Nizam. Each piece has a history of its maker, purchaser, and the occasion marked by it. What does it do? Such events are itched in the young minds of the rulers-to-be for perpetuating their rules. All Mughal kings, big and small, from Babur to Akbar to Bahadur Shah Zafar, have left royal chronicles of their rules.

Two months ago, I finished reading, *The White Mughals*, an incredible mix of history, sociology, anthropology, and romance of the 18th century India. It captures a period of declining Mughals and rising British. I read the book - like sipping scotch and taking notes, and urged my wife to read it too. After finishing it, she said, it was all history, and that is useless! I said, "That is why the Hindus have been ruled by nearly 100 foreigners from all over Asia and Europe.

The Hindus, in India, have no recent history to be proud of." Sadly, they are not even concerned about creating it at any level. History always begins from individuals and families. It is not to be found in books alone. History is strewn in imposing monuments, exquisite art works, battles won, forms of entertainments, folklores, and no less, in legendary romances.

(Oct 13, 2008)

NOTES AND COMMENTS

1. Satish: The last paragraph is really good. **Alok Kumar**

2. One needs to learn from history but not live in history. Even British royals are selling their heirlooms charging to see their palaces. Britain which was center on world in not a very distant past. Hindus have recent history both to be proud and ashamed off. Mahatma Gandhi and creation of Bangladesh are part of former and 1984 Delhi riots are part of later. **Rahul**

3. Very insightful again. I agree with you more than with Prabha. **Ved Sharma**

4. Brilliant article, thanks for sharing it. With best regards, **Ritu**

HISTORY, MATHEMATICS & HERITAGE

History is a unique subject. The makers of history are seldom its regular writers and readers. The paper brings out several dimensions of history of mathematics, in particular. There are pertinent questions - like those proving theorems have only a tunnel view of the history of their research problems. In general, the hardcore mathematicians have downplayed the history of mathematics as a subject. In academe, history of mathematics is neither a part of history departments, nor of mathematics departments. The fundamentals researches in such a discipline are never possible. There are only a couple of universities in the US that have positions earmarked for the history of mathematics. The paper throws light on its whys and hows.

History, in all its facets, is an index of a nation's total development. Whereas, mathematics may be studied independent of politics, humanities and literature, its history is a patch in the quilt that history is. In Indian context, the paper attempts to survey the history of mathematics after independence, before independence under the British, Muslims, and Hindu going back to medieval and forgotten past. It eventually poses the most crucial question on the necessary and sufficient conditions for the development and flourishing of mathematics in the smallest academic unit and a nation, at large.

The nursery of every academic discipline sits in the schools and young children. Mathematics Education has to find a respectable place in the colleges and universities. Mathematics Education or History of Mathematics should not be deemed as a place for the frustrated mathematicians. Mathematics is defined by it abstraction even in the fields that are considered applied. Hence mathematics meshes well in a society where the freedom to inquire, question an authority, a principle, and a book is guaranteed. Finally, the paper makes a bold connection of mathematics with Hindu heritage and religion.

(Abstract of a paper presented at the annual meeting of History of Mathematics and Heritage conference held in Imphal, Manipur, India - during Dec 19-21, 2008)

NOTES AND COMMENTS

GREENING OF THE DEMOCRACIES

Recently, it was reported that the White House has taken a top-level decision to support democracy all over the world. Whatever may have prompted this decision, it is welcomed with the hope that the relationships between India and USA will improve consequently. The US is the world's oldest democracy and India, the largest one. Yet, the ties between the two governments have been less than cordial. To an individual, who has lived in the US for twelve years, this situation has been unpleasant to watch. The US is a country of my adoption and India is the country of my origin, and my endeavor is that these two democracies move towards cooperation rather confrontation.

Generally, the relationships between two countries improve in two ways. One, if the two governments are able to map strategies to promote their defense and economic interests. That is why it is said that in politics there is no like friendship between two countries, but only conveniences. The other is the direct interaction between the two people due to geographical proximity or vibrant ideas.

At the people level, there is a noticeable admiration between the two nations. The increasing number of spiritual thinkers coming over to USA testifies to the curiosity Americans have for spiritual values. The life of affluence is compelling the Americans to seek new frontiers of mind and soul through Indian yoga and meditation. This pursuit of Indian philosophical thought actually stems from the democratic attitude of the people here. For millennia, India has been a sanctuary for all kinds of religious and political systems, and it continues to serve as a unique melting pot.

I have just returned to the US after spending two years in India. And what I saw in India- from the street level to the top institutional level, it surprised me. In the universities, where one comes across the youth and intelligentsia of a nation, one is swamped with Americana. Students proudly flaunt their jeans and liberal life styles through their awareness of latest trends in the US. Most graduate textbooks are written by Americans. A good number of faculty in every Indian university has visited some US university. Investigative journalism of Jack Anderson type is regarded very high in Indian press. Management of industries, which ran on clannish style until recently, is opening up to the American management concepts and techniques. Thus a whole new generation of Indians is coming up which would eventually yield influence in future.

All this has to be understood by the two governments, and it is high time, when Prime Minister (PM) Indira Gandhi visits the US at the end of this month - after 11 years. Directly, India and USA have no cause of conflict over ideology or boundaries in air, water and land. Some differences have been due to the sophisticated diplomacy of the US and blunt diplomacy of India. Let the two leaders set aside those pinprick areas. Instead, they should sign bilateral agreements which encourage technology. Climate, for any type of industry from tourism to computer chips, has never been so good in India, as today. Tourists from west, in particular, are visiting India in increasing number.

It may sound paradoxical that professionals, as turned out by Indian schools and institutes, find more satisfaction in going out to the States than staying back in India. For instance, most medical doctors would like to go the US right after graduation. One reason is that Indians accept several systems of medicine. Modern allopathy does not command absolute dominance, as it does in the US. Supply being more than the demand, which means exodus to the US. Therefore, if Americans invest in any viable venture in India, then besides availability of cheap labor, they shall have a highly competent force of professionals. That means not only saving in labor cost but also in professional payroll. To top it, there is no language problem. English is understood by Indian literates and its popularity has been increasing.

Last month, at a ceremony in New York to commemorate the 100th birth anniversary of Franklin D. Roosevelt (1882-1945), Mrs. Vijaylakshmi Pandit recalled his support for India's independence from the British. She added that there has been no comparable act of statesmanship towards India since then. Mrs. Pandit, being a sister of Jawaharlal Nehru, India's first PM, is the aunt of PM Gandhi. She served as India's ambassador to the US, USSR, Britain, and was the first woman President of the UN General Assembly.

Both President Reagan and PM Gandhi have not opened any dialogue in FDR spirit. The media on both sides has to play important roles while PM Gandhi stays in the US. Only then, the meetings between the oldest and the largest democracies in the world would be fruitful. It shall set the stage for Reagan administration's resolve to strengthen democracy all over the world.

(Aug 1982/Sep, 2011)

NOTES AND COMMENTS

THE QUAKES IN PUNJAB

Background

We spent two years (1980-1982) in India after living in USA for twelve years. A new wave of unrest was sweeping Punjab, a northwest state of India - having common border with Pakistani state of Punjab too. But a whole lot has taken place there since we returned. In daily newspapers and Indian publications in the US, reports and debates on chaos are filling the pages. To a person who has lived for good thirty years in Punjab, questions or answers for these events do not come out easily. The heart aches and the head reels. Nevertheless, in order to understand this burning socio-political problem and find any solution, a brief perspective of history is essential.

Hindu Sikh Ties

After the tortuous killing of Banda Bahadur (1670-1716), there was a vacuum in the newly born Khalsa leadership. Under the express orders of the waning Mughal king in Delhi, the Sikhs were literally hunted like animals - in the cities, in the villages, and even in the forests of Punjab. Despite such dangers, a pro Sikh wave was also rising up. The Khalsa baptization which the last Guru Gobind Singh had initiated in 1699 began to take place in many ordinary Hindu homes! Specifically, the first male children were 'given to the service of the Sikh Panth'. Despite this Sikh genocide (1746-66) which annihilated nearly 30% of the Sikh population, the number of Sikhs started swelling like mushrooms. Both Hindus and Sikhs were commonly seen as the members of the same family. There are many offshoots of this tradition. For example, if a couple was childless, or their children did not survive after birth, then they would invariably vow to place their first male child at the service of the Guru. So it is puzzling to figure out the causes that are creating a rift between the Hindus and Sikhs.

Bhinderwala and Sikh Rule

What has lead to the calls for Khalistan (means the land of the pure Sikhs) in the backdrop of recent hate campaign against the Hindus? Was Bhinderwala really a terrorist, or a soldier saint in the lineage of Banda Bahadur ? Did he whip hatred for the Hindus, as Hitler did for the Jews? Was he so much consumed with his mission that there was no question of his compromising? Certainly, he had captured the hearts of the Sikh youth, at large, and was systematically indoctrinating them on a radical course. His following was gaining momentum amongst the masses while he was trying to take control of different political organizations of the

Sikhs. Intellectuals had started accepting his ideology too. Moreover, a section of both retired and active army and civilian officers placed their services openly and indiscreetly at his disposal.

The Center mishandled Punjab affairs and the charismatic Bhinderwala capitalized on the political conditions to revive Khalsa supremacy as envisioned by the tenth Guru and his successors. Maharaja Ranjit Singh (1789-1839) had established the first Sikh Empire with Lahore (now in Pakistan) as its capital. However, its influence remained political and militaristic in nature. The official language continued to be Persian. The Sikh ethos was hardly planted. The British defeated the incompetent sons of Ranjit Singh, and by 1849, the Sikh empire was annexed into the British Raj.

By the 1930s, the British had known that they could not hold onto India for long. They wanted to leave India politically divided and economically emaciated, so that they could continue playing pivotal roles. For instance, they recognized autonomy for every constituent group - including Muslims, Sikhs, 500+ princes, and the scheduled castes amongst the Hindus. Whereas, the Muslims under Jinnah remained adamant for Pakistan, the Sikh leaders - like Master Tara Singh and Baldev Singh muffled their demand for Sikh homeland before India's freedom. As a matter of fact, they were prevailed upon by the towering spiritual and political leadership of Gandhi.

Post-independence

India is often acclaimed for winning her freedom by Gandhian principles of non-violence and without bloodshed. Ironically, it did not bode all well for the future. The freedom fighters of yesterday became overnight rulers. It was strange that vast India, not ruled by 80% Hindu population for nearly one thousand years fell into the hands of the inexperienced leaders in running it. Agitation in the states is the price the nation has been paying for poor decisions taken since 1947. For instance, after independence, the Sikh Punjabis were impatient to have their state and realize some form of self-rule. The Sikh sentiments were hurt when in 1955, on the recommendations of a States Organization Commission, several states were created based on regional languages, but Punjabi language was denied a state. It led to long agitations.

Error of the Heart

However, there were Hindu Punjabis who sacrificed their mother language in the 'wider interest' of the country. In the 1961 census, by declaring Hindi as their mother language, the Hindu Punjabis alienated themselves from the Sikhs. It was the judgmental error of the head on one side and of the heart on the other. Ever since, it has caused continual communal rifts with political repercussions. Finally, in1966, the present Punjab, which was long overdue, was created on linguistic grounds. But the Sikhs were not at peace politically. Their urge for more autonomy in running their affairs clashed with the central government which constitutionally has too much power. It is this festering conflict which has really raised its head under the guise of Khalistan.

Conclusion

As long as Akalis remained out of power in Punjab and at the Center, their agitations were limited in demands. But after having tasted political power during the Janta regime (1977-79), they cannot wait to come back. On the other hand, central government is coming out with measures to interfere in the affairs of the states. Recent events in Kashmir and Andhra Pradesh indicate that democracy in India is only spelled correctly.

Unless the Constitution is amended to reflect the history and culture of each state as per their relationship with the Center, such struggles may take uglier forms under new Bhinderwalas. Fortunately, the climate for constitutional amendment has never been as favorable as at present.

It has to be borne in mind that preconditions for a lasting peace and harmony lie in the change of heart and willingness to accommodate differences. Indian psyche is often governed by traditions, not by legislation. It is generally said that every big earthquake is soon followed by smaller ones before the crust is stabilized. Better preparedness for it alone can minimize the havoc.

(July 04, 1984)

PS – Sept, 2011

In Oct, 1984, Prime Minister Indira Gandhi was killed in a volley of gunshots by her two long-time Sikh bodyguards. It instantaneously sparked a wave of hate crimes against the Sikhs for the next couple of days in Delhi and surrounding areas. However, its communal repercussions have shaken Punjab for the next 20 years. Pakistan took full advantage of Hindu Sikh clashes in settling its scores for the loss of West Pakistan/Bangladesh in the 1971 war with India.

NOTES AND COMMENTS

INDIRA GANDHI MORTEM

Prime Minister Indira Gandhi is dead, assassinated by her two long-time Sikh security guards. Shockwaves of her murder are being felt all over the world. Some people are in grief and paralysed, but there are some, proponents of Khalistan in particular, who are rejoicing and claiming a vindication in this hour. It is time for all Indians to reflect deep over this tragedy and come out of stupor or euphoria in order to take charge of the present combustible situation.

There are all kinds of analyses leading up to this event. The quick explanation would be that the emotions were running high ever since the army entered the sacred Golden Temple to flush out the state terrorism as undisputedly directed from its premises. Bhinderwala died during that action, but not the ideas and ideals he stood for. He had successfully mobilized a section of the Sikh youth and intellectuals alike. Significant steps have been taken to placate the hurt feelings of the Sikhs, and lately, reasonable success was being reported on a political solution. However, it did not involve every disgruntled faction. The hardcore followers are pledged to take revenge for the death of Bhinderwala and the sacrilege of the Golden Temple.

PM Gandhi was singled out, and she had been receiving numerous threats to her life every day. Time will tell whether she was alone, or stood for some principles in the interest of the nation at large. But we have to guard ourselves against similar hard-core followers of Mrs. Gandhi that they do not turn loose and start any acts of retribution. That will be very dangerous for the nation in the long run.

The new leadership during the interim period before the general election or afterwards have to be cognizant that political problems like that of Kashmir, Punjab and Assam cannot be taken lightly for a long time. Fortunately, Assam did not resort to such violence though agitation has remained in the hands of the students for sometime. During the last five years, Assam has suffered much more economically than Punjab has suffered.

India has the best record of a stable political system amongst all the so-called third world countries. More violence and disturbances have taken place after independence that before it. The question remains, why? A deeper answer is that Indian mind, largely derived from the Hindus, is fundamentally individualistic i.e. anti-organizational in nature. Testimony to that is the number of dialects, languages, sects and religions that India continues to have for centuries. The number of political parties and the rate at which they are still being formed attest to the cardinal fact that, in nutshell, each individual is a party. This emphasis on individual growth in the name of self-realization has been nurtured by every ancient scripture through millennia. Mothers at homes have practiced this art in a scientific manner by serving food three times a day in a one-to-one manner.

Every family member is attended according to his taste, temperament and status. Collective eating at the table by the whole family on a daily basis is foreign to Indian custom and ethos.

Mahatma Gandhi wanted the Congress Party dissolved after independence. But his heir apparents kept Congress Party in the name of unity for political purposes. Gradually, it has led to the centralization of the government, which has meant less autonomy for the people and their states. Democratic model, which the Indian founding fathers chose, took into consideration the western frame of mind. Consequently, even the most minor demand for autonomy in running the affairs at the state level is considered a threat to the political unity. This center-state relations need to be amended in the Constitution in order to reflect the historical Indian psyche. The time has never been so ripe.

(Oct 31, 1984/June, 2011)

NOTES AND COMMENTS

A LESSON FOR OPPOSITION

Your analysis of the general elections in India was well written. You spared no words in addressing the opposition parties that the real cause of Congress' landslide victory was due to the split in opposition parties and their inability to have a common election platform. It was rightly pointed out that the opposition charges of rigging the ballots, excessive money spending and media manifestations were frivolous, and Rajiv's charisma and PM Gandhi's assassination were exaggerated. Certainly, the public, at large, was in panic over the breakdown of law and order after the murder of the PM. However, earlier to this national tragedy, life and property were unsafe in Punjab and Assam due to regional terrorists running amuck. Thus the public, sensing threat from outside and disintegration from within, voted for the Congress Party.

I would like to add another dimension to it. Emergence of Telugu Desam as the main opposition party is a landmark of the post election phenomenon. Earlier, the DMK and its variations have done exceedingly well. National Conference in Kashmir has a good track record of winning elections. Akali Dal in Punjab and a local party in Assam have great potential for winning in these states. The point is that Indian political tapestry is not merely black and white. Most of us living in the USA and Canada are sold out to the idea of a two-party system in a democratic set up. It does not make any sense to Indian socio-political conditions, where the culture thrives on a thought of unity in diversity! Does history or heritage of India have anything in common with the history of USA, Canada, Australia or New Zealand? These are recent resettlement countries, whereas India goes back to 5000 years in a continuous chronology. In western thinking, individual may be sacrificed for the organization, but in India, individual remains supreme.

Therefore, I foresee very healthy signs of crystallization of political parties at regional levels. The communist party has failed after 35 years. It has suffered breakups after breakups, and now is confined in Bengal and Kerala. In fact, each national party has undergone a series of breakups which is simply a sign of individualistic assertion! The Janta Party broke up when local character of the region and its leaders were bypassed.

The new trend is to respect the emergence of regional parties like the DMK and Telugu Desam. Once the public outlook is changed that the directives are to come from the local leaders and not from bosses at distant Delhi, a healthy coalition for central government would become a reality in near future. Indian mass psyche is guided by the character and personality of local leaders rather than by lofty principles stated in a monolithic manifesto.

(March 1985)

Post Script – Sept, 2011: Coalition governments have been ruling India since 1994, as no single party ever won absolute majority.

NOTES AND COMMENTS

RESERVATION POLICY & ITS AFTERMATH

Dr. Bhimrao Ambedkar, born in a scheduled caste family, was the chairman of the Committee that drafted of the Constitution of India, and Dr. Rajindra Prasad, a Gandhian Kayastha, was the chairman of the Constitutional Assembly which finally approved the draft for adoption. There was no question in the minds of the founding fathers that something urgent needs to be done for the depressed and oppressed classes amongst the Hindus. The British rulers had already incited them with a promise of a separate homeland within India! However, the towering influence of Gandhi on Indian politics did not let the British design take effect. However, Gandhi assured them of equality and fairness in free India.

If one checks the minutes of these committees, then one is struck by the absence of any acrimony during discussion. The article on job reservations for the members of scheduled castes and tribes went through the committees literally unchallenged. Similarly, there was no argument over the reservation period. Had Dr. Ambedkar put down 100 years instead of 20 years, then it would have sailed through too. Well, one may find fault for their lack of practical vision in this respect, as this reservation policy is tearing the country apart today. But a reference to the Constitution is pertinent. The founding fathers wanted to remind the future lawmakers that gross inequality and injustice had existed in some sections of Hindu society. It can also be removed by change of hearts rather than through repeated legislation at the center.

This lack of understanding on the part of present governments has caused serious problems of implementation of this reservation policy. For instance, if a member of a scheduled class gets into a medical college, army, or elite Indian Administrative Services, then his/her children continue getting the benefits of the present reservation policy. It perpetuates of the castes, based on birth – not on work. Later on, the reservation policy was extended to more backward classes and regions. Its implementation has brought out frauds of immeasurable consequences. People use forged documents to claim the benefits of these classes.

The present reservation policy has created a reverse discrimination as highlighted in some states, particularly in Tamil Nadu, where the son of a Brahmin with nearly 100% marks may be turned down for admission in a professional college, whereas, a member of reserved class, with 45% marks, may get in! These policies are being created indiscriminately to win elections at any cost. Democratic system which is meant to respond to every section of the populace is turning a mouthpiece of interested groups and influential lobbyists. It is time to stop legislating on this matter before it blows the country apart.

(April 24, 1985)

(**PS - Sept 2011**: India went up in flames during 1990 on Mandal Commission on reservations)

NOTES AND COMMENTS

POLITICIZATION OF ELITE SERVICES

The editorial by B. Krishna, as appeared in the *India Tribune* of April 20, is laudable for a historical perspective on the elite pre-independence, Indian Civil Service (ICS) and post independence, Indian Administrative Service (IAS). It should serve as a crash course on public administration for the generation of Indians growing up in the US.

Since independence quite a few changes have been made in the IAS - like the creation of a cadre of state/provincial administrative services, and other for the technocrats, in particular. Also, there have been a couple of administrative reform commissions. For nearly hundred years before independence, the ICS officers were kept too distant from the masses, as they only looked after the interests of the British Raj. It was essential to have a centralized cadre of top services.

In free India, things are different. Indian psyche functions at the individual and local levels. For instance, a posting of a 24-year old IAS officer, from a far-off state having different language and culture, is unproductive in the long run. India has to discover its own model of public services. The US model where some 40,000 key personnel change guards with new presidency, is out of question for India. Indian democracy functions at the grass root level. Recent elections clearly testify that a two-party model is a dream in India. Hence, any thrust on administrative reform has to focus at the state levels.

Politicization of bureaucracy is a bad omen for India. It is unfortunate that Indian political system has given unbridled authority to its lawmakers, MLAs and MPs. It is no exaggeration to say that an Indian legislator peddles his/her influence in the state day-to-day administrative affairs for more than even a US Senator. Since independence, more corruption in public life has been caused by the elected people than anything else.

Adding a touch of history, the British design of the ICS, as epitomized by the selection process of Rhoades Scholars, was excellent. It kept the British Empire growing. However, who does not remember earlier stories of corruption of the bureaucrats of East India Company in 18th century before India was transferred to the British government. Moreover, it was the impeachment trial of Governor General, Warren Hastings which kept the ICS officers, governor generals and viceroys of India above public scrutiny. Any system ripens for a while, but starts rotting eventually. In response to Gandhi's call of civil disobedience several ICS officers resigned from the British service, or became secretly sympathetic to Indian freedom movement. Nevertheless, they contributed to the fall of British Empire in India!

(May 03, 1985)

PS – Sept, 2011: Recent reports of corruption in India, at the individual, public, corporate and governmental levels, have been simply shocking.

NOTES AND COMMENTS

THE MUKTSAR MASSACRE

The daylight and point-blank massacre of fifteen Hindu bus passengers on July 26 by the so-called six Sikh gunmen near Muktsar has sent a chill into the hearts of Indians all over. The Sikh Gurus preached against injustice and fought against the atrocities of the Muslim rulers. Muktsar is a sacred place in Sikh history. In 1705, in order to redeem their honor, forty deserters (in 1704) of Khalsa, as baptized Sikhs were called by the 10th Guru Gobind Singh (1666-1708), died in a fierce battle of Muktsar. It is a travesty of history that the followers of that very Guru would publicly kill the unarmed Hindus in Muktsar.

Punjab has been under turmoil for the last eight years. The situation turned explosive ever since Indian army entered into the Golden Temple two years ago. The militant Akali leader, Sant Bhinderwala was killed along with of his followers. It has triggered a chain of unprecedented political murders. The political problem, started from some autonomy for Punjab, has now become intensely communal. The inept handling by politicians has worsened it. However, one does wonder, that when Rajeev Gandhi's government is going all out to resolve this crisis and there is a popularly elected Akali government in Punjab, then what kind of elements are destroying fabrics of a peace accord?

The answer is no longer hidden. Fifteen years ago, in 1971, India took advantage of the political crisis in East Pakistan, and largely midwived the birth of Bangladesh. How can the military rulers of Pakistan forget that humiliation, partition of Pakistan, and its permanent loss of Eastern recourses? The present tumult in Punjab is providing Pakistan an ideal opportunity to take that revenge and break India further.

Several reports have conclusively established that Pakistan is providing both men and material to the secessionist Sikhs in order to destabilize India. After the death of Bhinderwala, there is no one to guide his young militant followers often sheltered in Pakistan. This is evidenced from the number of wanton killings. The Pakistani Muslims, disguised as Sikhs, are generally involved in sensational murders. From the historic Hindu-Sikh bond, no political issue is strong enough to separate their blood.

A solution lies in Indian government acting on war footing towards any illegal activities on the border common with Pakistan. A few months ago, Benazir Bhutto openly charged President Zia playing the Khalistan game at the cost of human rights in Pakistan. If this leads to another war between India and Pakistan, then the good to come out of it would be that the common blood of the Hindus and the Sikhs would wash away the stigma of communal hatred between them.

(Aug 01, 1986)

PS - Oct, 2011: The Kargil war between India and Pakistan during May –June, 1999 was a part of Pakistani plan to break India from northwest too. The *Jehadis* crossed into India and with the support of Pakistani Army fought with Indian Army. President Bill Clinton personally intervened to stop this war from escalation. India should have pushed into Pakistan occupied Kashmir, where the 9/11 *Jehadis* were being trained and sheltered.

NOTES AND COMMENTS

PEOPLE AND POLITICS OF PRAYAG

Prayag (*YAJANA*/sacrifice), a holy city of the Hindus on the bank of the Ganga River, was named Allahabad (city of Allah) during the time of Mughal Emperor, Akbar. It was expanded by the British in the 19th century. However, nothing diminished its importance as a spiritual center of the Hindus. This is the backdrop my analysis of the outcome of a recent parliamentary bye-election in Allahabad, which was the focal point of all the bye-elections, held in India last month.

1. The outcome is a tribute to the Indian masses, for their individuality, that they could not be manipulated by the high-tech election machine of the Congress Party. They gave nearly as many votes to Sunil Shastri as to the other losing candidate Kashi Ram!

2. The thundering victory of VP Singh was entirely due to his clean political record built in the state of UP and the Center. It was the first time since the death of Jai Prakash Narain, that all major political parties got together in an election to fight the highly centralized administration of Rajeev Gandhi.

3. In 1984, Rajeev Gandhi and Congress Party won the general election – projecting him as 'Mr. Clean'. The public gave him the mandate to clean the sewer of institutional corruption. His record, so far, has been dismal. Those of us, who often visit India, notice rampant corruption in all walks of public and private sectors.

4. Another positive trend is that public is no longer going to vote on the waves of sympathy alone. Sunil Shastri is the son of the late PM Lal Bahadur Shastri. But he has not established any political record of significance. Last year, he left the cabinet of Veerbahadur Singh in support of VP Singh, and look at the turncoat, he fought against VP Singh!

5. The Congress caucus knew that they don't have any other candidate except Amitabh Bachhan who could possibly beat VP Singh. They played a bigger game. Shastri's name was made public only 30 minutes before the deadline for the filing of the nomination forms! They not only eliminated Shastri as a potential eyesore, but also got rid of CM Veerbahadar Singh on the ground of inefficiency. Since 1982, most state chief ministers are changed at the behest of the Center rather than by the MLAs on assembly floors.

6. The next general election is still 17 months away. That is a lot of time in the fast changing political life today. The future belongs to a party, or a coalition of parties, who have demonstrated a clean record of public service. The emergence of Ramakrishna Hedge in Karnataka and Jyoti Basu in Bengal,

are good signs for Indian politics. Rajeev still has time to set a few things in order.

7.   Finally, I may conclude on a note of 'prediction'. If Rajeev and his party are soundly defeated in the next general elections, then a bigger persecution will start against him than it took place against his mother, Indira Gandhi, who was even locked up overnight in Tihar jail. It has been reported in the press, by no less a person than Maneka Gandhi, that after the crushing election defeat in 1977, Indira Gandhi was advised to leave India and settle in Italy. This time, Rajeev would flee India and seek refuge with his Italian wife. Didn't the Shah of Iran and Marcos of Philippine leave their countries and after their being thrown out of power?

8.   The choice is clear. The spirit of Prayag has arisen! If VP Singh does not live up to his promise for the next 17 months, then he is going to be defeated by Amitabh Bachhan in the coming general elections. That is a long-term strategy of the Congress party to resurrect Amitabh and send VP Singh into political oblivion. The cleansing of Indian public life has to begin from the top, which was corrupted in the first place, during Indira Gandhi's regime. We, Indians living overseas, can definitely play a positive role at this juncture. Let us not miss it!

(July 04, 1988)

PS – Oct, 2011: The corruption in India has exploded like the cancerous cells in a human body. During the year, 2011, Swami Ramdev, a spiritual leader and Anna Hazare, a Gandhian raised the consciousness of the Indian masses nationwide – thus forcing the Government to take some measures. It is only a beginning.

NOTES AND COMMENTS

RECENT ELECTIONS IN INDIA AND ISRAEL

Parliamentary elections in India and Israel are just over. There are some very interesting parallels and contrasts that I thought of sharing with the readers of the *India Post*.

Coverage by the US media: It is so different! Israel is not much bigger than the smallest state of India, yet its election coverage has been overwhelming. There was no day-to-day coverage of Indian election scene. Whereas, during Israeli elections, even the local newspapers and TV networks covered it so extensively, but, there wasn't even a word in any local daily on Indian elections. Saffire's solitary syndicated column brought out the apathy of the US Govt. and media about India as a whole, and its election coverage in particular.

At the local level, the media went out of its way in contacting the Jewish community for soliciting their responses on the policies, impact of candidates, or the outcome of elections. Indian community in Las Vegas is quite sizable, but to the best of my knowledge, no one has been contacted about India's election.

India and Israel: Ever since Israel was created, Indian Government, as run by the Congress Party opposed Israel, and sided with all the Arabian countries - often at the cost of Indian public interest in the long run. It was during a short spell of the Janta Govt. (1977-79) with Vajpayee its Foreign Minister, that the first diplomatic channel was opened with Israel. The full recognition of Israel and diplomatic relations have yet to take place. The point is, it is the BJP which has greater national interest, and Israel is aware of it. But the US media and Govt. have yet to realize it without getting heat from Pakistan.

BJP and Likud Party: There is a great similarity between the BJP and Likud Party (LP) headed by the new Prime Minister, Benjamin Netanyahu. Both are tough on the internal security of their countries. The BJP held marches for bringing law and order in the strife ridden J&K. The LP has been tough on all terrorists no matter where they operate from, outside or inside Israel.

There are about 10% Arabs in Israel and in the recent election they (95%) reportedly voted for the defeated PM Shimon Peres. In India, Muslims form nearly 12% of the population and they have never voted for the BJP in a block. However, for the first time, they did not vote for the Congress Party which may have led to the loss of some Congress seats in the Parliament.

The LP is strong on the issue of Jewish settlements on the territories lost by the Arabs during three wars with Israel. India and Pakistan also fought three wars, but India always returned the occupied Pakistan territories. History is witness, if Pakistan ever won over any piece of Indian territory, then it is lost forever. Just like, it happened between Mohammed Gori and Prithviraj Chauhan some 1000 years ago! Look, China still occupies more than 100,000 square miles of India's territory taken after the 1962 war with India.

Coming back to the corresponding issue of illegal refugees coming in thousands from the Bangladesh, it is the BJP which wants them to go back. To the shock of the Assamese, some of these refugees have been granted Indian citizenships by the Congress Government. It has tilted the demographic balance against the natives!

Ironically, the media brands the BJP as communal and stirs fear amongst the Muslims despite the fact that the BJP ruled states never had any communal riots. Netanyahu has unequivocally declared, that a Palestinian state is a threat to Israel, must strengthen the Jewish settlements, and Jerusalem is non-negotiable with the Arabs. As compared with the LP, the BJP is moderate, and so is its leader, Vajpayee. With his resignation, he has set high standards of forming a government. Yet, the media is creating an image that belies the record. Image is everything!.

Lately, in the US elections individual Indians are making one of the largest election contributions and hold fund raising events. Yet, as a community, Indians are not that much even locally recognized. Some individuals do have an access to the White House, but it is the weight of the community that eventually counts. Perhaps this state of affairs of the US Indians reflects what India is perceived in the US scheme of things.

(June 01, 1996/Sep, 2011)

NOTES AND COMMENTS

THE ADVENT OF CHRISTIANITY IN INDIA

My mind stopped right away, as I read the following in the leading editorial of the *India Post* of Jan 8: "…Hindus and Christians have lived together in India for at least a millennium if not more." Accepting an historical point that Apostle Thomas came and settled in India in the 1st century AD, where he was welcomed by the Hindu king of Malabar Coast. He had sailed in with only tens of his followers, and this number did not mushroom into a thousand, even after a thousand year!

There is absolutely no record of any mass conversion of the Hindus to Christianity, or of Christian migration from Middle East before Islam swept that region in the 8th century. In fact, during the Islamic expansion, a lot more Parsis fled Iran and took shelter in India than the Christians did from this region. The first recorded visit of Christians from Europe was in the 16th century, when a physician employee of the East India Company was presented in the Delhi court of Mughal Emperor, Akbar, for consultation on a medical problem. In return, the East India Company was granted some trading privileges in a coastal region of Gujarat.

The population of Christians remained in hundreds and confined in the South, till East India Company established a foothold in India by the 17th century. After the disintegration of Mughal Empire in north, the East India Company established its suzerainty in Bengal, and hoards of missionaries started coming to India as soldiers of faith. Subsequently, Hindu masses and intellectuals like Raja Ram Mohan Roy came under the influence of Christianity.

Today, Christian population in India is more than 20 millions! How did this number grow from a few thousands only 400 hundred years ago, is a story of systematic conversion of the Hindus. For example, the number of Christians in unbifurcated Assam, at the time of partition, was hardly 1%, and today, in some Eastern states, it is nearly 90%! At no time, the British population in India was over 30,000, and most of them left India after its independence in 1947.

Recent clashes with Christians are engineered to destabilize the present BJP Govt. and malign the Hindu awakening after centuries of political slumber. However, a point has to be stressed that as long as the Hindus were being converted to Christians or Muslims, it was fine with the world. But if any Muslim or Christian voluntarily decides to re-convert to Hindu folds, then it flares up into communal riot and projected as a crime against Islam or Christianity.

There is no free market of religions, or two-way street! It is not out of place to point out that the numbers of the Hindus and Christians in the neighboring country, Pakistan, are diminishing to zero, and their social status deplorable.

(Jan 14, 1999/Sept, 2011)

NOTES AND COMMENTS

THE MAN OF THE MILLENNIUM CONTEST

In the Oct 8 issue of the *India Post* (IP), Publisher Japra has a kind of issued a call to the IP readers to consider Gandhi for this honor. One of its readers has virtually started a campaign for Gandhi's nomination!

In my understanding of Gandhi, if he suddenly comes alive, then he would feel sorry for the second coming! Most readers don't remember what Gandhi thought of himself. Of course, as the time goes by, it does matters no less, what others think of Gandhi. Currently, *Gandhi and the Mahatma,* a play from India touring the US, is portraying Gandhi as a lesser human being for his failures to properly bring up his sons, particularly, the eldest one, Harilal. Does anyone truly believe that if Harilal were alive today, he would cast his vote for Gandhi? Never, ever! So, does the public really care for Hari Lal, or Gandhi's failure as a father? Certainly not! Recently discovered documents on Einstein portray him as an abuser of his first wife. Also, he had no communications with his one professor son for some 25 years.

At this midpoint in polling, it is interesting to note Hitler garnering more votes than Gandhi. The current white supremacy movements and neo-Nazis, openly springing back into socio-political scenes in the US and Europe, are highlighting what Hitler did for his people and economy. He lifted Germany from the rubbles of the WW I to a state of pride and glory - all in a few years.

On deeper contemplation, it turns out that an individual or society remembers its great person or idea for its interested motives only, and projects some acts of greatness at the cost of the other. For instance, Jinnah may not be that well known outside Pakistan, but he is the father of nation, as he fought for its creation. In India, most people revere Gandhi for his leadership in its freedom movement. Without his leadership, a couple of more decades may have passed. His concept of non-violence has no impact in Islamic nations. For them, Gandhi is a non-entity, and so is he for organizations - like National Rifle Association in the USA, or elsewhere.

A lesson of history is that no one can win it all. The pubic memorializes the so-called heroes for their self-interest only. Nevertheless, the heroes may have paid very heavy prices on other fronts of life, including the life itself. An irony of human life is that, whereas, people worship persons like Buddha and Christ, but they also continue to remember and study the warriors - like Alexander and Changez Khan!

My personal word on this contest is that you vote for one who has impacted in an area that is very close and dear to you today. Let it be noted that in the search for the man of millennium, the names of the Sikh gurus - like that of Guru Nanak and

Guru Gobind Singh, are not seen in the partial list. That speaks a lot of the voters participating in these contests - frequently run by media for drawing readership.

(Oct 29, 1999/Oct, 2011)

NOTES AND COMMENTS

POLITICS AND NATIONAL AWARDS

The *India Journal* of Feb 11 has reported that sitar maestro Vilayat Khan has refused to accept the Padam Vibhushan award of the Government of India. It is the second highest civilian award in India. In the past, he had declined to accept Padam Shri and Padam Bhushan on similar grounds. He has decried politics in the process, particularly, when persons not as talented as him were recognized and awarded each time before him.

Politics is an integral part of any award system. Take for instance, the Nobel Prizes in Peace and Literature in particular. Some of the greatest giants in these fields have been denied these awards. In India, most of these awards have been influenced by the Congress Party and persons closer to its ideology. Many a great minds in various facets of public life have been ignored for such awards.

It is the first time in the last 4-5 years that one can notice the influence of the BJP Party and its supporters. They are trying to remove the inequity that has perpetuated for decades. With the result there is a lot more hue and cry over the awards than ever before. However, persons of the stature of Vilayat Khan will restore luster and glory to these awards by not accepting them. I salute him for his courage of conviction. Padam Vibhushan will remain smaller as long as he walks by it with his dignity.

(Feb 26, 2000)

NOTES AND COMMENTS

ON DENYING THE US AT WAR

My son, niece and younger daughter keep themselves well informed on social and political issues. We exchange e-mails, but once in a while, some sparks go off. It happened yesterday when my response to a presidential hopeful, John Dean's article evoked criticism of the Bush administration - on intelligence and Iraq's weapons of mass destruction. The two party politics is not of my taste, though I do participate in the process. I have never registered for any political party. I reasonably know what is good and what is bad for the US, and for that reason, at age 70+, I don't have to read a political columnist or listen to an anchorman anymore in order to understand the bare facts.

Is the US at war or not? This question is to be cleared up in the context of the events that are presently happening in Iraq. It is the **9/11 Attack** that compelled America to declare this war. If the four planes loaded with fuel and passengers had not hit the twin towers of WTC, Pentagon, and missed the White House, nothing would have happened to the regimes of the Talibans (Pure Islamists) in Afghanistan and of Saddam in Iraq.

Moreover, if the decision to ground all the airlines had been delayed only by a couple of hours, then the Sears Tower in Chicago, Space Needle in Seattle, Bank of America building in San Francisco and LAX and Dallas airports would also have also turned into burning infernos. The media and the democrats, vehemently criticizing President Bush for not coming on TV on 09/11 to comfort the nation, shut up when it was discovered that the President was a target in the air. The **9/11 Attack** was worse than the Pearl Harbor/Hawaii Attack by Japan, in 1944.

When a nation is at war, the daily life is affected. On a personal note, the classrooms which remained unlocked for 24 hours before 9/11 are now electronically locked up soon after the last classes are over. I have a special key to open the rooms for my students. Air travel has become very frustrating. Often, my wife says, "Why do they declare different color alerts when nothing happens?" I tell her, "Nothing **seems** to happen because of the heightened security measures!" According to a recent FBI/CIA release, since 9/11 through 01/ 2003, more than 700 acts of sabotage have been thwarted and aborted. It has saved many lives and properties! I salute these heroes working behind the scenes.

This enemy is not like the red communists of Soviet Union with different political ideologies. This enemy is not like faced in WW I and II, where old geopolitical hegemony of Germany dominated the Europe. It is not like Japan that wanted to take over natural resources of Southeast Asia. This enemy is very spread out. It is driven by Islamic fascism of world domination.

On scanning the world history, I just could not find an enemy like this. In early 2001, the Talibans exploded 2000-year-old and 250 tall Buddhist monuments - protected by the UN as Heritage of Mankind, and despite all the pleas, appeals and protests across the world. It was actually a clarion call to the world of bigger explosions to come soon! At that time, the Muslim and non-Muslim youth - like the Walkers, from all over the world, were getting fighters' training in that region. The worst has happened in Kashmir where many thousand Hindus and Sikhs have been killed and driven out of Kashmir. Kashmir is now ethnically cleansed!

A couple of days after the **9/11 Attack**, I tried to estimate the number of hard-core enemy infiltration in the US, when it was discovered that there were 19 men, all Muslims, in those four attacks**.** Assuming their average stay in the US is five years and an individual has lived in five different cities, then by any calculations, any one terrorist must have interacted with at least 100 persons in the places they lived, stores they shopped, mosques they prayed, offices they worked, and sites they visited etc. My most conservative guess was 10,000 on close operators in the US alone. Not even 500 suspects are in the custody, as of today! The US supporters of this enemy, in a couple of millions of Muslim population in the US, are embedded in the neighborhoods, offices, universities, colleges, and even in the political systems.

In war, it is not just a victory that matters, but a total annihilation of the enemy and its roots. It reminds me of events in the history of India during the 11th century. Mahmood Gazani attacked India eighteen times and was defeated 17 times by Prithvi Raj Chauhan. Prithvi Raj made a big mistake 17 times of not chasing and killing Gazani. For his mistake, India has paid a heavy price. In the 18th attempt, Mahmood Gazani finally won. The first thing he did was to behead Prithviraj Raj, and laid the foundation of a series of Muslim occupations in western India.

The Hindus, having no sense of history, are repeating the same national mistakes - whether living in India or the USA. The Indian Parliament House, the symbol of a democratic government was attacked by the same enemy in Dec 2001. A couple of hundred members of parliament escaped their slaughter. India did not declare a war on Pakistan, as the US did on Afghanistan. Nor, India has militarily supported the US!

(June 21, 2003)

PS – Oct, 2011: If Iraq did not have any weapons of mass destruction, then why Saddam let so many UN resolutions pass against his nuclear arsenals. Why did he stop the entry or expel the UN inspectors on more than one occasion? If it was a bluff, then he could have called it off before the attacks were launched on Iraq. He could have saved his life and his regime. Some still believe that the weapons were smuggled out of Iraq. Nevertheless, this question will be settled by the scholars when all the documents are declassified in Iraq, UN, UK and the US and made available for academic research.

NOTES AND COMMENTS

A PERSPECTIVE ON HOMELAND SECURITY

Tonight, I spoke in *Provocateurs Club* of Las Vegas toastmasters on historical perspective on homeland security. It started with the US Bill of Rights, the first ten Amendments to the US Constitution, enacted in 1791. There is little that people do it today the way it was done more than 200 years ago. For instance, one may wonder at the relevance of the two amendments - #7 right of a jury trial for an amount exceeding $20 and the other #3 on not forcing a homeowner to house a soldier in it.

The most talked First Amendment includes religion. It says: that the Congress shall not make laws to **establish** a religion nor **prohibit** people to freely exercise one. It must be noted that Christian Church has been the backbone of all the European colonies, and the US colony was no exception. It became a 'Christian' country. The freedom that the Protestants and other church denominations did not have in Europe was now protected in the US. The early colonizers forced and 'lured' their black slaves and native Indians into Christianity. At that time the First Amendment was not addressed to the Hindus, Muslims, or Buddhist etc. to have the same equality! Moreover, in the US of 1776, there was no Hindu, Muslim, or Buddhist population.

India's prosperity, through the 10th century, attracted people from all over - like the US is doing today. Material prosperity eventually softens the later generations. **When national issues are often discussed from ethical, moral and universal grounds, then it tolls the decline of an affluent society.** They forget how their ancestors fought with their blood and sweat in building a great nation. The worst sign of decline is when a later generation turns apologetic for any perceived act of injustice by their forefathers 100 - 200 years ago. It is terrible.

The Hindu rulers of the 10th century India treated the Arab traders with generosity and warmth. Realizing the passivity in the Hindu way of life, Mohamed Gori alone invaded and plundered west India seventeen times. What they did to the grand Hindu temples, monuments, and women is so chilling that it dwarfs the **9/11 Attack on America**. For instance, in one raid on Mathura, a holy city of the Hindus, its magnificent temples were razed and set on fire. **It took seven days to melt the huge gold idols into ingots so that they could be carted away to Arabia.**

Hundreds of such attacks eventually changed the demographic landscape of north India for the next 1000 years. The weakened Hindus accepted Muslim atrocities as destined, and waited for better days in the next birth! They did not stand up and fought to protect their own homeland. **The foreign invaders destroyed their will to live in dignity for the next one thousand years.**

I also asserted that the enemy of the US is embedded in the US population. The **Patriot Bills** needs full legislative and public support. Currently, the US borders are porous and internet and cellular technology have made the world virtually borderless. The **Bill of Rights** has to be interpreted in the context of modern times. 200 hundred years ago, no one had forethought that the US would face the attacks - like Pearl Harbor and 9/11.

After two major speeches, there was a very healthy discussion for 90 minutes in which opinions were freely expressed under a moderator. That also gave me an opportunity to add a few comments of clarification and elaboration. I reminded that India has miserably failed to protect its homeland since 1989, as it could not stop the 99.99 % ethnic cleansing of the Hindus and Sikhs from Kashmir.

Incidentally, the present enemies of the Indian way of life and the American way of life are the same Islamic Jihadis. In Dec 2001, they attacked the Indian Parliament. A massacre or capture for ransom of 200 Members of Parliament was miraculously averted. India did not even take one hundredth of measures what the USA has already implemented for its homeland security. Had India gone after the terrorists in Pakistan in 2001 - like the US did it in Afghanistan, then India and USA would have snuffed out the terrorist networks.

India failed again, when a couple of days ago, it refused to send its troops to Iraq to join the USA in its re-construction. The Hindus, ethnically dominant in India, have never learnt a lesson from their own history. That is why they are condemned to repeat it every fifty years. However, this is a lesson for the US public and the US Government too. Once this enemy wins, it will change the conquered landscape forever.

It was a great evening!

(July 19, 2003)

PS - Oct 2011: During the Bush Administration (2001 – 2009), the US did not have any other major act of Islamic terrorism on its soil. However, quite a few attacks have taken place during the Obama Administration before the killing of Osama bin Ladin in May, 2011. However, in India, according to a report, 50 terrorist attacks take place every year! The Nov 2008 attack in Mumbai killed nearly 200 people and paralyzed the entire nation.

NOTES AND COMMENTS

CONGRESS PARTY HAS LOST!

December 04 is going to be a momentous day in Indian politics. Congress Party lost in four out of five state assembly elections. Yes, it is the Congress Party that has lost - BJP (Bharatiya Janta Party) did not win. About two weeks before the elections, 63-year old, Sharad Pawar, a renegade of the Congress Party, itching to come back, said, "I will accept Priyanka Gandhi as the Prime Minister (PM), but not Sonia Gandhi. It shows how the Congress Party and its stalwarts have become bankrupt in their leadership vision.

Priyanka, 31 years old, has not contributed to any national issue. Yet, some Congress leaders are lining up behind her, as if her Gandhi persona can bring the party back to power. Neither the Congress Party is left with any leader, nor do they appreciate what Sonia Gandhi has done for it. Six years ago, the Party brass pressed Sonia Gandhi to take over the party reins. Now that she has established a track record, the leaders want her out before she becomes the PM! Because of the squabbles and having no charismatic field commanders in the states, the Congress Party has badly lost this round of state elections.

If BJP gloats on having won more seats in each state, including Delhi, then they are mistaken. The General Elections are coming up in 2004. It won't be surprising if BJP loses parliament seats in the same states where they have just won assembly seats. The reason being this victory belongs to the NDA (National Democratic Alliance). Six year ago, this experiment of coalition government hardly had lasted one year. But after a fresh mandate in 1999, the NDA has been moving unchallenged for the last two years. All inner fights have become a thing of past. It has set an example that a rainbow of parties can have a common agenda for the progress of the country. Their record is incredible, particularly, if one compares it with any past five years of Congress Party in power.

India's foreign exchange reserve has been the largest in history and its currency - rupee, never so strong. Achievements due to liberalization, privatization, deregulation and denationalization are too numerous to state. The credits go to the leadership of Vajpayee and his rainbow coalition, the NDA. However, the BJP has a very long way to go. At present, it is primarily a party of urban Hindu traders. The Hindus remain divided and distributed amongst several socialistic and communist parties. Muslims stay miles away from the BJP. In the name of secularism, Congress governments have been anti Hindus, but pro Muslims and pro Christians. It has finally backfired on Congress. On the other hand, the BJP has yet to do anything for the Hindus. The 2004 parliamentary elections may turn a new page of history, if BJP absolutely comes in power. **My prediction: NOT YET!**

(Dec 04, 2003)

PS – Oct, 2011: In 2004, the BJP/NDA lost their 1999 mandate. Another coalition of parties, the UPA (United Progressive Alliance) elected Manmohan Singh of Congress Party, as PM. The UPA won again in 2009.

NOTES AND COMMENTS

1. It is incredible that many of your predictions have been proved correct. As far as I am concerned in my view it won't be a politician who will do something for our country. **Subhash Sood**
    I wrote: This article was published in the India Post/San Francisco. You see one need not be an astrologer to predict. However, understanding of events of past and present is very essential. All the leaders who lost had personal astrologers! Thanks

2. I feel that the mistake of leaving its traditional agenda of promoting Hinduism as a strong nationalist movement and too much pampering non-Hindu voters by promises and financial handouts, BJP has disillusioned Hindu voters (who form 80% of Indian population). Promising to appoint a million or so Urdu teachers, high increase in direct and indirect subsidy for Haj pilgrimage (as against raising fees for Hindu pilgrims to Amarnath ji, Mansaarovar, etc.), setting up of minority finance corporations where the interest rates are highly subsidized (around one-third of what is charged by other governmental development financial institutions), nominating left oriented intellectuals to various educational and cultural bodies (this irritated the nationalist intellectuals of high credentials who were ideologically and functionally supporters of the Hindu/Sangh parivar at all time), pampering of Muslims at every stage by tall promises and their funding/implementation (even Sikhs were ignored and their religious pilgrimages were not supported by the government in any visible manner). **Nigam**

THE GROWING POWER OF A RELIGION

Yesterday, I was amazed and appalled to read the reports of worldwide Friday protests against the upcoming French legislation banning Muslim headscarves for women. There are now 5 million Muslims in France - out of its population of 60 millions. At one time, not too long ago, the Muslim population was mathematically zero. The protests are being organized in all the major cities of France and European countries. Middle Eastern countries are expected to do it. Surprisingly, the protest rallies are taking place in cities of India including Kashmir! When I read about Kashmir I said it is now all Muslim, as the terror tactics since 1989 has ethnically cleansed Kashmir of all the Hindus and Sikhs.

There are three obvious components of this issue. One, the legislation has not become a law. Two, the proposed legislation also applies to the skull caps of the Jews and Christian crosses. Three, **the Jews and Christians are not protesting against it!** It is certain that the Muslims won't stop migrating to France even after this legislation becomes a law. Modern France, predominantly a Christian country, yet the French government is banning the Christian crosses! Can anyone think of any one thing that applies equally to all religious denominations in any Muslim country in the world? In Saudi Arabia one cannot even carry the holy Gita publicly. They are all autocratic societies - none is democratic! In fact, the Muslim nations are not made for democracy. Islam is all about unquestioned obedience to the laws enunciated in Koran and Haddis.

For the last 25 years, the Muslim migration to the European countries has been phenomenal. In Belgium and Germany, they make a bigger proportion of population. **It is no different from Muslim armies marching west out of the deserts of Middle East in the 7th and 8th century.** The strategy of Muslim terrorists is to take advantage of the democratic rules of law in European countries in order to gain political and social bases. Once they are politically strong, they can take over the whole country by force. The most tolerant Hindus of India in the 9th century were run over by a few thousand Muslim marauders. Once they took over the western India, gradually the entire country came under their grip for centuries. From a zero Muslim population a 1000 years ago in India, they are over 150 millions in the truncated India even after 1947 carving out of 130 millions in Pakistan and 120 millions in Bangladesh!

I strongly believe that the laws of religious freedom in the US and Europe were enacted at a time when they had no non-Christian populations. It was essentially to protect the religious freedom of various Christian churches starting to emerge after the Church Reformation. Hence, it does not give other religions the same rights and privileges.

The non-Muslin nations of the world have to understand the strategies of Islamic terrorists. Instead of banning head scarves, skull caps, etc. the laws should be amended to clarify the religious freedom. **Otherwise, these countries will meet the same fate that India met, and will be taken over from within and without in a short time**.

(Jan 17, 2004)

NOTES AND COMMENTS

1. Great article...you know more history so I cannot comment on that but it reads well and I certainly saw the Hindu cleansing in Srinagar. The people I met and stayed with had to flee the year after I was there...for their lives! **Rene'**

2. I am a broadminded person basically. I liked Muslims even in childhood. However this faith breeds contempt and fortifies hatred, violent streaks, and compulsive tendencies.
    You should send this article to President of France and USA and to Queen of England, and heads of States in Netherlands, Germany, Austria, Switzerland, Denmark, Sweden, Norway, Australia, and New Zealand. This faith has not produced any philosopher of any worth. Science itself does not progress on its people. **Subhash Sood**

VAJPAYEE MUST STEP DOWN

It has been two days! Vajpayee has not yet taken any moral or strategic responsibility for this election defeat. He called for early elections costing the tax payers crores of rupees. The worst is the stance of the BJP Party President, Venkaikah Naidu. He should have been the first to submit the resignation. I can't believe that Vajpayee wants to continue as the Leader of the Opposition. **The lust for political power is the mother of all lusts!**

In the US, the CEO of a company gets the first axe for corporate losses in public relation. The coaches of professional sports, making millions of dollars, are fired in the middle of a season, if the team starts sliding down. At the end of every sports season, nearly 25 % of the coaches are fired, or they resign themselves. If a coach does not take the responsibility, then the fans, media and management go after him. No business in the US is as competitive as professional sports.

This principle is also the driving force in the US public life. The problem with the BJP is dual. The party members, being largely Hindus, do not go after the blood. There are timid attempts to fix blame on some one as a sacrificial lamb. It is terrible. The leadership studies tell that if a leader owns up responsibility, then it quickly percolates at every level. On the other hand, when the underlings find their leaders dodging the bullets, they too shrug and demure accountability.

Sometimes, it appears that the lack of leadership is the main reason for sticking up with the status quo. Hindus relatively do not have leadership traits. Vajpayee has been elevated at a pedestal that no one dares to touch him. I do not know whether he has really nurtured any coterie of leaders. After the Nov 2003 assembly elections, Mahajan, Jaitley and Swaraj were projected as the next generation of BJP leadership. They were so much hyped that they lost their judgment! On the success of the assembly elections, the BJP called the parliamentary elections six months earlier.

The Hindus are conditioned to obedience towards their elders under every circumstance. It is, in fact, a corollary of their long subjugation for centuries. This approach may keep an uneasy peace at home, but in politics it does not yield power. **Political power comes through the barrel of a gun, or with edge of sword**. That is the only principle of succession in politics. A new leadership has to claim a stake, stand up, and wrest the power. **This is a moment of reality check for the old and new guards of the BJP.**

Yesterday, I wrote to a BJP diehard, that the entire top brass of the Party has to step down. They better undertake *PADYATRAS* (walking on foot). The undertaken *RATHYATRAS* (chariot runs) were on highways, not in the byways of villages.

They should traverse the entire country before the next elections. Gandhi did it, Vinoba did it. Reddy just did it, and trounced Chandrababu Naidu, the self proclaimed CEO of Andhra Pradesh.

(May 15, 2004)

NOTES AND COMMENTS

Yes, as part of our democratic traditions and constitutional requirements, Vajpayee has submitted his resignation which has been accepted by the President. Sonia Gandhi is being sworn in tomorrow. I am reminded of a couplet by Sarojini Naidu which I read in my school days: AND PEACE TO THE VANQUISHED AND HOPE TO THE STRONG, FOR ME O' MY MASTER THE RAPTURE OF SONG.

Unfortunately all of us find fault with others and indulge in blame game (within the family and outside)and do not reflect on our own shortcomings, limitations, lack of efforts and actions, poor planning and mis-deployment of our precious time and other resources to face the realities and challenges in our life. BJP is no exception. Quite often we get drunk in our small successes and embark on big missions/ projects without appropriate thinking, planning and preparations; even ignoring our own manpower base, its quality, competency, capability and seriousness. Chamchas, who loiter around as 'close advisors, considerably reduce one's own independent thinking and poison ears, eyes and even the mental makeup. Bajpai, left to himself, has emerged as a real leader of worldwide standing; compare him to Bush, Tony Blair, or any other personality of today (Governmental leaders of Germany, Japan, France, Italy, Russia, Korea or any other country) He has been in the national mainstream of politics from his childhood; was jailed in Quit India movement when he was just 17 years of age. He has been, since then behaving in a dignified manners (leave aside a few slips of the tongue which all of us have; also consider his age and not so good health to handle political work of the type which we see today everywhere in India). Thanks: **NIGAM**

TALES OF MONARCHY

For the last couple of days, the media coverage of two political events has occupied a space in my mind. One is the 80th birth anniversary of the British Queen Elizabeth. A reporter added that in 15 more years, she will break Queen Victoria's record of 64-year reign (1837-1901). It is a sign of world acceptance of British monarchy in social, cultural and political aspects of life. Historically, the monarchy has kept Britain dynamically unified, as do the Union Jack (flag) and God Save The Queen (anthem).

The other event is the surge in violent protests against the Nepalese King Gyanendra. Unfortunately, the worldwide media is projecting the Nepalese king and Nepalese monarchy synonymously one. If King Gyanendra is incompetent, corrupt, incapable to rule and defend the country, then he must abdicate, or be thrown out. His excessive power may be curtained. But the abolition of the Nepalese monarchy must be opposed.

Varied forms of monarchy exist in several countries of Europe, Africa, and in almost every Muslim country. It is prevalent in some Buddhist countries of South East Asia. A unique observation about Nepal is its political freedom during the last millennium that India lost to scores of foreign invaders. After independence in 1947, India adopted a socialistic system. Nehru, the first Prime Minister of India and the contemporary kings Tribhuvan and Mahendra of Nepal never got along well. However, I always foresee closer ties between India and Nepal, as seen between the US and UK.

For a perspective, it is better to have a brief survey of the region during the last 200 years. By the turn of the 19th century, the British were secured from the East and South of India. In the North and West they used diplomacy: **Make a peace treaty when enemy is strong and break it when enemy is weak.** Maharaja Ranjit Singh, the founder of the Sikh Empire 'blundered' in accepting (1809, Amritsar Treaty) Sutlej River as the Eastern boundary of his empire. Soon after his death in 1839, the British annexed Punjab in 1849 when his incompetent sons were thrown out in quick succession.

The history of the Hindu kings of Nepal and India goes back in ancient times due to their common scriptures and heritage. Like Maharaja Ranjit Singh, a Nepalese king in the 19th century tried to extend its northern boundary into Tibet and China to control over Mount Kailash and Manasrover Lake, the time immemorial places of Hindu pilgrimage. But a defeat and treaty with the Chinese cut it short.

The Nepalese monarchy admirably preserved its identity during the 19th century when the bigger kingdoms in India were falling before the Tsunami expansion of the British Empire. The British treaty with Nepal in 1816 thwarted Nepal's expansion in South and West. Under the second treaty, the British started recruiting the Nepalese martial race, **Gurkhas** into the British/Indian Army (as the Mughals did with the Rajputs under Akbar). The ultra loyal **Gurkhas** fought for the British in India (with their Hindu brethren), Europe and Africa for nearly 150 years! A paradox is whereas, the Hindu kings of Nepal ruled with militancy, how come this edge was lost to the Hindus of India?

In recent times, the Nepalese monarchy did not champion the Hindu causes abroad. They have, rather, projected a subdued image of Hinduism. The Muslims fleeing Mumbai after the communal riots in 1993, felt safer in Hindu Nepal than in secular India. India's polices toward Nepal were exploited both by China and Pakistan. During the 1970s, Nepal was flooded with cheaper Chinese goods. But along with it came the seeds of Lenin and Mao ideologies of anti-monarchy (the anti-thesis of Hinduism) that are booming in Nepal today!

Recently, Nepal became the only place in the world, where Islamic and communist ideologies have colluded against India and the Nepalese monarchy. The open border of Nepal has become a haven for the Islamic terrorists to plot against India from the Nepalese soil. The hijacking of Air India planes and other acts of terrorism are traced back to Nepal. Yet, the Indian political parties have not acted globally to counter them. Kathmandu and Delhi may be apart, but their people are far closer, as they have been bound in marriages, jobs and businesses for centuries.

Every folk tale of India begins with a king. For millennia, the Hindus have been inspired by great lord kings - Raam and Krishna. The present attitude of Indian masses is a backlash against the licentious and treacherous princes who supported the British rule in India. Naturally, Indians don't have much sympathy for monarchy in general. At the other end, whereas, the countries like USA and USSR have heavily invested, say, in India's educational enterprise, the Nepalese monarchy has openly done little to patronize any Indian university.

Nevertheless, it is high time that the Indians stand by the Nepalese monarchy at this juncture and Indian government rightly use its diplomacy and resources. **There has been never been a move to abolish the British monarchy**. Last week, the assets of Queen Elizabeth were ranked Number 192 amongst the richest persons in Britain (India born, Laxmi Mittal is Number 1). It does not upset the public. In the new world countries, monarchy may be archaic, but in old countries, it nurtures great institutions that ultimately make the backbone of a great nation.

Is there a monarchy in future for India where Hindus adore power figures even in their numerous gods and goddesses? Nehru was a populist 'dictatorial' Prime Minister. Indira Gandhi tried and failed. But the fate denied it to Sanjay Gandhi! The meteoric rise of Italy born, Sonia Gandhi, as the most powerful figure in Indian politics today, indicates that a scion of Nehru-Gandhi dynasty may emerge as a future 'king' of India.

(April 23, 2006)

NOTES AND COMMENTS

Satish ji, nice one! I am with your view in this article most of the times. Just to add a few things.

- Nepalese people, in general, are not against monarchy per se, but they felt hopeless after Gyanendra's takeover. He was never a popular figure and people suspected him for killing King Birendra and his family. More than that, his son is so hopeless that people lost hope in Monarchy in Nepal.
- If we read Nepal's history, Malla, and Lichhibi kings did great jobs in building temples and spreading Hinduism. In early Shah Kingdom, only a few Kings exercised their absolute power and did great jobs, but in later years, Ranas ruled Nepal as their proxies. The new history of Shah Kingdom began with King Tribhuvan (the grandfather of Gyanendra). Yes, they did not do anything that paralleled with Lichhabi kings of Nepal. No patronage to any universities.. no patronage to any temples... nothing like Thai king, who is a great scholar of Hindu epics.
- Yes, Nepal became a place for Kashmiri Muslims and what not. Nepalese governments (even under absolute monarchy!) could not see long-term impact of letting them settle in Nepal.
- Nepalese kings colluded with Maoists early on to weaken other political parties. But it boomeranged.
- If there is anyone to blame for Gyanendra to lose his throne despite general support to monarchy in Nepal, it is he himself and his son.

Nepal is at the verge of being a playground for many religions and there are massive religious conversions. This conversion is not something out of free mind. It is also not due to 'untouchability' or other social factors. It is merely based on financial basis. People are lured for that!

I know, you know very well about Nepalese history. But I just tried to highlight my general observation/opinion. Best regards, **Mahesh**

TIME TO REACH OUT TO ISRAEL

Recently, a forwarded e-mail has listed over 40 remarkable achievements of the Israelis. By and large, one should be very discriminating about the internet news. Since the 1950s, as political awareness started occupying my mind, I wondered at the existence of no diplomatic ties between India and Israel. The two are 4000 miles apart and never had any conflict. Here are some interesting facts about India and Israel:

1. Israel was created in 1948. In 1947, nearly one third of India/Hindustan was carved out for the Muslims, as a new country, Pakistan (land of the pure). It was a condition of 'price' for independence.
2. The Jews have the longest history of continuous living in Hindustan.
3. Hindustan is the only land in the world, where the Jews were never persecuted.
4. The oldest stately synagogue in Asia, perhaps outside Israel, is in Cochin, India.
5. India is the only country, where the least number of Jews have migrated to Israel.
6. India and Israel fought wars with their neighbors right after they came into existence.
7. The 6.5 million Jews died in one holocaust **outside Israel**. But more than 20 millions
   Hindus died in several holocausts **within India,** under the Muslim and British rules.
8. Whereas, Israel has extended its territorial control since 1948, India has lost its parts to China in 1962 War. The Islamic Jehadis control Kashmir after the ethnic cleansing of the Hindus and Sikhs in recent times. The secular Indian Government is ashamed to admit it.
9. Hinduism and Judaism are the oldest religions in the world.
10. India is the only museum/tolerant of all religions and cults in the world.

It is time to cultivate closer ties between the Hindus and Jews at the individual and corporate levels without waiting for the governments to give any lead. The Hindu Diaspora, particularly in the US and Canada, can make history in this direction.

There being no private capital in India for at least two decades after independence, there were no contacts between the Hindus in India and Jews in Israel. On the other hand, the attitude of the Hindus towards the Muslim sentiments is of unwanted 'magnanimity' for winning them over, and fear of Muslim reprisal and their historic atrocities. No matter how many Muslims occupy the highest seats - like that of President and Chief Justice of India, it is never enough.

Israel has offered its technology and encouraged Indian students to study in Israel, but the Congress led governments always cooled them down. Reason, it would offend the Muslims! The first diplomatic connection between India and Israel was set up in 1977 - during the Janta Party rule.

Since 1989, the Islamic terrorism in India has been on the rise dramatically. Neither, the Indian government, nor any Hindu organization has supported the US in its 2001 War against the Islamo-fascists who brought down 9/11/2001 to the USA, and Kargil, 12/11/2001 (Indian Parliament), Godhara massacre, and regular blasts including 11/28/2008 (Mumbai), to India. The Hindus have to wake up and align with other friends including Jews, and conversely. Unfortunately, the 80% Hindu population of India, being distributed in every political party in India, have little clout in Indian Government.

(Aug 03, 2006/Sep, 2010)

NOTES AND COMMENTS

1. That's all very important information. Most of which is new to me. Thank you. **Dutchie**

2. Dear Dr. Bhatnagar: India and Israel jointly work on various programs and will discuss with you when I see you next time. **Venkatrao**

WASTED CHIVALRY

I never met Virneder Singh. Only a month ago, his elder brother, Narinder, a friend and colleague of my nephew, told me about his serving in Indian Army as a major. Knowing my travel pleasures, particularly in unusual places, he insisted that I visit Virender in Kashmir. Today, at 9 AM, on Dewali Day, Virender, at the age of 30, became a dead target of the Muslim terrorists coming to fight there from all over the world.

In 1998, my sister, brother-in-law, and I spent four days in Srinagar after completing the Amarnath pilgrimage. The devastation of Hindu temples, properties, and their exodus (later of the Sikhs too) from Kashmir Valley shocked us. We had taken this trip with confidence, as Shiv Sena Superemo, Bal Thackeray had warned these terrorists that any attack on Hindu pilgrims will stop the Muslims going to the Hajj through Mumbai.

No words of consolation came out of my mouth, when I saw Narinder. As he was getting into the car for the out-of-town funeral, I could only mutter that it was your test time. My mind was possessed with festering Kashmir. For the last 18 years, Indian Government has been running a losing war. The shadows of Kashmir are falling on Afghanistan and Iraq too. In the US, some generals and Secretary of Defense were forced to resign for their failures. But no one in India has paid a price for the colossal blunders in Kashmir.

The Muslim fighters have adopted the time-tested methods of ethnic cleansing and Madrassa education. A few years ago, Imams of 50,000 masjids, running the madrassas in Pakistan, overwhelming rejected the introduction of science in the curricula. The madrassas are the Harvards and Oxfords for turning out the best fighters in the world.

Indian army in Kashmir and the US forces in Afghanistan and Iraq are fighting with their hands tied at their backs. They can only engage the enemy when attacked first. The deaths of the terrorists are splashed all over. It is unbelievable that the Hindu journalists of English media support and abet the Muslim terrorists out of fear and cowardice.

During the Amaranth trek, we saw many despondent soldiers and officers counting their days to leave Kashmir. Virender was under transfer order to leave Kashmir only after a day. His wife was waiting with his 3-year old son. The situation of Indian army borders insanity. The battles are controlled by the generals sitting in high tech command centers, and by the politicians eyeing on the next election - rather than the next generation.

Every day, the soldiers and officers are shot like sitting ducks for the staggered prizes on their heads. It is seldom reported, as they die unsung. They are not heroes, as they are not given free reins to fight and prove their chivalry. It is like a college where professors do not teach the students, or of a hospital, where physicians don't treat the patients? That seems to be the state of Indian Army in Kashmir!

(Nov 09, 2007/India)

NOTES AND COMMENTS

1. Coming to the other piece," WASTED CHIVALRY", you are perhaps right in observing that India is fighting a losing battle in Kashmir. The problem lies largely in the vote-bank politics. Otherwise, forcing liberal education in Madrassas on the pain of closing them down and cutting of the sources of funding of militancy will weaken insurgency in Kashmir. Mr. Jagmohan as the Governor of Kashmir tried to do so and all of us know what happened to him. He was unceremoniously recalled by the Government of India. **SR Wadhwa**

2. "Wasted Chivalry" is really good, you have pointed facts in a short and crisp manner... Looking forward for more insights like these from you...Regards. **Gargi**

JODHAA AND JALAAL

Yesterday, I watched the 210-minute long Hindi movie, *Jodhaa Akbar* without taking a break. Ever since my wife saw it two weeks ago, she wanted me to watch it for my interest in history. Also, public protests against it had aroused my curiosity. During the movie, the only entry made on the clipboard was on the Hindu Raja, Hem Chandra of UP and Delhi. Despite Hem Chandra's well-equipped army and its size, 2-3 times that of Akbar, he lost the war, his head and his kingdom in the Second Battle of Panipat, in 1556. Had he won - like the Afghan chieftain, Sher Shah Suri did in 1540 over Humanyu, Akbar's father, the history of North India would have been different.

The movie has dramatized a new love story between the Rajput Princess, Jodhaa Bai and the 3rd Mughal King, Jalaal-uddin Mohammed, known as Akbar (means Great). The postfix, 'uddin' of the name and ending, Mohammad, are parts of every Mughal king's full name. Jodhaa Bai, raised in a puritan Hindu culture of the 16th century Rajasthan, is far removed from the romantic folk tales of Anarkali and Salim, or Rupmati and Baz Bahadur. Movies are periodically produced on historic romances. Here the big difference is that Anarkali and Rupmati were commoners.

Is there anything offensive in the script to hurt the sensibilities of the Hindus? Yes, it is the over glorification of Akbar and his justified rule over Hindustan. With hindsight, Akbar cannot be blamed either for his ruthlessness or diplomacy in building a vast empire. The Hindus were dis-united, their armies overmatched in weaponry, and they had forgotten the Chanakya doctrine (*Neeti*) of chase-and-annihilate-the-enemy. Unfortunately, these factors have not yet changed!

According to Abdul Fazl, the chronicler of Akabarnama, Akbar's harem had 3000 concubines. The British historians, Blochman mentioned 7 wives and Beveridge, 300. Jodhaa Bai remained his chief queen who bore Nur-uddin Mohammad, known as Jahangir, successor to the throne. According to the *Wikipedia*, Akbar had three sons and six daughters from his 4 queens. Almost every Rajput kingdom had sent a *Dola* (daughter and dowry) to Akbar's palace.

Conquering new lands and expanding empires is synonymous with taking over the resources of the vanquished including their wealth and women. Back in the 4th century BC, Alexander married daughters of some kings he defeated. The passionate urges that fire up in a man for the prized women also drive him to the battlefields. **It is puzzling how this connection got lost over the Hindus.** The Hindu epics of Ramayana and Mahabharata have numerous instances of wars over beautiful women. Successive defeats of the Hindu kings since the 11th century dropped a pall of defeatist mentality over Hindu life, in general.

Twisted Hindu morality, cowardice-cum-non-violence and inability to stop strangers entering their homes, are due to collective defeatist mentality. The norms of morality are different for rich and poor and for rulers and the ruled. **The first love legends of the Hindus will be born only when they are Victors in a War**. For instance, the Hindus have to conquer back nearly one million Sq KM territory lost to China in the 1962 war, and re-populate a million Hindus and Sikhs ethnically cleansed from Kashmir since 1989 - heralding the beginning of a new Hindustan.

(Mar 09, 2008)

NOTE AND COMMENTS

1. I have not seen the movie. I have been reading about it in papers and some mentioned she was not married to Akbar, although there is her palace at Fatehpur Sikri.
    You know Hindus are still not united. The regionalism was the downfall of Hindus and it seems we are heading the same way. Muslims are so organized because of their practice of going to mosques every day. It is impossible to get Hindus together in such a large measure. **HNB**

2. Bhai Shri Satish Ji, Sasneh Namaste!
    Allow me to say in ONE word, your undernoted write-up is EXCELLENT and a right analysis.
    Unless we, Hindus get United, forgetting our petty quarrels & Recover & re-conquer our lost territories from China & Pakistan & unless we are able to re-established our Kashmiri Pundits back into Kashmir & till we regain our self Confidence & re-start believing in our strength, we shall continue to be hopeless lot of people, namely Hindus on this earth & we shall continue to receive beatings from the enemies as well as from Invaders like Temurs, Khiljis, Nadir shahs & Mughals etc who have been enjoying our women & we whether as commoners or as Indian Hindu Royalties, had become simply cowards , giving away our women & everything to such cruel Invaders, like Akbar, Aurangzeb & other Muslim Rulers or British Rulers of this impotent country. Best regards, Sincerely Yours, **S C Gupta**.

OBAMA ONTO OMAN

I was in Al-Diyar Hotel in Nizwa, Oman when I witnessed the inauguration of Barrack Hussein Obama, the first Afro-American President of the USA. This event is historic for more than one account. Look at the odds: He was born to a white mother, who married a Muslim graduate student from Kenya. The father went back to Kenya leaving 2-year old Barrack behind. The mother, who was his second or third wife, re-married another Muslim graduate student - from Indonesia. During five formative years, Obama lived in Indonesia, one of the crucibles of Islamic terrorism today.

All this was flashing my mind, as I was watching the inauguration ceremonies on TV. The mind was buffeted by so many thoughts - a sign itself of a great event that the entire world was watching with great anticipation and expectation. The multiple TV coverage, in a small country like Oman, is an index of Obama's worldwide popularity. The live hysteria on the streets of Washington DC, in particular, is unprecedented in terms of the number of people and the expression of their emotions.

Obama's election has strengthened popular clichés – like, the US, a land of opportunities - one can be what one wants to be - have dreams and realize them in the US. Have I realized mine in 40 years? Oh yes, far beyond the material possessions and pleasures, I am discovering myself in my 60's. Many friends, relatives, and institutions who have been assisted - could not be done, otherwise. Warren Buffet once said that one of three reasons for his success in life is to be born in USA.

Obama's inauguration is a celebration of the US immigrant character, a hallmark of great American Civilization. Coming from the USA, a 300-year old land of the immigrants, I am here in ancient Oman teaching for a semester. It is known as the land of Sinbad, one of the greatest sailors in the world. However, some think of him as a myth. In great nations, myths become facts; in lost lands, facts become myths.

With western discovery of oil (called black liquid gold) in gulf countries, lately, the petro dollars have been pouring. With growing energy needs, speculation raised the oil prices to dizzying heights. Already, I have seen the mud dwellings of the natives in Oman and Dubai. They are now living in palatial homes in their lifetimes. The world is in awe at mega construction projects undertaken by Dubai, in particular.

The Gulf countries make a different world, as shaped by Islam. While watching the celebration, I thought of many Indians in Gulf region, who have spent 40-50 years in these countries. But they are excluded from political life. The proportion of natives vs. expatriates in countries - like Dubai and Oman, is close to 1:4. Yet, the natives control all strategic departments. Essentially, once a non-Omani, is always a non-Omani.

A paradox of human drama is that people are happy to come to Gulf area, as they are for the USA. In Oman, the expatriates earn money, remit it, and go back to their home countries after a certain period. With unchecked terrorists' blasts, India needs to adopt new immigrant and citizenship policies. There is no one model for nations to become great. But India cannot rise up without the will of the Hindus, the major stakeholders.

(Jan 22, 2009/Oman)

NOTES AND COMMENTS

MUSCAT MUSEUM & MORE

A museum is an index of a nation's present state, its traditions and history. Visiting a national museum is a must on my itinerary. Today, I 'knocked out' the Omani National Museum in Muscat. Often, I am the last person to leave a museum, but today I have established a new record of being the first one to enter and the last one to walk out.

The visitors to a museum tell a lot about themselves, as they do about the place. The sole receptionist-cum-curator told me that the hours were kept limited, because the Omanis seldom come. Today, besides me, there was a European couple - only three people during 9 AM-1 PM hours. **Sophistication in life's many pursuits does not come as rapidly as sudden wealth may come**. Gulf countries provide unique examples in history where entire nations went from rags to riches in one lifetime.

Naturally, my thoughts went back to the US Smithsonian museums in Washington DC. It is a complex of a dozen buildings comprising the US National Museum. One cannot see it all in one month! It symbolizes the US; a great civilization. Muscat museum is hardly bigger than the collection an average American living in a 3500 sq ft home.

A week ago, I was disappointed to see the signs at museum entrances that the afternoon hours, from 4-6 PM, were canceled. I had taxied from Nizwa, 175 KM away. Today, I was inside the museum by 10 AM, and was excited with anticipation. The excitement was not on visual plane, but intellectual one. It is what I have described it, as an inverse mathematical modeling in history of mathematics - establishing mathematical knowledge from ancient artifacts. Modern books are only 500 years old.

In fairness to the Muscat museum, I was told, than the national museum, in a new building, opens up in 2010, and that will be vastly better. The focus of my recent researches, in history of mathematics, is on the geographical region comprising Oman, Yemen and UAE. However, I could not make any mathematical connections. Many ceramic jars and crockery were Chinese and Japanese. They were on display because they were owned by the Omani royalty or wealthy.

Mathematics brings ultimate precision and perfection in its work, so do mathematical applications to a society. The finishing of any artifacts measures the quality of materials, tools and workmanship. It was nothing high then; it is no different today. During one-month stay in Oman so far, I have seen structural fissures in new buildings and hotels – like, cracked tiles of glossy floors and broken out furniture in classrooms and offices. Though, nothing is more than a couple of years old.

The most interesting item in the museum is a copy of Prophet Muhammad's letter to the rulers of Oman. The rulers submitted to him. Oman is one of the first and fewer countries in the world to be Islamicized without warfare. The receptionist told me such copies were found in India, Baluchistan and Afghanistan. But the original is lost or not traceable! Look at the irony of my second visit, as I pulled out the camera to take its picture, its battery was dead!

The political colonization of the 18th century may be over, but West Europeans continue to colonize the world. All the archaeological work in Oman is done by the Germans and Danish. No wonder, hoards of German tourists are seen in the hotel I am staying. Of course, there are French, British and Italians too. Ordinary European tourists are doing what their ancestors started 4-5 centuries ago. A young German couple, riding bikes in Dubai and Oman, told me of having met a 60-year old German physician crisscrossing the desert on a bike alone - from Dubai to Salalah - covering 3000 KM. It is not just to test the limits of physical endurance, but to truly realize a spiritual experience.

A small room was displaying a moon rock and flag that the astronauts carried for each nation. I remember having seen such a moon nugget in 1973 - displayed in the lobby of IU's Lily Library. On the other hand, ancient Omani sailors went far and wide in oceans. It appears that knowledge of building boats did not improve with time. It was interesting to note their knowledge of wood fiber, and the teak wood for the boats was imported from India.

The workmanship in Omani wooden boxes with hundreds of decorative brass studs made them extremely strong but nothing mathematical comes out. They are used in the drawing room for display and storage of items. The one my maternal grandfather had was older and better. Omanis, living in tribes, are warring. It is symbolized by its national insignia of two swords and dagger tucked in a waist belt. The Sikh insignia is remarkably similar!

A collection of locks, keys and bolts on the doors had rudimentary mechanical actions. They are massive. Locks and keys operate on arithmetic functions in computer jargon. It is the knowledge of these functions that creates complex electronic system used in homes and vaults of the banks worldwide. However, they are mostly American.

A showcase contained the medals, stripes and ribbons given by the British Government to the rulers for their assistance, loyalty, or permitting the preaching of Christianity in their Sultanates. It reminds me of the Americans awarding honorary doctorates and ranks in the in the US military to individuals who have taken politically correct decisions. The basic instincts of the humans are the same; the styles change with time.

So far, Oman has yet to produce a first tangible mathematical nugget. I have engaged my students in this project too and eagerly wait to see their efforts. On looking out for them in the coins, it was amusing to note that till 1968, Omani used French/Austrian coins!

During this researching I hit upon a romantic story of a German, a commerce representative in Zanzibar, and its royal princess. They eloped away to Aden and married in 1867, but lived in Germany. It has been the story of all empire builders going after the beautiful women, as they go after new challenges, **Once an adventurer is always an adventurer in any arena - be it physical, intellectual or financial etc...**

(Feb 26, 2009/Oman)

NOTES AND COMMENTS

GURDWARA VS. HINDU TEMPLE

"I don't want to go the temples - no interest in them," thus responded Vinod, when her younger sister asked, if he would like to see the beautiful Hindu Temple of Las Vegas. Vinod and I are known for each other for over 30 years. Yesterday, he, along with family, arrived from Florida for a week. He is 68, and has been a successful engineer in life.

Vinod's remarks silently sent my mind to races. Is there something disgusting about the Hindu Temples? Why Hindus stay away from them? During growing years, hardly we ever went to a temple as family. Here, I am not discriminating between the idol-less Arya Samaj temples and the ones, where the deities are enshrined. Hindu temples in the US are seats of multiple gods and goddesses - signifying emerging unity amongst the Hindus from different Indian states. Also, my focus is on the community temples, not on the tiny ones hidden in home nooks and closets.

Exactly, a week ago on June 03, I had a 3-hour stopover in London, while returning from Oman. As I came out of Heathrow Airport, Harpal, also known for over 30 years, asked me, "Uncle, would you like to spend time in a South Hall gurdwara?" "Sure," I said. The drive took only 15 minutes. The Singh Sabha Gurdwara is perhaps the largest gurdwara in the UK. The non-stop *LANGAR* (free kitchen) is served on the floor right below the main hall where Guru Granth Sahib is seated. Irresistibly, I settled down by a pillar and let the *Shabads* (the holy verses) permeate my being, as I contemplated over the epochal role of gurdwaras in Sikh history.

At the entrance of the main hall, a huge notice board had a picture of martyr Sant Jarnail Singh Bhinderwala and a program to commemorate the 25th anniversary of Blue Star Operation. The notice claimed that 250,000 Sikh men, women and children died in various encounters, now called as Sikh Holocaust. In statistics, it is taught that the numbers do not lie, but its first part is: whose numbers are they? **The world only remembers, what you don't let the world forget it**.

In that atmosphere, I said that in next 50 years, Bhinderwala II will emerge. He will have the same vision of Khalistan, but will not join his forces with the Muslims of Pakistan. The Hindus of Punjab, not ready 50 years ago, will eventually become militant. Recent BJP and Akali combine will change the equation. After all, what is a Khalistan without Nankana Sahib, the birthplace of Guru Nanak and Lahore, the capital of the first Sikh Empire under Maharaja Ranjit Singh? Such a conversation went on inside the Gurdwara while partaking the *prasada*.

The Hindu temples in the US can revive the pre-Islamic traditions of the temples when the 'entire city used to be in the temple'; not the other way around, as seen today. Some remnants of the present Ranganathan Temple in Trichi points out as to how integral it was in Hindu way of life. All public issues were processed through the temples. **The Hindu temples have met a real holocaust in northwest India**. In Punjab, at the time of independence, there was not even single Hindu temple that was 50 years old. The size of a temple is an index of the political clout of its community. It is also a place of celebration of family events, showcasing the talents of the youth, and recognizing contributions of the adults. **Spirituality and sociability are inseparable.**

(June 11, 2009)

NOTES AND COMMENTS

SUBBARAO & NOBEL PEACE PRIZES 101

In Las Vegas, a popular saying is that unless you put a coin in a machine, you won't hit a jackpot. Participation is key to winning any competition. Also, without a competition, an award is not worth it. Generally, universal recognitions - like Nobel Prizes, are bestowed through a network of supporters. For historical reasons, Indians, the Hindus in particular, have shied away from competitions for varied reasons - from individual attitude of extreme humility to a unique brand of centrism. Collectively, it never generated any mass support. No wonder, that most laurels - from the Olympics to the Nobels, in every human arena, are garnered by the westerners. They are the ones who start up the playing fields, intensely compete for the awards; and are never satisfied with mere participation.

I look forward to the month of October to learn about new Nobel Prize winners. It is also tied up with my teaching courses/seminars on history of mathematics and its non-European roots. Thus, mathematics is approached as a converging limit of religions, politics, and histories. This paradigm is apt for understanding the winners of the Nobel Peace Prizes. They are controversial and largely questionable, and often have only tangential connection with peace - locally or globally. Having followed the lifetime work of octogenarian Gandhian, S. N. Subbarao (affectionately known as Bhaiji) for nearly 30 years, he is the most deserving person for the 2010 Nobel Peace Prize. He is a true Gandhian-in-action - not in scholarship, name, or belonging to any scion.

According to Alfred Nobel's will, the Peace Prize should be awarded "*to the person who shall have done the most or the best work for fraternity between nations, for the abolition or reduction of standing armies and for the holding and promotion of peace congresses*." The will, perhaps, written in 1895, the first five awards were started in 1901. The committee, taking a wide interpretation of Nobel's guidelines, expanded them to include efforts to combat poverty, disease and climate changes. Also, the number of awardees has gone from one to multiple, and from the individuals to organizations.

One can well understand Nobel's reasons for instituting awards in chemistry, physics and medicine. He was a man of applied sciences. Eventually, he turned his innovations into industrial production of dynamite and other explosives. Literature aside, it may be out of his subconscious guilt that he set up a Peace Prize. He sold explosives to anyone without any consideration for peace. Ironically, his dynamites continue to explode all over the world for bringing 'peace', as some army generals 'fight' for peace. On the other hand, Subbarao has quietly transformed the hearts of a million people for peace and harmony in India and abroad. One may Google or Yahoo his name for knowing his work.

A cursory analysis of Peace Laureates forms an interesting landscape. There are nineteen years when Peace Prizes were not awarded, particularly during the wars, when peace was needed most. What does it tell about the human psyche; is it more for war or peace? I think it was/will remain equally for both!

The Nobel Prize in Economics, first awarded in 1969, was set up by the Central Bank of Sweden in the memory of Alfred Nobel. I bet the Nobel Foundation must have transferred million$$ to this Bank. The omission of mathematics has stories including the juiciest one in which prominent Swedish mathematician, Mittag Leffler had a liaison with Alfred's lady, or conversely. **Nobel's will has clearly ruled out mathematicians ever getting this honor!** It is no surprise, as a woman drives every man in a short or long run. Incidentally, Nobel's third lady friend won the fifth Nobel Peace Prize in 1905!

The Peace Prizes, during the first 2-3 decades, mostly went to the Scandinavian countries and individuals. The Prizes then being widely unknown, it was like a blind man, distributing goodies and ending up with his own folks. So far, 20 organizations and 96 individuals have received Peace Prizes. It has been jointly shared 23 times. The 1994 Peace Prize was divided between Arafat, Rabin and Peres! The 1973 Prize was also shared by three including Henry Kissinger. But his Vietnamese counterpart, Tho, refused to accept it. Once in a while, declining an award enhances the stature of the decliner.

Nevertheless, with its lofty traditions, the Nobel Prizes reign supreme in the world in areas given out. Despite 200-year old history of women's suffrage and women's rights movements, only 12 women have been Peace Laureates. Men fight and go to war, and often over women. At the end of the day, men end up getting peace awards!

The omission of Peace Prize to Gandhi, the apostle of non-violence, has been widely discussed. He was nominated in 1937, 1938, 1939, 1947, and finally a few days before his assassination in January, 1948. The omission has been publicly regretted by members of Nobel Committees. In 1948, the year of Gandhi's death, the Nobel Committee declined to award a prize on the ground that "*there was no suitable living candidate that year*". Later on, when the Dalai Lama was awarded the Peace Prize in 1989, the Committee Chairman said that this was "in part a tribute to the memory of Mahatma Gandhi." **However, Subbarao's winning the Prize shall do full justice to Gandhi's omission.**

Sometimes, the world of men is stranger than fiction. Recently, nomination records from 1901 to 1955 have been released to the public. It was discovered that Adolf Hitler was nominated in 1939 by a member of the Swedish Parliament. Other 'infamous' nominees included Joseph Stalin and Benito Mussolini. This trio is responsible for the killing of over 15 million people! Further, they inspired several Maos, Pol-Pots, and Idi Amins to extend their legacies in poor Asian, African and Latin American countries.

The Peace Prize has been awarded only six times to individuals/organizations outside the western world. Seven times, it has recognized Christian archbishops and Christian organizations - like YMCA. It also includes Mother Teresa, missionary physician Albert Schweitzer, and Martin Luther King, inspired by Gandhi. The citations clearly state their Christian faith. Elie Wiesel (1986) won it mainly for educating the world about the Jewish Holocaust. Non-violence approaches of Buddhist Laureates Dalai Lama and Aung S. Kye (1991) are derivatives of Gandhian thoughts. **Summing up, nominating Subbarao for the Peace Prize is also recognizing India's ancient heritage**.

(Aug 12, 2009)

NOTES AND COMMENTS

1. Dear Sh. Bhatnagar Ji, Your latest reflection is very interesting. Let your efforts succeed and a new chapter in the field of Social work begins. Ameen! Today, I wrote to friends in Turkey, Pakistan and Nepal for submitting BhaiJi's nomination. With regards, Your brother, **Gurdev**

2. Thanks. Great history about Noble Peace Prize. **Inder Singh**, President Global Organization of People of Indian Origin, GOPIO

3. Excellent piece!! –**Harpreet**

4. There is a lot of politics behind awarding Nobel prizes. For example, Gandhi did not get the prize because the Swedish did not want to offend the British that were illegally occupying the country. Again Al Gore got the prize not as much for himself; the Europeans wanted to embarrass George Bush.
   Then again there is another reason in awarding Nobel prizes – particularly the peace prize. All the important Nobel prizes are won by Americans and Europeans. The non-white world has had practically 0% contribution to science, economics and technology in the last 1000 years and therefore has won few, if any, prizes. So to inject an amount of balance and assume some humility against the "mediocre" 3rd world populations, , the Swedish give Nobel peace prizes to third world nationals like Mandela, Mohd. Yunus, Dalai Lama, Mother Teresa, et al. –**Samesh Bararoo**

SETTLING OF INDIANS IN THE US: AN OVERVIEW

BRIEF EARLY HISTORY

The history of immigration of the Indians into the United States (US) can be traced back to the turn of the twentieth century, when some enterprising Indians, Punjabis in particular, crossed the US border from Canada to grab for themselves a piece of the new found gold and silver bonanza in northern California and Nevada. The status of Indians in Canada at that time was that of indentured labor. The British, with the connivance of the princely rulers of India, had used force, enticement and threats, largely upon the village folks, to leave India and labor in the British colonies in Africa, Latin America, Caribbean and Fiji islands. They, however, kept them out of white Australia and New Zealand. At that time, Indian masses considered going overseas as some kind of an irreligious act - a belief mentioned in Gandhi's autobiography.

The Indians in the US have gone through a lot of changes in their fortune. Simply put: what they achieved through sheer hard work, they lost it for lack of any political representation. Immigration and citizenship laws were conveniently changed to force them cross borders into Canada in the north, or into Mexico in the south. Those who stayed back continued as the lowest paid farm labor stripped of any ownership rights. It may be added that these laws were, mainly directed earlier towards Chinese and Japanese, who had emigrated in tens of thousands in the middle of the nineteenth century. Also, their application on Indians was a bit controversial from a legal point of view – in the sense that some classified Indians as Caucasian, and others not.

It was after WW II, followed by the great American affluence and relaxed US immigration policy initiated by President Truman that Indians started coming here. Those who were already here began to surface up in owning up their farms. It was out of this stock of immigrants that the first Indian, Dilip Singh Saund was elected to the US Congress twice. He married a white woman, a crucial factor in the political aspirations of an Indian. Incidentally, Saud, with MA from India, came to the US for Math PhD.

A historical remark on the early immigration is also in order here. The US Census Bureau has records of the number of immigrants from India since 1820. The numbers until the beginning of the 20th century are generally in tens, and often zeros. On data analysis, it is found that the immigrants during this early period were not ethnic Indians, but the British officers. After completing the service tenure in India, some preferred to immigrate to the US rather than going back to England. Whenever, the direct British/European quota was exhausted, they used small non-European quota. The US immigration never objected it!

IMMIGRATION IN THE SIXTIES

It was the drastic change in the US Immigration Act pushed during the Kennedy Administration that Indians started immigrating into the United States in significant numbers. The white and non-white immigration quotas were removed. However, it was not an absolute open door policy. There were restrictions, as only Indian professionals of high caliber including mainly doctors, engineers and technicians could immigrate. Those who came to USA on student visas were able to change their status to that of immigrants once they had obtained doctorate degrees and sometimes even after master's degrees. Others could get the immigrant status by investing a certain amount in a US business, or marrying a US citizen, or a permanent resident. These openings quickly started swelling Indian population. However, this phase did not last for long.

The oil crisis of 1971 hit the US economy for the first time after the great depression of 1930s. The unemployment rate hit all time high and the Americans could not tolerate non-citizens, particularly the non-white holding any high paying jobs. The Immigration Act, therefore, was amended again in 1972 which removed the blanket clearance for the professionals. Since then, only professionals certified by the US Department of Labor are cleared for immigration in the areas of shortage of qualified people among the US citizens. Investment limit for the business was also raised to half a million dollars - making it nearly impossible for an individual to come up with such a huge cash.

THE AFFLUENT MINORITY

It is remarkable that just within 20-25 years, the Indians population in the US soared up to half a million. According to a recent survey, Indians, as an ethnic group in the US, have the highest per capita income. It is also contributed to the exodus of wealthy Indian businessmen and professionals from African countries and Hong Kong due to persecution and political uncertainties. They had the options of going back to India or settling in England, as they held British passports. By and large, Indians being family oriented, they lost no time in getting their close relatives and even friends, if possible, from India.

With a prominent rise of the Indian community and other oriental groups, the US Congress initiated another round of restrictive immigration measures. At present, there are two bills in the House and the Senate, which if passed, will not allow immigration to certain blood relatives beyond a certain age and marital status. Prompted by such impending legislation, the Indians have started becoming US citizens, primarily to get their relatives from India. Still, there is a large number of Indians who do not want to become US citizens, as it amounts to giving up Indian citizenship. It is commonly seen that in a family, one spouse is a US citizen and the other holding onto Indian citizenship. Recently, there has been a considerable lobbying in for dual citizenship rights. Strangely enough, the opposition to dual citizenship is stemming from the Indian government.

THE INDIAN HERITAGE

If there is a single factor which keeps Indians so distinct from other ethnic groups, then it is great Indian heritage and traditions. Unity in diversity is main fabric of Indian culture. It is more a cliché in India, but it becomes a living concept in a far off land. The positive outcome is that Indians are able to continue their life styles in food, dress (particularly women), beliefs and customs. The construction of gurdwaras and temples of various Hindu deities all over the US, testifies to the sprouting of Indian religions in a new soil. It appears that the spiritual spadework, done by Swami Vivekananda in the beginning of the 20th century and later on by a few other saints like Swami Ram Tirath and Yogananda Paramahansa, is bearing the fruit now. Spiritual knowledge is the greatest gift of India to the rest of the world. During the last two decades, the US masses and intelligentsia alike have been greatly influenced by the Indian ethos as expounded by Maharishi Mahesh, Srila Prabhupad, Krishnamurti and Yogi Harbhajan Singh. Rajneesh/ Osho, though ended up getting notoriety, nevertheless, has left an historical mark on the US landscape.

THE FIRST GENERATION

The negative offshoot of the traditional and close-knit living is that Indians have not yet participated in the mainstream life of the US. The first generation of Indian immigrants were quite fixed in their beliefs and remained occupied in building their careers and newfound fortune. Therefore, they never participated in the local, civic, and political process - staying away from politics, since in India, it was considered a pursuit of the "ruffian" or the "rich". Consequently, the great melting pot of cultures, as the US is considered, has not yet absorbed the Indians to any significant extent.

Besides, the first generation of Indians always had a lingering conviction that after having earned sufficient money, professional experience, or retirement, they would go back to India. I call this social behavior as "Marcopolian". Marco Polo returned to his native village near Venice after earning all the riches and fame in the service of the Chinese emperor Kublai Khan. Despite his great services to the Chinese nation, he did not become an integral part of the Chinese society at large. Naturally, his urge to return to his native village continued to grow stronger. And when he did come back after 25 years, he was forgotten by his own people! Most of the first generation of Indian immigrants experience the same plight, though on a smaller scale, when they visit India every two or three years. The ties with India being emotional, each India visit makes their amalgamation in the mainstream USA more difficult.

THE SECOND GENERATION

In the history of rising civilization of the world, another social behavior emerges - the intellectuals, without strong spiritual moorings, go wherever their work is rewarded. The first generation of Indians, who were by and large professionals in various walks of life, found their reasons of staying in the US much stronger than reasons for leaving it mainly because of social alienation. They have now their children for whom India has very different meaning from their own. The same emotional bond which pulled the first generation towards India, is now holding them to the US for the sake of their children and grandchildren!

There is going to be no en masse reverse immigration to India. A few Indians, who did return to India for social and other reasons, came back to the US after some time. Besides, their mental image of India when they lived there had also undergone a great transformation due to urbanization and industrialization. Indians, professionally well settled here, have lost patience necessary to adjust back to bureaucratic Indian life.

There is also another feature regarding the second generation of Indian immigrants, that there are lots of immigrants who are basically non-professionals. They are in the US because of their parents, spouses, brothers and sisters, who came first. This factor is significantly changing the tapestry of Indian ethnic group. Indians are now also seen doing all sorts of menial and petty jobs on one end and small lucrative businesses on the other end - unheard in the sixties and seventies. The family problems of divorces, drugs, alcohol, school/college dropouts, and disregard for high performance in education are also more and more becoming common occurrences rather than exceptions amongst Indians who are now in the second generation.

THE NEW SOCIO-POLITICAL THINKING

In the backdrop of all these realities, a new wave of socio-political thinking has emerged amongst the Indians. It has several fronts. During the last 5-7 years, the Indians have started consolidating into political organizations of their own which are generally bipartisan. Most active amongst them are Indo-American Forum for Political Education, National Federation of Asians Indian Organizations, and the Association of Indians in America. Indo-American Forum for political Education was founded five years ago by Dr. Joy Cherian, who was recently nominated by President Reagan to the Equal Opportunity Commission. The US Senate has just confirmed his appointment.

A nationwide Indo-American Democratic organization has been launched this fall. In order to have a greater political clout in the American politics, Indians have also joined the Asian American Voter Coalition with Philippines, Chinese and Japanese. In contrast with India, this reflects a different aspect of the Indians in the US in that they have, to some extent, put aside their trait of strong individualistic ambitions in large interest of the community. Realization is emerging that the US is now their new home, and they have to make their future here. It certainly does not mean that India is ever going to be forgotten. Both at the individual and the organized levels, Indians have been donating time, money and expertise to institutions and other causes in India. This participation can be measured by the equity held by them in many industrial ventures and the non-resident accounts.

Other dimensions of Indians settling in the US can be understood by the rising number of them making names for themselves in media, business and other enterprises. There are at least ten weekly Indian publications in the US today, owned and run by the Indians. The leading ones are: the *India Aboard* (New York, 1968), the first Indian publication started by Gopal Raju, the *India Tribune* (Chicago, 1976) and the *India West* (San Francisco, 1974). According to a recent syndicated article, newspaper stands in New York are monopolized by the Indians there.

On a similar note, a few years ago, a national stir was caused by the rapidity with which Indians, particularly the Guajarati Patels, were taking control of the motel business in the US. This prompted an investigation by the Immigration and Naturalization Service. However, it could not find anything illegal in their ventures. The secret of their success lies in the hard work by the entire family, accompanied by a very frugal living. Chatwal of Bombay Place chain of restaurants and Tandon in computer industry have taken full advantage of the American opportunities to become multi-millionaires. They are new sources of inspiration to young Indian entrepreneurs in diverse fields.

Another measure of Indian life in the US is the number of ongoing cultural activities across the country, on small and large scale. Groups of film stars, dancers and other artists from India frequently tour major cities in the US. This provides entertainment and culture continuity. On a note of concern is the emergence of some scattered anti-Indians sentiments in the US. The most vocal opponents are known as ' Dot busters' in the state of New Jersey. Indian women wearing **BINDI** on their foreheads, as a part of their makeup or religious sentiments, have been the targets of hate group. Primarily, they resent the fact that in some US cities, Indians are controlling the total economy. There have been several violent attacks over the last couple of years. The impact of such events is also pushing Indians into political activities.

A CONCLUDING REMARK

Just as Indians never forget their roots in India, no matter how many generation pass, so must also not the people of India, as it happened to the Indians particularly in Guyana, Surinam, Fiji and Caribbean islands. In the US, since the days *Gadar* party was formed in San Francisco, Indians in the US have played monumental roles in the social and political events in India. It is an irony of history that in response to the clarion call by the *Gadar* party, the forefathers of the present California Sikhs had left the US to fight and die for the freedom of India in 1914. Today, the Indian government is charging that the Khalistan secessionist movement is supported from aboard! Therefore, besides Indian government, the social, religious and political leaders in India should have active liaisons with overseas Indians. India can always harness this source for any political, cultural and economic advantage. Of course, the converse has always been true.

(Oct 02, 1991/July, 2011)

NOTES AND COMMENTS

THE *GADAR* MEMORIAL CENTER: A PERISCOPE

(A Reflective Letter to Jagmohan Kaushal, a social activist of Bathinda, India)

The experience of this visit has to be conveyed through letter writing, my most effective mode of expression. Some people are at their best in public speaking and some in other literary genre -like poetry, drama and novel. But for me, you know, it has been through letters. Once my energies are focused on the addressee, I can transcend to a state of *Pen Yoga* - using that person as a vehicle that you are now. So be ready for a ride of your life! Thus, it may be published in the *Sahi Buniyad* as the longest letter ever written to an editor. By the way, in the New Year, the Editorial Board may like to consider publications of certain articles in English, as they are received. I do appreciate your translation efforts into Punjabi. But, as you know, unless a translator understands author's thought processes, nuances of an expression may be missed.

Ever since I decided to visit our son Avnish in Oakland area this year, I was determined this time not to miss visiting the Gadar Memorial Center in San Francisco (SF). Prior to arriving in SF, I had gathered some information about it from the website of Indian Embassy in US. The site has a brief history of the Hindustan Gadar Party and its Memorial Center, including directions to reach there. However, it did not have any information about its opening hours. The Memorial is an hour drive from Castro Valley where Avnish lives. Anyway, assuming that the place is likely to be closed on weekends, I called two phone numbers noted from the web site, but got no response. I tried to contact the Indian Consulate that I thought may have information about it, but no one picked up the phone either. The Consulate phone information service needs to be public oriented. Even in the US, Indian Consulate bureaucracy is no different from what one encounters in any government office in India. **I have it partially figured it out, that in India, most people thrive in chaos as it breeds bribery, which they would lose in an orderly competition.**

I had to give up on Gadar Memorial for that day and, instead, spent some time in San Francisco Museum of Modern Arts. Next day, my daughter-in-law, Anna having it her off day, felt a little obligated to show me around. Usually, in my travels I stay like a free bird without letting the hosts ever feel my presence. Years ago, I made it a point to make sure that my stay does not interfere with the essential routines of my hosts.

I did want Anna to have some idea of the place that is so high on my tourist priority. My son and Anna are second generation Indian Americans who are either born in US, or came with parents at a very young age. Both were less than a year old when their parents came to the US. Anna asked me to call the Memorial Center for its opening hours. Early frustration not gone yet, I told her it really did not matter even if it was closed, as I would be just satisfied by looking at that building. That strangely quieted her.

We set off with a map in my hand and she doing the driving all the way into the congested SF areas. Without any problem, we were there at the Wood Street. The building numbers not properly marked, we missed the House Number 5 when we drove by it. But when the sequence of numbers kept increasing, we realized it that we had to turn back to locate it. May be it happened due to my excitement. Buildings on the Street are older, 2-3 storey high, and most have a common wall on one side. It is in a busy district. On the top of the building words **Gadar Memorial** are written in small letters with an insignia of Government of India. There is no public parking near the Memorial, but I told Anna to park the car right in front of the garage door that was on the first floor leading to its basement.

Rushing out of the car while a gush of emotions welling up, I ran up a small flight of stairs. There appears to be a huge basement and garage on the first floor, but the main structure is on the second floor. Lo and behold, I go up to find both big glass doors locked up! There was some light in a side room. We knocked up several times, but for no avail. I knew what Anna was thinking and she knew what was going on in my mind. But we did not say a word to each other. I pensively stood there looking far and near from a small balcony out in front of the main doors.

For a few minutes I closely examined whatever I could see through the glass doors. Thinking that this was going to be a futile trip, I asked Anna to take my picture standing up in front of the Memorial sign. After a while, I came down with a heavy heart and footsteps - still trying to absorb the vibrations of the events that the building had witnessed, I looked its side byways. There was no opening between it and the house on the left. However, I noticed a gap between it and the house on the right. I climbed up a single brick boundary wall and raised my heels as high as I could in my small frame. I noticed a small wheel chair ramp leading to the back of the house. I was thrilled at this opportunity to be able to walk on the soil where I visualized hundreds of martyrs and Gadar Party supporters must have stepped upon. There was a small area in the backyard with a wooden plank fence in common with a dwelling on the other side. I breathed the air, and some physics laws tell that I must have inhaled some atoms of that Gadar era!

In a strange ponderous gait in the back yard while Anna waiting outside, I was trying not to miss even a square inch of this space. At the lowest level of the outside wall were inset small glass windows for the daylight to filter into the basement. It was all filled with boxes, heaps of papers and files in a haphazard manner. From a few strewn pieces that I could read, it seemed an old record of passport/ visa applications. The SF Consulate may be using this basement as a warehouse. It may be a fire hazard to keep records in the Consulate Office in violation of fire regulations. It reminded me how in India people kept old newspaper piled for years before selling them away to junk buyers. In the US, it is illegal to store flammable materials in homes.

At that time I was also wondering whether the Consulate had some records of the Gadar Party mixed up with it. It would be a shame if such a thing had taken place. I am not sure if some room in the basement has a few boxes containing the Gadar material. But all this was a guessing game running through my mind. It was just about then, that Anna called, "Dad, there is a man going up to open the building." **I felt as if some prayer was answered, or the power of my faith has materialized this person.** I went back to the front and again hurriedly climbed up the steps. Anna was already there. An Indian, about 35 years of age, respectfully showed us in. He told of his job in the Consulate Office - within walking distance from the Memorial, and after lunch he would be going back.

I was feeling a little nonplused at the whole situation while standing in the main hall where great many meetings must have taken place since 1917. It appeared the man was either a peon or a domestic servant of a consular. He is given a small room for living on the 2nd floor of the Memorial. Besides this small room, the second floor has two restrooms, a kitchen, lobby, and a big meeting hall with a low 9' ceiling. On noticing him hurriedly eating, I shared my snacks with him that I always carry in a shoulder bag during my hikes and excursions. On informing him about my interest in the Gadar Party, he suddenly said, "You can stay here as long as you want. Just close the outside glass doors when you leave as the doors have self-locking system." I was delighted and moved by his gesture of trust. In a customary Las Vegas life style, I tried to tip him. With folded hands he declined to accept it. In the US, no employee will ever assume such a responsibility. But at the same time every public institution in the US has clearly posted hours of operation. Neither there was a sign outside, nor was this man aware of its functioning. In a few minutes, he was on his way out, as quietly he had showed up.

Feeling assured of my stay in the hall, I felt a new wave of excitement sweeping over me, and Anna kept wondering what kind of place it was that she had not even heard of it during her two years of living there. I was pacing around the hall. She may have noted me behaving like a child suddenly brought in a toy store, but is unable to make up the mind on which toy to pick up. **I really felt overwhelmed by its vibrations, as if in a previous birth I was connected with this environment and now was trying to recognize my old things**. I briefly explained it to Anna what this place was all about. Since it was too much to expect her sit there and watch me absorbed in work for a couple of hours, and parking being a severe problem, I suggested her to do some shopping and return here to pick me up at 4 PM. Dutifully, she left me alone.

Though left all alone, yet I felt surrounded by these immortals. It is at such moments that one realizes the difference between the longevity of a human being in a physical form and legacy left behind with great ideals. Stretched to an extreme, certainly after a thousand years perhaps names of one or two of them may survive in some books. **Nevertheless, the quality of an individual life is always measured by the amelioration brought in life around it**.

I was still going back and forth looking at pictures, books in the shelves and material in showcases that were lined along the walls of the hall. At the entrance there was a visitor's register wherein I proudly entered our names. There were about 100 plastic chairs stacked up for functions and meetings here, or at the consulate. First, I had thought of writing this letter right from the Memorial itself, but soon realized it was too much to do it. **My pen won't be able to keep up with the pace and gush of my thoughts that was going to pour out**. So I decided to take a full stock of all the contents and note them down on a few sheets of papers that I carried from home. I did not find any writing paper in the Memorial after I ran out mine!

There are 21 framed pictures of the Gadar Party leaders and martyrs on two opposite walls of the main hall, and of Gandhi's alone on the front wall. We all know how Gandhi's path of achieving independence was absolutely different from the *Gadaris* (Actually they were called *Gadari Babas*), yet he loved and respected them. It was Gandhi's incredible leadership that Indian masses and intelligentsia followed him. There is no picture on the fourth wall where the two entrance doors are attached.

Twenty-two open bookshelves have an assortment of books and four showcases display some Gadar Party material. Initially I thought all the books might be of that era. However, after a careful examination of 6-7 bookshelves, it was not difficult to rule out that most of the books were recent publications and acquisitions. Noticeable were a few books, first published 200 years ago, to be classified now in the categories of rare books. I still had no way of checking what if any Gadar documents were stored in a basement area. Under the guest register, a small chest of drawers has card classification system of these books. It was a bit amusing to see such an archaic book classification system in the most high tech country! My another thought was that with open shelves, no checkout system, and no regular open hours, this collection is likely to wither away.

Well, I was to make the best use of my limited time. While looking at those pictures, I felt as if they were also peering at me. It was an eerie feeling - like one gets in a cemetery, but I soon got over it. No one, unaware of their heroic deeds, would pay any attention to their ordinary facial features. **Ordinary looking people appear extraordinary because of their great deeds and sacrifices**. Therefore, the first thing I decided was to pay my homage and respect to each one by standing before each picture for a few seconds and take notes of whatever I see or comes to my mind. Here is the list of those bravest of the brave sons of India who are still alive! While walking by the picture gallery, a few fundamental questions came up to my mind:

What is the relevance of their story today?
Why the youth of India should ever know it?
Why the readers of the *SAHI BUNIYAD* should care about them?
What are the historical lessons of such a movement?

I pondered over these questions as I browsed. Every age has its own fights for freedom - from an individual to societal levels. Certainly, the youth in India do not have to fight against the British today the way the *Gadaris* did. But look what is happening to the integrity, secularity and solidarity of India. There is a real fight going on for the protection of Indian ethos and values. It has been intensely waging in Jammu and Kashmir (J&K) and in the entire Northeast (NE). Who is stopping the youth of Punjab and other states from going into Kashmir and NE and fight for the protection of the Hindus and Sikhs who have been forced to flee from those areas where they had lived for over 125 years? **The problem of Hindus' safe return to their homes and hearths in Kashmir is even bigger than what the Gadaris faced**! Nearly 96% of Hindu population in Kashmir has been kicked out in since 1989, and in some NE states 90 % of the population is converted to religions foreign to Indian soil. All this has happened after independence in 1947!

Ethnic cleansing is a modern clandestine war. Success in Kashmir has emboldened the enemy to push their operations in Jammu, Himachal and Uttaranchal states. Enemy infiltration in Punjab since the 1980s has been going full blast, and now working its way along the western border states of Rajasthan and Gujarat. Emboldened by successful outcomes in Kashmir, Bangladesh has also unleashed its fury on the Hindus. Hundreds of Hindus are fleeing into India every day. More powerful forces of Taliban, Al Qaida and international Islamic organizations have joined Pakistan and Bangladesh in this clandestine ethnic cleansing. Hindu population in Pakistan that was nearly 20 % at the time of partition in 1947 is now less than 1 %. Both financial support and fighters are coming from every country of the world, wherever the Muslims live.

A statistical figure tells that during the last 10 years only one in 100,000 Indians, including ministers from other states, has visited Kashmir Valley, and much less the NE! How can Kashmir be claimed as a part of India when Indians from other Indian states cannot safely visit it - forget about buying any land, house, establish business, or settle there after retirement? After all, what is the definition of a region being a part of a country? Such are the current issues at the national level to be raised and at every local level. Indian youth waits to be shown a path by an inspired leadership. Otherwise, once the Kashmir issue is made international, J & K will be constitutionally lost to India. On this issue, India is at the mercy of USA and Russia today. Ethnic cleansing has prepared the groundwork. **Batches of brave Hindus have to enter Kashmir with Kashmiri Hindus, and not leave it until demographic landscape is restored.**

Coming back on the Memorial track here is a 'panorama' of pictures. The dates in parentheses across some names are the dates of their **kissing the British gallows** while singing *Bande Mataram* so that coming generations can live in freedom. The comments in the Italics are mine.

1. Dr. Mathura Singh (27/3/1917) Russians handed him over to the British where he had escaped from India. (*It indicates that Russian Czars were opposed to India's freedom fight as they were to their own workers' movement. The irony is that the British in the 1920s wanted to take control of Afghanistan in order to check Russian expansion in South. In the 1980s, the Soviet Union wanted to control Afghanistan for the same reasons! Now in the 2000s with the US help both the West and Russia may succeed!*)
2. Harnam Singh Sialkot (17/11/1915)
3. Bhai Bhag Singh murdered by an Indian hireling of the British. (*Imagine what it would have taken for Indians in British army or police to shoot/betray their civilian friends, neighbours, brothers, cousins and fathers? Does it not really establish some unique superiority of the British mind and institutions in winning such a strong loyalty from Indians by and large? **These unanswered questions are relevant in any organization today***)
4. Ajit Singh (*uncle/Chacha of the Bhagat Singh*)
5. Baba Ram Singh Kuka
6. Udham Singh Kassil
7. Mewa Singh
8. Rahmat Ali Shah (26/3/1915)
9. Lala Lajapat Rai (***The only leader popular in India, UK and USA***)
10. Jagat Singh Sur Singh (Sur Singh is a village) (16/11/1915)
11. Bhagat Singh (*The*)
12. Kartar Singh Saraba (17/11/15)
13. Baba Sohan Singh Bhakana
14. Udham Singh (*The*)
15. Pandit Ram Chandra Bhardwaj
16. V. G. Pingle of Maharashtra (17/11/1915) (*One wonders how a person from Maharashtra would join the Gadar Party. I have no other information about his life. But my guess is that a passionate person no matter where he lives, would stand up against any tyranny*)
17. Baba Waisakhi Singh
18. Baba Prithi Singh Azad
19. Pandit Jagat Ram
20. Sohan Lal Pathak (20/2/1919)
21. Lala Hardayal (*who was mysteriously killed in Nov. 1947 while traveling in ship going to India, after independence He had a doctorate from Oxford, and came to USA as a visiting professor at Stanford University*)

Before I resume the heart of the showcased material, let me briefly get back to the books placed in 22 shelves. Most books are written in Hindi and English dealing with literature (including children), history, politics including works and speeches of leaders such as Radhakrishnan and Nehru. There are reference books too - like the collected works of Gandhi. What impressed me was a set of fifty volumes that Macaulay edited in 1850's on **The Sacred books of the East**. In 1960, nearly after 100 years, Motilal Benarsidas has re-published them with a foreword by the then President Radhakrishnan. Also, there are volumes on the framing of Indian Constitution and India Penal Code - a strange assortment of titles indeed.

A few books of history and reference must have value as rare manuscripts. Indians see little monetary value in antiques. May be it is the Hindu belief that every old thing including their bodies are to be discarded in favour of new ones. What a contrast with the West! On the contrary, a belief in **one life to live** makes a person see value in everything, thus enhancing the quality of present life.

As I said earlier, with a primitive index of books and the absence of supervision, their safety and usage are all up in the air. If they are not properly taken care, the collection may be wasted. Indian Embassy should link up with a US university where there is research activity in Indian history, and place this collection in its library. In the meanwhile, the Embassy should involve volunteers to come and assist in Memorial operation and care taking. Americans love to volunteer their time to the libraries. **Library is an index of comparing West with East**. Indian staff members coming to Embassy and consulates for 2-3 years have hardly any time and interest in the Center. Another viable option is to involve Indian community in raising money for an endowed university chair in **Modern Indian History**, and this collection can go along with it.

Now I turn to the **Heart of the Center**, the four showcases displaying some pamphlets, documents and booklets. I was really in awe in extending my hand to reach out and touch the material. **They were alive in their own way, and kind of challenged me to comprehend the magnitude**. At DNA level, they are very much alive. Like enumerating pictures, I decided to pay my respect to each item within my time frame. Each and every document must have been held by at least one member of the *Gadar* Party. Initially, it was irresistible not to browse the documents in some detail, but I had a race with time too.

1. *India's Voice* 9/43. (In this small monthly, an author quotes the *San Francisco Chronicle* of 16/11/1942: Sikhs were traditionally loyal to the British, were not opposing in 1857, they sided with the British---) *My thoughts immediately went back to the specific turn of events in the 1857 Independence War of India, or Indian Mutiny when the troops of princely states of Patiala and Nabha went out in support of the British army to fight the nationalist forces in Kanpur and Meerut. It absolutely turned the tide of that war. Who knows without this support, the British may have suffered heavier losses and conceded some political concession?* **Indians were not organized and strong enough to throw the British out of India**. *In three months, the British were*

also able to move additional forces from their colonies, Malay and Indonesia. For this loyalty, the British increased proportional representation of Sikhs in the British Army. During the WWI, the Sikhs won the highest number valiant awards.

After quelling the 1857 uprising, the British tyranny on Indians at every economic and political front was doubled and quadrupled. The terrible famines in the erstwhile regions of Bengal, Orissa and South Bihar were the direct result of economic emaciation of Indian peasantry.

However, after 50 years of the Mutiny, a greater number of Gadar Party members were Sikhs. They were also at the forefront in convincing Indians in the British army and police to quit and disobey the orders of the British officers against the nationalist Indians.

2. A framed form for joining the Gadar Party, in Gurumukhi. (*Very interesting*)
3. A booklet of patriotic songs in Hindi (*Handwritten*)
4. An Urdu publication, *HINDUSTAN KI GWAHI* (Evidence of India)
5. An English pamphlet, *Unlawful Government of India and Mahatma Gandhi* by Ras Behari Bose based in Japan. It was a part of the Indian Section of Eastern Oppressed peoples Association. It is a powerfully written piece on the detention of Gandhi. (20/07/1930). *It also establishes an active network with revolutionaries in Japan and Far East*)
6-7. Punjabi Booklets, *AZADI DI GOONJ*, Number 5, 12. (It was noted in # 12, that in 1930 Civil Disobedience Movement, an entire army battalion was court-martialed for their refusal to fire on Indian protesters. *It provides a rare example of Indians in British army and police not obeying commands against Indian freedom fighters. In civilian life such instances are numerous.*
8. *History of India* in Urdu by Bhai Parmanand, MA 1918, 350 pages; a history professor.
9. A booklet, *A few facts about the British Rule in India*, June 1915. (*It is really heart rending to read it*. In one place an **English man** is quoted "In 1901 the poverty and suffering of the people are such as to defy description". One of the several data reads as:
    Plague deaths from 1897-1903: 7,251,257, more than 7 million! (***The world will never forget the victims of German holocaust of Jews. Today, Indians know more about what happened to the Jews in Germany, but hardly aware of a bigger holocaust of the Hindus in India itself!***)
10. *The United States of India*, monthly, 11/1924 devoted to the economic, social and intellectual independence of India. (*It may be noted that the Gadar Party had positive images of the United States of America not only in finding a similar name of free India, but also for of its institutional models. A big map in the lobby of the Memorial also titles India as the United States of India. I **have always wondered at the prudence of the founding fathers of Indian Constitution to name free India as Bharat or Bharatvarash. I have never heard an Indian commoner or a leader in private or public using this name!***

*It is invariably called Hind, Hindustan, or India. Hindustan is the only justified name as it is and has been the only land of the Hindus. It is only in the land of the Hindus that foreigners, including Muslims, Christians, Parsis and Jews etc. have/can come and flourish, but not conversely. Since by the 1930s, the leaders and masses were aware of the British policies of creating divisions between the Hindus, Muslims and Sikhs, that the Gadar Party must have agreed on this name, the **United States of India**.*

11. *India against Britain* by Ram Chandra, Editor, 01/11/1916 (*It was interesting to note in it that like Afghanistan, **both Nepal and Bhutan had defeated British forces three times**! That is why they were never colonized by the British. How many Indians today even in the academe, know of this fact?* Also noted was that the living conditions in princely states were better than in the British provinces of India.

12. Framed picture poster of Yugantar Ashram, the name of first headquarters of the ***Hindustan Gadar Party*** (full name of the *Gadar Party*) started at 436 Hill Street, SF (in Hindi).

13-14   *GULAMI DA ZAHAR* (Poison of Slavery) in Punjabi and Urdu by Lala Hardayal, 1919.

*Coming from a Delhi Kayastha family, Hardayal's name was proudly mentioned in our family when I was growing up in BTI. It was while teaching in Panjab University Evening College, Shimla that I first read his famous book, **Hints for Self-Culture**, a guide for the making of a new class of Indian intellectuals. The book still continues to influence me. For several years in India, I gifted copies of this book on various occasions. It is time that some private company or government undertakes a mass printing of this great book.*

Reflecting on the Gadar Movement, I strongly believe that had the Gadar Party drawn only a couple of intellectual giants and leaders like Lala Hardayal, then this movement would have become a parallel force to the Gandhian Movement. Its new cadre today would not have let the national defense and integration problems come to this pass today.

14. In Punjabi, handwritten *Constitution of the Gadar Party*, 29 pages.

15. *India's Voice* 1/1944 (*Paper has turned brown and brittle with age*)

16-21.   Punjabi booklets, *Gadar Di Goonj* numbers 2, 3, 4, 6, 7 and 14. *One is unnumbered.*

22. *ANK DI GWAHI* in Punjabi.

23. An Urdu pamphlet, *NEEM HAKIM KHATRA JAAN*   (A quack endangers life)

24. A pamphlet from China (*It indicates a collaboration with Chinese groups against the British*)

25. A pamphlet in German. (*Germany has always sided with India*)

26. In Punjabi, *GAYATRI MANTRA*

28. In Punjabi, Russia in 1914.

29. A booklet on Baba Hari Singh Oswal

30-31. Hindi and Punjabi versions of the magazine, *GADARI RASALA, ANKO KI GAWAHI* (Evidence of Data)

32. *HINDUSTAN KA GADAR* in Punjabi (*Gadar* was a powerful weekly publication of the Party, besides its numerous other publications.)

32. First anniversary issue of *Gadar Ki Salegrah*, in Urdu (in 1917 the Party headquarters moved to 5 Wood Street, and was known as *Gadar Ashram* owing to its intense activities)

33. Poster in Urdu in a cardboard form

34. *Gadar*, a newsletter of the Gadar Memorial Center dated **15 August 1993**. (*I don't know how current this publication is, and how much it is connected with the historical weekly the Gadar of the Hindustan Gadar Party. But their mailing address is 5 Wood Street, SF. However, its activities have not been reported or heard anywhere. After independence, the Party headquarters eventually was taken over by the SF Consulate office of the Government of India. Since March 1975, it is now the office of the Gadar Memorial Center, perhaps the only one outside India.*)

It is obvious that the Gadar Party was very active in all kinds of publications in many languages, and mixing them whenever necessary. That is one lesson to draw. It is a shame that soon after independence so much was damaged in riots over language issues in India. In public service, message and its spirit should not be sacrificed for the sake of a language. As I finish writing generally one-line descriptions of these materials, my appetite after browsing a few of them has been sharpened. Next time when I visit SF, I'll spend more time and carefully study a few items, provided the collection remains intact and accessible!

Talking of visiting the Memorial in future tells me to go back to its Visitor's Register. I was a little curious about the number and the types of people who had signed in it so far. The current register has only been maintained since 1982. Groups of names signed in one ink indicate that when people come on certain functions they also write in their names in it. Otherwise, there are gaps of weeks between two sign-up days. It is possible that some people may not like to sign up, though the register is prominently placed. In a random count, I figured not more than 2000 visitors coming during the last 19 years! Included in the list are names of some Government of India ministers visiting the Center during their US trips. By and large, majority of visitors are from California come for the obvious reason of their ancestral associations.

After winding up my deep and comprehensive survey of the main hall, I came out in the lobby. It is a small area. A door at one end of the lobby was locked up. It leads to the basement. There are five framed posters and a few memorial plaques when this building was officially dedicated on 19 March 1975. Inscribed in a plaque is the name of Didar Singh Bains of Yuba City as Chief Patron of the Memorial. In other patron categories the names that I could recognize are of Yogi Bhajan Singh, Dr. Gobind Behari Lal and Dr. George Sudarshan. Inscribed in plaques are names of patrons hailing from Yuba City, California, that I call it as a citadel of *Punjabiyat,* in the USA.

On a lobby wall common with kitchen is a big map of **United States of India that includes present Pakistan, united Kashmir, Burma, Sri Lanka and other small territories**. Two other walls display a framed poster in Urdu appealing to Indians not to fight with the Chinese. Suddenly I thought of the 1950s when the mood of *HINDI CHEENI BHAI BHAI* foreign policy turned around into a stab in the back by the Chinese assault on India in Oct 1962. This shock was too much for the Prime Minister Nehru to bear that he died of a brain hemorrhage in May 1964.

A photo of the members of freedom fighters for India *Jatha* 1924 includes a picture of Raja Mahindra Pratap of Vrindaban. It really took me by surprise as all along Indians have viewed nearly 00 Indian princes as stooges of the British Empire. But reading about him showed that there are always some exceptions. For Raja's opposition to the British policies, he was denied passport to leave India. It is an intriguing story how he reached Germany where he joined the German forces. The British confiscated all his royal property in India. Later, he became an ardent supporter of the Gadar Party.

A framed poster titles: Remember Our Gadar Heroes. It is written there: **that the Gadar Party was started 8 years before the Non-Cooperation Movement of Gandhi and 4 years before the Russian Revolution**. Names of the founding members are: Lala Hardayal, Ram Chandra Bhardwaj and Baba Sohan Singh Bhaken. A weekly *Gadar* was launched on 1/11/1913 from Yugantar Ashram, 436 Hill Road. It was published in several languages. During 1915-16, the figures of 400 members hanged and 5000 life imprisoned are noted.

It is an awesome feeling to be a part of this history. History is not a cookbook of recipes. Yet, those who don't know their history are condemned to repeat it – is so true. A point is the continuous transformation of human problems in all its aspects. **Yet, standing up and staking your life for your ideals and values, providing inspiring leadership in crises and working in a united way, are the qualities that are always called upon in any age and national crisis**. With such heavy thoughts I walked out of the glass doors of the Gadar Memorial, making sure that they were securely locked up.

An afterthought on Gadar Party is that the Government of India with the collaboration of overseas Indian communities should establish Gadar Studies Centers in Vancouver (Canada) and London (UK) where the Gadar movement had its wings. The first Indian Ambassador At Large, **Dr. Bhisham Agnihotri is ideally positioned to explore such projects with Indian Diaspora.**

The most urgent need is to save the display items from natural decay, mishandling and neglect. The entire collection can be electronically saved on a single hard disc. Readers interested in this project should convey their concern to the Indian Embassy/Consulates in USA and the Ministry of Foreign Affairs in India. However, any individual having a better plan of action for the preservation of this history of freedom and comments is free to contact me at my E-mail address: viabti1968@ yahoo.com. A committee of concerned individuals can bring quick results.

In conclusion, I must say that I finished this letter in 4-5 long sittings. First round of editing took six times the time of putting it all together. In a long hand, I definitely save time, but then the text cannot be continuously edited and polished. Anyway, now I send it you for your inspired comments. I am sure you did enjoy this historic ride!

(Dec 20, 2001/July, 2011)

PS: Footnotes for general readers
Gadar is an Urdu word adopted in Punjabi also. It is equivalent to the word revolution in English. A traitor in Urdu would be transliterated in English as *Gaddaar*, which is also adopted in Punjabi language. An English reader must see the big difference in meanings caused by this subtle difference in spelling.

NOTES AND COMMENTS

YUBA CITY: A CITADEL OF PUNJABIYAT IN USA

Introduction

Yuba City (YC), California, is an emerging symbol of Sikh Diaspora. It is like Southall of England and Vancouver of Canada, where *Punjabiyat* pervades the air. YC is not the earliest Punjabi settlement in the US, but it has become the most dominant one. Over the last 75 years it has spread the image of Punjab outside India. In a relative short period, a lot of folklore has woven around the Punjabi community in YC. My first visit to YC was nearly 20 years ago, and this one was in Dec 2001. The article attempts to weave a unique braid of personal pleasantries with issues pertaining to education, history, sociology, and politics that I have personally lived through. It oscillates between high and dry concepts, and popular myths and notions in order to keep the reading interest high.

Punjabiyat

It is pertinent to have some understanding of the notion of *Punjabiyat,* the fountainhead of all the subtitles in this article. Pondering upon it, one would realize that it is not *Punjabipan* that stands for the mundane characteristics of the Punjabi people. Let me, however, quickly add that I am not getting further into it by defining Punjabi! The only place of unambiguous definitions is in the realm of mathematics. There are always gray areas in other fields of human endeavour. *Punjabiyat* does include Punjabi language, Sikh religion, life styles, history and cultural values. However, it still remains incomplete. It is only when all these ingredients and other intangibles crystallized with chivalry, courage, and war victories of Punjabis into the making of first Sikh Empire under Maharaja Ranjit Singh that the *Punjabiyat* defined itself. A kingdom turns into an empire when foreign powers appoint their emissaries in it.

The world only remembers the empire builders, and masses follow their life styles and accept their religions. Again, empire here is limited in a political setting - measured by the extent of its geographical boundaries. However, history abounds with instances when superiority of thought in religion and science has led to great political empires. *HINDUTVA* is a similar concept. But what presently the VHP (Vishwa Hindu Parishad) and BJP (Bharatiya Janta Party) are talking about HINDUTVA is without the major ingredient of any war victory! When was the last Hindu Empire builder in the history of the world? Also, as a subtheme, I am posing deep intellectual and educational questions in the very first paragraph to the readership.

Dignity in Teaching

Now I resume my trip to YC spiced with insights and observations as they stand out. It was a beautiful crisp December day, when we set out from Oakland. My son and his friends drove me there. I have known a friendly couple in YC who migrated to California from Patiala in 1976. After living for a couple of years on a farm in Fresno area, they moved to YC in 1979. The couple has found a niche in their professions and also in socio-cultural life of the city. Harpal Chahal, who was a political science professor in Khalsa College, Patiala, has made a remarkable adjustment in teaching at middle and high school levels.

In India, it is considered somewhat of lower status to teach in schools vs. teaching in colleges. The universities sit at the top of an academic pyramid. Within a school or college, it gets worse, as it is more prestigious to teach higher classes! I remember how inflated or deflated were the egos of the teachers solely based on classes they taught. **Teaching status is measured by the content of knowledge acquired to teach, not by teacher's ability to communicate the material to students**. It is a reflection of social caste system that India has been strongly clinging for ages. Despite this background, Harpal has showed an uncommon ability to make a switch. He was always satisfied and happy in school teaching for over 20 years. (The couple retired in 2003 and 2005)

Determination of Salary

In the US, school teaching is considered as challenging as university teaching. Hence the salary differential is not significant. It is one's aptitude for teaching at a particular level that determines the professional entry. Both of my daughters are school teachers. The older one decided to teach in an elementary school ten years ago, as she loves to deal with the young kids. The younger one, who recently started teaching ESL (English as a Second Language) in a middle school, is not paid more for it.

In India, there is fixed pay scale for every one teaching irrespective of subject. In the US, salary is negotiated despite a salary range. It is governed by the market principles of demand and supply. Good schools and universities pay more to attract good teachers and professors. It is common amongst universities to attract Nobel Prize winners on their faculty. By and large, a math teacher gets a higher salary than does a social studies teacher. Special education (for mentally deficient) teachers get a higher salary for the challenges they face every day.

Substitute Teaching and Teacher Aides

There is a significant population of Punjabi children in central California where the Chahals have lived. Under the California State laws, if the number of particular minority students is at least 10%, then at least one bilingual teacher is hired for that class. This formula may not be followed exactly at present. Nevertheless, that is how both husband and wife were able to put their foot in the door. Harpal's wife, Surinder was a high school teacher in Patiala. Let me add that they did not get into the teaching profession as soon as they landed on the US soil. For a year or two, they picked up the fruits in California farms. It is a tough manual job and they were not used to doing it in Patiala. But they were determined to make their entry into the teaching profession.

While starting in temporary or unpaid volunteer positions as teacher aides and substitute teachers, they also took a few evening and summer courses for getting teaching certification. Substitute teaching is a concept that is still foreign to Indian education system. There is a general policy in US schools and colleges, that students must be provided instruction for a certain minimum number of days in an academic year. If a school teacher has to miss classes for a few days due to sickness, accident or professional conferences, then substitute teachers are called in to cover those classes. Every school district maintains a panel of substitute teachers. Occasionally, substitute teachers walk into classes with a short notice of a couple of hours. Substitute teachers may be retired teachers, housewives, and other persons who do not want to work full-time for various reasons. The system is not - like in India, where the students are left unattended to create boisterous scenes and disturbance for other classes. There is a tidy payment waiting at the end of the school day. Teacher aides are often volunteers or student teachers under training who assist regular teachers in upkeep and teaching of classes.

In a university setting, there is no department of substitute teaching, partly because not many people can walk in to teach at a college level. Here it works by honor system. To give a personal touch, during the last 30 years, I have not missed my classes for more than 8 days. So what I did was to request some colleagues to cover my classes, and I covered when they had to miss theirs. Once a colleague was hospitalized for four weeks, three of us taught his classes without any remuneration. It is time to introduce a modified system in Indian schools. It also brings community members in school environments. Students also respond well to such an involvement. Some times working as a teacher aide and substitute teacher can lead into a permanent position. However, volunteering is a hallmark of American life.

Honor System

Let me add that no official record is kept when a professor misses for a day, though it is in full knowledge of the department chairman. Neither any colleague, nor I have ever submitted leave applications for any sickness or going out of town. It is paramount to think how a system alone brings an overall integrity. And it applies to every facet of education and business life in USA. Imagine an everyday scenario in the US: a person, who teaches a course, writes its final exam, prints its copies, supervises the exam, grades all papers, and assigns the final course grades. It is nothing like in India - external and internal paper setters, exam preparation weeks, cheating, and police like supervision of the students. It is such a national scourge. And it stems from an inherent mutual suspicion. **Honor system is the heart of American education, and no wonder it is the most sought after education system in the world today.**

Indian system certainly has a colonial vestige to it. The British never trusted their subjects. Though British are long gone, but in all erstwhile colonies, by and large, the British systems are still continuing. At this rate, it will take another 50 years for an educational system to be in tune with present needs of a nation and its cultural heritage. There are some positive signs of changes in India, but the monolithic government control on education and the lack of public faith in its ability to run things on their own, is keeping the pace in check.

Education beyond the Classrooms

Chahals moved ahead with hard work, sincerity, along with their Punjabi guts and initiative. In a few years, Surinder was promoted up in school administration and put in charge of minority children in the district. It is quite an achievement for an Indian woman without any US degree of higher education. For a person coming from any Asian country, India in particular, I strongly recommend that everyone should go to a college, or join US Army, Air Force, Navy, or Marine. Serving in any wing of the US armed forces gives one a total sense of US life - from its history to the present life style and expectations. The main advantage lies in full acceptance by the community. The basic training is not tough for the Punjabis, and service contract of 3-5 years is quickly over. But its benefits are for life long.

Studies and Work

Without knowing the nuances of the US life, success in retaining a job and upward mobility is limited. I have known so many of my own relatives who did not do well as they could. Since coming to the US on immigration visas, they were right away eligible to work and apply for any job. However, those who come on non-immigrant visas like tourists or students, and wish to settle in the US, generally they get into a college and finish a degree. Another point that Indians can rarely fathom is that college degree particularly bachelor's means always working and studying together. Doing study all day and not working even for 10 hours in a week is not looked upon nicely! In India, it is studies, studies, and studies! Also, **the excessive number of reviews of material before exams smothers creative and original thinking at a prime time of life**. The maxim in US life is to work through your studies.

Scholar Athletes

An ideal American student is a distinguished scholar in classroom, a great athlete in field, and a volunteer in community. There are many state and national awards recognizing these qualities. Heisman trophy is one of the most prestigious awards for colleges and universities. Recently, it has been instituted at high school levels too. Look at the Western leaders in government, business and other organizations. They are a combination of all three characteristics in some proportion. After all, if you have not used your brain hard enough to solve tough problems, have not felt your heart jumping out of your chest in competitive sports, and have not related with community problems in an effective manner, then how will you ever make a mark in the society? India has a long way to go to bridge a gulf between sports and academics.

During my recent visit to India, after noticing lack of play areas in a school, I remarked to a group of students and teachers that students can always find play space enough to do sit-ups, push-ups and 40-meter sprints. They alone will make a great physique. In one private school, a huge playground was seldom used for sports! Competitions must be encouraged in such sporting activities requiring little resources. It pained me to see the young kids going to tuitions right after their long school days! All work and no play will slow down both intellectual and physical growth. This culture has to change.

Work Ethics and Dignity of labor

Part of Chahals' success is due to the fact that both of them came from families of educators and professionals. However, that is not enough. Harpal's elder brother, an English professor in the same college, also migrated to the USA. But he and his wife returned to India in a few months. They just could not accept working hard in the beginning. The US is a land of opportunity for the opportunistic as well as entrepreneurs. Initially, one should be willing to work three times harder than in India, at any available job. I remember Chako, an Indian finishing his doctorate at Indiana University while working as sewage sample collector as his part time job. Literally, it meant putting dips through manholes to collect samples of human waste. I was new in the US then, and could not believe it. May be his being a Kerala Christian had something to do with his willingness to do this job. Will a Hindu do it? Mind you, his hourly wage was higher, based on the principle of demand and supply!

On a personal note, during summer months, I cleaned vacant apartments including toilets. The big difference is that in India there may not be any reward for hard work in one's lifetime. Perhaps some Indians don't mind being unrewarded, provided, somehow it is 'guaranteed' in the next birth. They take a skewed understanding of the *Gita* of not caring about the fruits of actions. But in the US the rewards for creativity and hard work are quick. I have known persons doubling their salaries with the same employer in 4-5 years.

Successful Community

Yuba City has a population of nearly 50,000 and lies only 50 feet above the sea level. There is a general misconception about the size of Punjabi population in the city. YC, being often in news, gives an impression as if Punjabi population is over 50%; in fact it is only 10%. But the impact of the Punjabis on local economy is very high. Chahals told that nearly the entire local economy is in the hands of Punjabis. Take, for instance, land far and around YC - Punjabis own it all! Punjabis own all Seven-Eleven convenience stores and gas service stations. Of course, they own restaurants, retail shops of all kind of goods and services. They are many Punjabi physicians and engineers with every specialization. That is a considerable wealth.

Chahals proudly told how they made a net profit of $200,000 from a farm sale after five years. But this is peanuts as compared with many Punjabis who have made millions in real estate. Before the sprouting of recent rich Indians in high tech industries, Didar Singh Baines of YC was considered one of the richest Indians in the US. No wonder, leaders from India or in the US trek through YC to raise funds and gather political support for their causes.

Pride and Place of worship

In YC, there are two gurdwaras, one Hindu temple and one Masjid. I did not have the time to visit any place. I often tell in gatherings that owning a million-dollar home is indeed a great achievement at an individual level. Only a few people may care to know who is living out there. **But a million dollar place of worship establishes the identity of the entire community**. Then the whole world recognizes the community.

That suddenly shifts my thoughts in a high gear to cities and hill stations of India. Way back at the turn of 20th century, in some places like Shimla and Missouri, a few British who came there, built great churches in the most central locations. Some churches were built in the 1860s when the British had not yet taken a full control of that part of India! In my hometown Bathinda (BTI), a hundred-year-old imposing church, in railway colony, still stands. Hardly any British lived there, but I recall a few locals converted to Christianity. Conversion, by and large, is a one-way street. From the religion of the king and the powerful, the force of religion moves down in a social hierarchy.

Prosperity in Adventure

Over tea, I asked Chahals if they knew some Punjabis who remembered stories of the Hindustan Gadar Party. I was told that most of those Punjabis lived in San Francisco or nearby rural area of Stockton. YC is mostly populated by two types of Punjabis. Punjabis in the 1890s came down from Canada into USA when they heard of Gold Rush in Sierra Mountains of California. In Canada, Punjabis were shipped as indentured labor. They were free to work and move anywhere after the contracted five year period. YC was not their destination. It was a complex change of the US laws enacted in the 1920s that forced Punjabis into hiding and marrying Mexican women in order to retain their residency and possession of lands. Currently, the Punjabis in YC include generations of those Punjabis, and Indian immigrants coming under the immigration laws of 1960s.

Before the 1960s, very few professionals moved in YC. It is after the 1960's with the waves of Punjabi immigration from India that the demographic landscape of YC has changed. It is because of the wealth and opportunities in the US that people in villages of Punjab are always willing to sell their lands, properties, and take loans in order to enter into USA illegally! Everyday there are reports of scams and swindles of human smuggling - how the travel agents literally drop and desert them in some European and South American countries. **Bigger the risk, bigger the award, is the way that defines Punjabi spirit**. I have heard stories of illegal Punjabis making a great success in the US.

Punjabi Love for Land

However, one should not get the impression that in YC one would be noticing Punjabis strolling around in bunches as one sees people in the bazaars and roads in a typical Indian city. Loitering is considered indecent in US, and in some places it is unlawful beyond certain hours in public places. However, as we were driving to Yuba City the open spaces of the region were very captivating. The soil is very rich and water is plentiful for any crop to grow. There are all kinds of fruit orchards. The climate is perfect. Farmers harvest two crops at a time, as the fruit trees are much spaced apart. At this time of the year when leaves had fallen off, one could see all kinds of geometrical patterns formed by various symmetries needed in planting of trees. I was really mesmerized by grids of parallel lines for miles together! Ownership of a 100-acre farm is typical. I have known a few owning over 1000 acres. It reminded me of Punjab, as I used to ride in a bus or train with green fields on both sides of the road or railway lines.

While chatting with them, I presented Chahals a copy of the *Sahi Buniyad* a bimonthly educational publication from Bathinda, and stressed the importance Gurmukhi script in *Pujabiyat*. They briefly looked over and wrote a cheque for its subscription.

Prestige and work

It is but natural for the readers to think that given an opportunity to go USA, anyone can be successful. Even PM Vajpayee quipped in his speech at a reception given by American Indians during his last visit to New York. As I mentioned earlier, that is not true, but it has to be reiterated. My brother-in-law came on immigration visa twice, but he returned to India each time after short stays. So many Indians have lost their pride and identity for not working hard. Manual work in India is still looked down upon. I remember the 1950s when people in India bragged about their jobs or of their loved ones in which no work was done for the pay they were drawing. Work was only done as a favor for bribe money.

That was the culture in which India won its freedom and it still dominates in all state and central government services. Americans love to do a variety of work with their own hands. A typical American is an excellent carpenter, auto mechanic, plumber, painter, gardener, and dishwasher at home. **When more work is to be done Americans invent machines, but rich Indians like to hire more domestic servants**. New machines symbolize a superior intellect of that society. On the other hand, the availability of domestic servants stands for an oppressed and exploited class in that society.

Insight into a common scenario

Let me continue with this thought to a little climax. In the US, any two persons standing for a service will reflexively form a line showing courtesy to each other. In contrast, Indians in India take pride in breaking lines. **Social influence and prestige is measured by your ability to go ahead in a line by any means**. There are many such things that are different and are rooted in our history and cultural ethics. That is why any outright attempt to transplant a US system in India has not been successful. Eventually, India shall find its own models of management.

Pride in Heritage

Since the 1980s, YC has assumed importance for its active role in the US and Indian politics. Punjabi Sikhs are extremely organized. After the **9/11 Attack on the USA**, a male Sikh was shot dead in Arizona for mistaken identity. Chahals told me that not a single incident of hate towards Sikhs has taken place in YC. Frequently, parades and processions are held on various celebrations of *GURUPURABS*. This year, 50,000 people from YC and neighboring states participated in the procession on Guru Granth Sahib Divas - celebrated on the first Sunday of Nov each year. It was a spectacular!

Gurdwaras are central to social and political life of the community. Everyday there is some activity and Punjabis take an active interest. Politicians of every shade pass through YC for financial support. However, so far no Punjabi in recent times has sought an elected office from this region since Dalip Singh Saund served in the US House in 1960's, from Imperial Valley. Such a day is not far off in the life of YC. In British Columbia, Canada some Punjabis have won top electoral positions.

Compiling YC History

I suggested to Chahals to compile anecdotes on early Punjabi settlers and Indian visitors in the YC. He told that there are still people who remember Partap Singh Kairon and Jai Prakash Narain who used to come down to YC to work on the farms in summer months for earning money. Short time that I had in YC, I did not get a chance to meet local Punjabis. This article may pave a way for thinking in this direction. Chahals told about the availability of generous educational grants to buy and develop materials for minority students. A monograph on the Punjabis in YC is a feasible project that I intend to push and pursue. In fact, compilation of a series of monographs on Indian communities in major US cities should be encouraged and supported by Indian media and organizations.

Non-Punjabi Life Style

Let me add that such domination by any other linguist and cultural region of India is not found within and outside India. **Nearly half a million Indians were shipped out as indentured labor in some 60 British colonies in Africa, Southeast Asia, South America, Canada, and Pacific islands, including Fiji.** Gujaratis and Tamilians in African countries did eventually prosper, but they did not participate in local political systems. They ran away to UK, India, and other places from the despotic regimes of Idi Amin and his ilk. Since the 1980s, Gujaratis, in particular, have become the target of hate crimes in New Jersey, USA, where they literally control small businesses. They make all financial gains in the state, but they do not participate in its civic or political life. Since Hindu women wearing **BINDIS** became targets of random attacks in New Jersey, this hate crime movement is called Dot Buster.

Tamilians in Southeast Asian countries are still at the lowest rung of the society identified with the most menial jobs. Beharis and UPeans, sent to Latin America and West Indies who despite being in majority in some sparsely populated lands, have not made a political impact. **Does anyone know why people from Bengal and neighboring Bihar and Orissa were not shipped out to the colonies?** My answer is that they were so much physically emaciated with famines and plagues of previous years that they had no physical strength left to do any manual labor! It was the result of punitive economic policies that the British imposed on India after quashing the 1857 Mutiny.

A Model of Indian Life

The main reason of the Sikh dominance is their pride, faith, and practice of Sikh religion. Chahals are very active in gurdwara affairs. Since the **9/11 Attack on America**, Harpal Chahal has given lectures in nearby places on Sikh religion and its way of life - how it is different from the Hindu religion, and how Sikhs are different from Afghanis. Afghani Muslim men in particular have a tremendous resemblance with the Sikhs due to turbans and flowing beards. Gurdwaras are the heart and soul of the Khalsa way of life. Surinder Chahal often teaches classes in a gurdwara about the US life style to the newly arrived Punjabi women from India. It is a great civic service.

Gurdwara is not just a place of worship. It is also a place where congregations celebrate birthdays, weddings, and discuss social and political issues affecting them. It is in contrast to the Hindu temples where the devotees come and go in different directions after an hour of listening in Sanskrit language that the priests do not fully understand it. There is a dichotomy between the life within in the precincts of a Hindu temple and outside. Modern gurdwaras have made Sikh life a seamless culture. It is a place where spiritual, material, intellectual, and all social outlooks converge for the total uplift of the community. Despite local autonomy in gurdwara management, the presence of an apex central authority over all the gurdwaras in matters of the observance of Sikh piety, has also played a unifying role in the Sikh community within India and abroad.

(March 16, 2002/June 2011)

NOTES AND COMMENTS

1. Dear Dr. Satish Bhatnagar: I find your article, YUBA CITY: A CITADEL OF *PUNJABIYAT* IN USA very inspiring, to say the least. I would like to know a bit a more about you, the only thing I know from this article is that you are a Professor of Mathematics, but if you did not reveal it, my guess would have been that you had a solid background in social sciences, that you do. It seems to be based on experience, not just on books. I am also guessing that you are deeply committed for the betterment of India. I would also like to know about the project or projects you are involved with in India or abroad. My name is Ram Chaudhari, and I live in upstate New York. Hope to hear from you, **Ram Chaudhari**.

SOME LESSONS OF *GADAR* MOVEMENT

(**Note**: The salient points of a paper were presented at one-day conference (June 01, 2003, Santa Clara, CA) on the occasion of the 90ᵗʰ anniversary of *Gadar* Movement)

A sense of history that the West has it, India, where 80 % are the Hindus, never had it. **George Santayana famous line, "Those who do not learn from their history are condemned to repeat it**", so aptly applies to India's period of the last one thousand years, when examined in blocks of 40-50 years. In the US, hardly a week goes by when some event of WW I or WW II is not highlighted on a TV channel, book, movie, novel, commentary for public consumption. Such efforts keep the collective mind focused, and the nation effectively responds when an event like Sept 11 ever hits it.

In contrast, the *Gadar* movement, four years older than the **Russian Revolution** and eight years older than Gandhi's **Non-Cooperation Movement**, but it is nearly forgotten amongst the Indians born after the 1960s. Therefore, I take this opportunity to thank the organizers in rekindling awareness about this movement of great historic proportions.

During visits to my hometown Bathinda, some friends often asked me to get information on a *Gadari*, Bishan Singh Hind. It was only 18 months ago, that I first visited the ***Gadar*** Memorial Center in San Francisco. Certainly, he is not one of the 21 persons whose framed pictures are displayed on its wall. But who knows the existence of any records of the ***Gadar*** Party? I pose it as an open question. This paper is an extract of the article that I wrote after visiting the Center.

Every age has its own fights for freedom - from an individual to national level. Indian youth and leaders do not have any fight with the British today. But look what is happening to the integrity, secularity, sovereignty and solidarity of India. There is an ongoing fight to preserve Indian ethos and values.

The war is intense in Jammu and Kashmir (J&K) and in the entire Northeast (NE). Who is stopping the youth from marching into J&K and NE and fight for the protection of the Hindus and Sikhs? Where is a leadership? The Hindus and Sikhs have fled from areas in J&K where they have lived since the reign of Maharaja Ranjit Singh!

The problem, of displaced Hindus and Sikhs returning to Kashmir, is bigger than the problem the *Gadaris* faced in freeing India. Nearly 96% of Hindu/ Sikh population in Kashmir has been kicked out of it since 1989, and in some NE states 90 % of the population converted to religions foreign to Indian soil. Since

1947 the borders of India have shrunk, and its ancient heritage threatened. Here is a gist of major thoughts that are distilled:

1. When men are **willing to lay their lives**, then ordinary people can meet any challenge.
2. Without a **cultivated core leadership**, any following eventually loses its steam.
3. Having full support from **non-Indian dominant** group is paramount.
4. Men **rise above their religion and region** when the common cause is greater.

The following are some of the present day problems of India that cry for *Gadar* approach:
1. Demographic shift and ethnic cleansing of Hindus in Kashmir, and now in Bangladesh
2. Occupation of Indian territory by China
3. Combating and countering mounting anti-India acts of terrorism

If the *Gadar* Party had only a couple of leaders of the stature of Lala Hardayal, then this movement would have complemented the Gandhian movement, and most militant problems of free India today would never have cropped up.

(May 20, 2003)

NOTES AND COMMENTS

MY SECOND VISIT TO THE GADAR CENTER

[**Background Note**: This article turns out a sequel to the one I wrote in 2003. However, that was in the form of a letter to my friend and editor of an educational magazine, the **SAHI BUNIYAD**. Later on, it was posted on a few websites. Its one version was presented in the first **Gadar Conference** held in San Jose in June 2003. My interest in the Gadar Movement is a natural consequence of being born and raised in Punjab. Also, I remember when the San Francisco Gadar Memorial Center was opened in 1975. Though I have come to SF several times, but missed visiting the Center. The Center has no regular opening hours, and is not included in any list of tourist places. It was during my Y-2000 visit to India that a friend told me of a Gadari who had died in Bathinda, at age 95. He wanted me to check out the records. It sharpened my desire, and by a twist of mysterious circumstances, I first visited the Center in Dec 2002. It was one of the most overwhelming experiences of my life - expressed in a 6000-word letter.

In the meanwhile, a metamorphous has taken place in me. The skill cultivated over 40 years, in writing all kinds of letters, is now channeled into various *Reflections*. My forte lies in dressing bare historical facts with colorful narration and passion. Using my perception, I daringly interpolate and extrapolate historical events with other contemporary events as well as the present ones. That enhances the significance of history for better understanding of the present.]

Yesterday, while I was being driven to the Gadar Memorial Center, San Francisco, I asked myself - why am I attracted towards it? The answer that came out is that **one is generally drawn towards a place or person associated with sacrifices and service to the people above self**. Of course, for one who is not familiar - like my wife and children, the Center means little, unless they read about it. That is another reason of my continued research in this direction to periodically inform and educate people of a glorious chapter in the history of modern India. I consider it my social obligation.

A unique feature of the Gadar Movement was uncanny unity brought amongst the Punjabi Hindus, Sikhs and Muslims. However, it should be understood that at least 90 % members of the Gadar Party were Sikhs from rural areas of Punjab. It was a turn of the 20th century, and the British gauged the danger of this unity. They did not want the 1857 unity between the Hindus and Muslims become a reality again. Religion based political parties, like Muslim League, Akali Dal and Hindu Mahasabha were encouraged by the British legislation on ethnic representation in late 1920s. Eventually, the Divide and Rule was enshrined as an open policy of the British.

In my opinion, the unity was consciously driven by the desire to regain the lost empires. For the Muslims, the loss of the Mughal Empire was in a natural course of rise and fall of empires after 200 years. But, for the Sikhs it was too short to enjoy the fruits of the Sikh Empire that stretched the entire region west of Sutlej River and extending in north beyond Kashmir.

The builder of Sikh kingdom, Maharaja Ranjit Singh, was no doubt a great king, but he lacked a vision of a long term Sikh Empire. He did not follow the succession secret of the Sikh Gurus. He forgot how Guru Gobind Singh placed the Sikh politico-military leadership in the hands of Banda Singh Bahadur. Otherwise, Ranjit Singh would have been succeeded by one his able generals, like Hari Singh Nalwa rather than by weakling sons who lost the empire to the British within ten years after the death of Ranjit Singh. Since then the Sikhs have been hungry in controlling their own political destiny. Perhaps, in Manmohan Singh becoming the first Sikh Prime Minister of India, a larger dream of Sikh community may have been realized!

Though I had only a couple of hours in the Center, but my work was cut out. There are four small display shelves containing original documents of the Gadar Party. I am sure a significant record of its publications and correspondence is lying scattered in the attics of the descendents of the Gadaris. They should search and save it before rotten away, or accidentally trashed. By maintaining a comprehensive website on the Gadar Movement (www.lib.ucdavis.edu/punjab), Tejinder Singh Sibia has done a great service to the researchers and general community.

Listed below are the abstracts of some documents and pamphlets that I browsed. They are all from only one of the four showcases. The time was not enough for a full reading:

1. *AZADI DI GUNJ* (**Echoes of Freedom**) Number 14. It is published in Gurmukhi with touches of Urdu. **Obviously, the Gadar Party was not hung up on any language**. Only the spread of the message was important. One of the two cartoons depicts an English enjoying watching a Hindu and Muslim fight. In the other, a British soldier is shown flogging an Indian. That captures the atrocities of famine and hunger caused by heavy taxation on Indians. Also, there is a soulful rendering of a poem by M S Dukhia with a title, *GAL NAL NAHIH MULK AZAD HUNDE* (Countries Don't Become Free With Idle Talks.)

   This four-page pamphlet is in a porous condition like most documents. The least the SF Consulate can do is to have all the documents scanned on a disc and save this small archive for posterity and research scholars. Through this open article I volunteer to pay for its expenses incurred for this purpose.

2. *GADAR DI GUNJ* (**Echoes of Revolution**) Number 1 and 7; Year 1931. 15, 000 copies of Number 1 and 25, 000 of Number 7 were published and distributed free. Number 1 has all poems in its 28 pages, and so does Number

7 in its 24 pages. All of them exhort to fight for the freedom of the country. Poetry can come from the heart of even an uneducated person, and reach the heart of every man. Whereas, the ideas in prose are a product of a cultivated mind.

It may be noted that the population of the Punjabis around the 1900s was very small in California. Legally, Indians could not enter into USA. Thousands of hardy rural Punjabis were shipped as indentured labor in the 1880s over a period of ten years to sweat out in the farms and factories in harsh cold regions of Canada. When the news of Gold Rush in Northern California and Nevada spread out, some of the adventurous ones crossed over into the USA. However, they were pushed out of the mountainous mining areas. Gradually, they settled in the farmlands of central California.

3. *RAJASI MANTRA* (Royal Mantra) Its subtitle is *Things to Remember by Baba Nihal Singh.* Though the script is Gurmukhi, but it is mixed with Hindustani. It is in a narrative form and dwells on 110 small observations - including the concepts of *HALAL KHORE* (Sincere persons) and *HARAM KHORE* (Bastards); Another focal point is; Remember Your Heroes.

For this reason, I have always admired the Sikh tradition of paying homage in every **ARDAAS** (public benediction) to the men and women who sacrificed their lives for their religion. Also, most Gurdwaras maintain a gallery of portraits of such heroes. I wish the Hindus at least start recognizing their leaders.

4. *HINDUSTAN GADAR,* "**The only revolutionary paper within and outside India**." These words are written on this 4-page poster type pamphlet published in Gurmukhi containing pictures and poems. The most moving and inspiring lines are by Madan Lal Dhingra that he wrote during his trial. He was hanged on August 17, 1909.

"I admitted the other day that I tried to shed the English blood as a humble revenge for the inhuman hangings and deportations of patriotic Indian youth. In this attempt, I have consulted none, but my conscience. I have conspired with none but my own duty. I believe that a nation held down by foreign bayonets is in perceptual state of war. Since open battle is rendered impossible to a disarmed race, I attack by surprise. Since guns were denied to me, I drew my pistol and fired.

As a Hindoo, I feel that a wrong to my country is an insult to God. Her Cause is the Cause of Shri Ram. Her service is the service of Shri Krishna. Poor in wealth and intellect someone like myself has nothing else to offer to Mother but his own blood and so I have sacrificed the same on her altar.

The only lesson required in India is at present is to learn how to die. The only way to teach it is by dying ourselves. Therefore, I die and glory to my martyrdom. This war will continue between India and England so long as Hindoos and English race last (if this present unnatural relation does not change)

My only prayer to God is that I may be reborn to the same Mother and I have to re-die in the same sacred Cause till the Cause is successful and stands free for the good of humanity and to the glory of God."

I have read these immortal words before and they always evoke a surge of emotions. For a moment, I could not continue reading the documents. I had to stop, get up from the sofa and coffee table where I was working. On pondering over, it reminded me a famous line of Rev. Martin Luther King Jr. **"Life is not worth it, if you are not willing to die for anything."**

I have not been a keen observer of changes in the arrangement of objects around me, whether in my own home, or elsewhere. Though I had been in the Center Hall for an hour, I did not notice that the only picture on the front hall, of Mahatma Gandhi, was not there as I saw it in Y-2002. Replacing it was a painting or picture of three stripes in colors with two Khalsa dagger emblem in the center. It has no description, but my guess is that it may be a flag of the Gadar Party. Unquestionably, this picture fits right into the spirit that pervades the hall. If any reader knows anything about this picture, then I would appreciate hearing. Slowly and reverentially, I marched past the photograph of each freedom fighter and martyr.

I resumed my examination of the worn-out documents that still ignite my thoughts on the present state of the events whether in India and the USA.

5. *GULAMI KA ZAHAR, GULAM KI ATMA* (**Poison of Slavery, Soul of the Slave**)
This is a 16-page undated comprehensive essay in Urdu by Lala Hardayal (1884-1939), one of the greatest intellectual giants of India and a founder of the Gadar Party. **A movement without masses is ineffective as one without thinkers and leaders in it.**

This essay is divided in two parts. The first part, **Poison of Slavery** deals with origins and reasons that lead to the slavery of India. Hardayal is also known for a great rational mind in the tradition of European thinkers who certainly influenced his thoughts during his stay in Europe. **The essay is a masterpiece and needs to be re-published in every Indian language by the Government of India and private publishers**. His penetrating observations and courage of conviction show a side of a fighting genius. It is very much relevant for the Indians today.

Hardayal scrutinizes the popular folk tales of India, social practices, and beliefs in Ramayana, Mahabharata and Bhagavatam. It was such a joy and inspiration to read it, though my Urdu is rudimentary and only home taught. In the second part that takes only 4-5 pages, He dissects thinking of Indians who have become of slaves of the British in body and mind. Near the conclusion he forcefully writes, **"Oil can be extracted from a rock, but a slave has no soul!"**

Reading a good portion of this essay and its tone, and myself being a toastmaster, I am sure Hardayal must have been a great orator and rebel rouser of his time. He must be like Anthony of Caesar era. No wonders, the British, through pressure on the US government, had Hardayal evicted from the USA. He held a faculty position with Stanford University. He came to the USA in 1912, but in 1914, he moved to Germany and Switzerland, where he organized similar parties and raised arms and money.

6.   GADARI RASALA #3 *ANKA DI GWAHI* (**Statistics Speak Up**)
    It is published both in Urdu and Gurmukhi containing shocking statistics taken from the British Gazetteer. Its 48 pages are filled with various data from the year 1881 through 1916. It is divided into the following 14 categories through which the British Empire was hemorrhaging Indians. Only a line or two are picked up from the text:
    1. **Land Taxation income** 2. **Income from canals.** 3. **Salt Taxation.** This is very revealing. Through this punitive tax the British were able to extract a pound of flesh from every Indian. Twenty years later, Gandhi found in Salt Taxation a perfect handle to defy the British Raj. There is an amazing piece of history how some Rajasthan princes catapulted before the British in levying salt tax on the salt from the Sambhar Lake in Rajputana. Once the British had their agents posted in each princely state the status of princes was not better than the British pets. 4. **Income from forest resource** 5. **Expenses on Army.** 6. **Expenses on Police.** It reveals how the size of the police and army increased after 1857, and the way they used Indians soldiers and cops against Indians. 7. **Plague deaths in Punjab.** There is a breakdown of figures in each district of Punjab. How plague and some fever took a heavy toll children under 10 years. 8. **Plague deaths in India. Between 1896-1912. Nearly 6.7 million people died according to the official British reports.** The unofficial figures are nearly 12 millions!

In some parts of Bengal, Orissa and Bihar the emaciation of body went on for a few generations that their physical condition became a vernacular phrase. On noticing any one devouring a meal, I remember my mother admonishing, "Look, how he is eating like a hungry Bengali!" What bewilders me is a benign neglect by Indians themselves of this condition. Is it because for the Hindus, death is like change of clothes for the soul? With such an outlook who would care about the

Hindus dying of plague, famine, or in massacres! This apathy over their tragedies amongst the Hindus continues even today, though on a different scale.

9. **Export of Wheat**. 10. **Income of Indians**. Even according to one British officer the per capita income of Indians was very low. 11. **Police Department** 12. **Income and purpose of rail**. The Railways were for the purpose of moving the goods, or army as urgently needed. 13. **1911 Census of India**. The average age of a man was 22.5 years and of a woman 23 years in comparison with the European man at 47 and woman at 50.

7. First annual issue of Yugantatar Ashram in Urdu dated Nov 1, 1913. It is another valuable document for preservation.

While stretching my legs, I briefly glanced at the books in nearly 20 full bookshelves. They contain some useless books like World Almanac 1970 and India 1977 etc. It reminded me how in the US libraries out-of-date books are taken off the shelves every few years, and put on sales for raising funds for the libraries. Without a community involvement, the SF Consulate has no incentive to undertake such a project.

I wanted to do more research, but the Center was to be closed. It was through a special arrangement with the Indian Consulate Office that I had gotten this admission.

(July 03, 2004)

NOTES AND COMMENTS

1.   I enjoyed reading the article. **Inder Singh**

2.   You are great. The article is very inspiring. My profound regards. **Sham**

KOMAGATA MARU: THE FIRST MARITIME REVOLT

[Note: My strength is unconventional in analyzing old data and bringing out new findings. When the focus is on a tree, I can see its muscular grandeur. And when it is on the forest, then I see its panoramic beauty. A historical event is a valuable study only, if it can be connected with the present life. Therefore, sociology, politics and psychology are richly blended with folklores and anecdotes to bring liveliness for the discriminating readers. The scholarly jargons are avoided.

The story of Komagata Maru is braided and meshed with various other themes and sub-themes. This article is replete with astute observations and daring conclusions, but supported by facts and figures. In many places, a need for elaboration may be felt, but I maintain a very condensed style. The memories and thoughts were stirred up after watching a 90-minute documentary, **Continuous Journey** on Komagata Maru during the 11th Punjabi American Festival, held in Yuba City, California on Sunday, May 29, 2005. I especially went there to see this movie.]

The Symbol

Komagata Maru virtually symbolizes the hopes and aspiration of poverty stricken, politically persecuted, and yet adventurous ordinary Punjabis. It is the story of 376 Punjabis who left the shores of India at the turn of the 20th century by, perhaps, selling their lands or borrowing money. In fact, this practice continues even to the present times! Let it be emphasized that it was not an organized departure. It happened in ones and twos from India to the British controlled seaports, particularly, of Hong Kong and Singapore.

Freedom and Dignity

A basic question rises - how come the Punjabis were the pioneers in the pursuit of better life? The answer is simple; **the Sikhs were the last to lose their very first Sikh empire**! Chatrapati Shivaji's successors in the 18th century extended the Maratha Empire over the declining Mughals in north. But they were defeated in the Third Battle of Panipat (1761) by the forces of Afghani/Irani Ahmad Shah Abdali/ Durrani. Unfortunately, the Marathas did not get support from the Hindus of the region, or the Hindus dared not go against the Mughal rulers. On the other hand, the vast Sikh empire under Maharaja Ranjit Singh hardly lasted ten years after his death. When Dalip Singh succeeded, the British broke the treaty signed with Ranjit Singh, and fully annexed Punjab by 1849. From the empire builders, the Sikhs were suddenly like the birds with clipped wings.

It is during the foreign travels, that Indians realized the indignities they suffered in their homeland India. Even today, the Indian passports do not command due respect. One finds it out in unpleasant situations encountered - either when stranded during a flight or in need of a transit visa at a foreign airport. The overseas Punjabis in 1914 were neither citizens of a free India, nor they got the equal treatment legally available to the British subjects. This story is not a part of present history textbooks, though India has been free for nearly 50 years. Ironically, it is not taught in the schools and colleges of Punjab, though the Sikhs have ruled it for over 40 years.

A Bold Venture

The ***CONTINUOUS JOURNEY*** is the first documentary movie on Komagata Maru. Just before the movie, I was introduced to Ali Kazimi, its director and producer. He seemed in his 40s and made a few background remarks before the movie rolled in. It took eight years, and he spent 50% of his own money. The main financial support came from the South Asian Heritage Foundation of Canada.

For a moment, I really wondered at a Muslim making a movie like this. Then Sir Richard Attenborough, the director and producer of the classic movie, *Gandhi* flashed up in my mind. Also, in the same breath crossed the name of Rahi Masoom Raza who wrote the stirring dialogues of the popular TV serial on Hindu epic, the *Mahabharata*. In the world of men, you cannot sweep the entire race on one person's beliefs.

Afterwards, I told Kazimi, "The movie is powerful, the background music great, and your deep voice narrating most events is perfect." The famous Bollywood actor, Naseeruddin Shah also lent his voice. My voice has the least commercial value! Above all, the archival research undertaken was a labor of love. You cannot cut corners in some projects.

Freedom after Indentured labor

Punjabis were brought as indentured labor in Canada since the 1880s. Its cold climate required robust labor force. The news of the 1890 gold rush and lumber factories in northern Nevada and California prompted some Sikhs to cross the border into the US states of Washington, Oregon and California. The hard working Punjabis were pushed out of mining of which they had little knowledge. But the farming regions of Fresno and Imperial Valley attracted them. Soon the word of a better quality of life in Canada and USA spread in Punjab. It was a combination of economic opportunities and desire to live in freedom that triggered an early trickle of Punjabis into North America.

Gathering Storm

Gurdit Singh, a business entrepreneur in Hong Kong chartered the Japanese ship Komagata Maru for taking the Punjabis into Canada. This ship was built in Germany in 1898, sold to Sicily, and then to Japan. That is how it got the Japanese name. In Japanese language, Maru means 'ship' and Komagata is a popular name like Elizabeth in English. From the official documents, it is evident that Gurdit Singh was fully conversant with the British immigration laws in the colonies and political ramification of his enterprise. Before sailing, he also took the legal advice from his English attorneys in Hong Kong.

As soon as the ship neared Vancouver harbor in British Columbia, the Canadian media went up in arms against Indians. The daily newspaper headlines were like, **"The Hindu invasion of Canada Imminent!"**. A subsequent search of the passengers produced not even a single weapon. It was a time when the unwritten policy of the Canadian Government was Canada for only the White Anglo Sextons. In 1907, the Canadian immigration policy was essentially amended to exclude Indians who flourished, once the five-year period of indentured labor was over. It was finally corrected in 1948. In near future, the Canadian Government would apologize to the Punjabis for this historic discrimination.

Empire Building

After decimating most Canadian natives and corralling the rest in open prisons, called Indian reservations, the Whites naturally wanted to reap all the advantages for themselves. It is a universal strategy of the victors. Whenever, the Greeks, Afghanis, Arabs, Iranians, Turks and Mughals carved out parts of India as their hegemony, they had their brethren from homelands follow them into key positions – particularly, in military, civil administration, and law and order. After all, the white Canadians were not supposed to welcome new Punjabis from India! **But the crux was of legality.**

The then British Prime Minister went on record in supporting a ban on the entry of Indians in Canada by saying that 'the Hindus have not contributed anything to the human race in the last 2000 years'. **In recent times, the US TV evangelist Billy Graham and presidential hopeful Pat Buchanan have also made similar statements against the Hindus**. However, the Hindus have not waged any media blitz against such libels.

It is no wonder that the Canadian federal and provincial governments, immigration authorities, and courts were all stacked up against the Indians stranded in a ship - 1 KM away from the shore of Vancouver. The Shore Committee, formed out of a small community of 2000 Indians in Vancouver, was able to hire a white attorney, Edward. He did a good job at the risk of his own life and that of his family. Whatever legal grounds he presented, were eventually rejected by the court system.

Komagata Maru and the Gadar Party

About the same time the Gadar Party was formed in 1914 in San Francisco. It was not too far from the Canadian waters. It requires further research as to what role did the Gadar Party play during the Komagata standoff. After nearly two months when food and water ran out in Komagata Maru, the white Canadian militia under the ruse of supplying provisions clashed with the demoralized passengers. **This is the first maritime revolt of Indians**. A couple of Indians were killed and a few injured. The passengers, being at a high point, had an advantage in hurling the objects down on the boat. The militia retreated back to the coast. Some compromise was made.

Integrating Media

My thought went onto Gandhi who assiduously used the British controlled media to his advantage in every agitation he undertook in South Africa and India. Eventually, he became the darling of the western media. It was the media reporting on British police beating the unarmed and peaceful *Satyagrahis* (persons steadfast on truth) that shook the conscience of the West. As compared with some Indian scenarios, such as *Salt Satyagrah*, Komagata Maru was a very big stage. But there was no media reporting on behalf of the Indians! Thus, Komagata Maru saga lies buried and nearly forgotten in the annals of Indian history.

Hindu Individualism

The Hindus, including the Rajputs, have displayed individual acts of heroism. Often, they lacked in leadership. **Courage as a trait, one is born with, but leadership is institutionally cultivated.** A few years ago, while talking with a liberal British professor of history, I said, "On a one-to-one basis, for every smart British, there was a smarter Hindu even in the 18th century India. But the Hindus immediately lose this edge as soon as the corresponding groups are compared. Perhaps any group of two English men was stronger than every group of two Hindus in a population of 330 millions! The British ruled India because of the inherent divisiveness amongst the Hindus. If it were not the British, then French or Dutch would have taken over India." He was speechless.

Tolerance defines Hinduism

In every media reporting and government communiqués on Komagata Maru, the word used for Indians was Hindus. Kazimi remarked that Hindustan being the name of the country during the Mughal period, so its people were called Hindus. Islam and Christianity, of foreign soil, had taken roots in India by the 19th century. I rolled back to the pages of history when India was a 100% Hindu nation. Its hallmark was tolerance for other religious practices. The erstwhile Hindu kings and princes let the Jews, Christians of St. Thomas and Parsees come and live in freedom and flourish in India. In recent history, the European trading companies and Christian missionaries established their posts and churches on the coast of India. Islam alone entered India with sword.

I am convinced that the ideal of secularism can only become a reality under the Hindu religious states. The current practice and interpretation of secularism in India are anti-Hindus. More communal riots have erupted since the 1947 partition of India than 100 years before it. This was aptly acknowledged by a Muslim leader in 1993 when the Muslims fled to Nepal after the communal riots in Mumbai. He said, "The Muslims are safer in the Hindu kingdom of Nepal than in secular India!"

Perennial Causes

There are two main reasons for the failure of any militant course by Indians against the British. They surfaced up in Komagata Maru episode in 1914 and in the case of the *Gadaris* (means revolutionaries) returning in another ship from the US to India and that too in 1914. One, the US and the Canadian governments openly colluded with the British in spying over the meetings and infiltrating its membership. Neither the Gadar Party in San Francisco nor the Shore Committee in Vancouver had taken measures to counter against massive espionage by the government machineries. The declassified documents show how easy it was for the Americans and Canadians to exchange information between authorities in USA/Canada, England and India.

The other reason is the presence of *Jaichands* (means proverbial traitors) amongst the Hindus. They betray by essentially thinking for themselves rather than of the nation at large. The documentary revealed how two members of the Shore Committee turned out disloyal. In the ultimate analysis, this recurring historical fact boils down to religion. **Hinduism giving ultimate freedom in the pursuit of life and happiness, an individual is more likely to watch his own interest at the cost of his society.** At the other end, Islam instills community over individual. That is why no one has betrayed Osama Bin Ladin in four years even for a $50 million bounty put on his head by the US Government! The *Jehad* works on absolute loyalty to Islam.

Some Demographic Findings

It is pertinent to examine some demographic data on 376 Indian passengers in Komagata Maru. The website: **http://people.lib.ucdavis.edu/tss/punjab/ districtlist.html**, the most comprehensive and reliable source of material on the Gadar Party and Komagata Maru and Punjabi issues is professionally maintained by Tejinder Singh Sibia of UC Davis. The list has 372 passengers. Perhaps, four kids were not included. It has only three pieces of data on each person, namely,

first name, **district** and **village**. That interestingly shows that the village identity, becoming extinct today, was strong 100 years ago than of the last name. At least, 95% Indians lived in the villages at that time vs. 75 % today.

All the 372 passengers were from Punjab. The united Punjab, before the 1947 partition of India, had 19 districts. Some districts were at least twice the size of present districts in India. Six of them went to Pakistan. Ambala and Hissar are parts of a new state of Haryana carved out of Punjab in 1965. The maximum number of 74 Punjabis came from Ferozepur District. Four districts had only one person each. It included Faridkot District that covered my hometown Bathinda!

From the names, 20 are clearly identified as Muslims; 18 of which came from one district Shahpur. It may be noted that in the late 19th century, particularly after the 1857 Indian Revolt, the Hindus and Muslims had come close, as they fought against the British. Many Hindus had names like Ram Bakhash, Iqbal, Ram Deen etc. This list has 4-5 such names.

Hindu and Sikh Identity

It is very difficult to differentiate between the Hindus and Sikhs from their first names. As a matter of fact, in a popular parlance, the Hindus in Punjab are still referred as *MONAY* (means clean-shaven) and Sikhs as *KESDHARI* (means retaining hair). Historically, nearly 100% of the first few generations of *KHALSA* (baptized/*Amaratdhari* Sikhs) came out of the Hindus.

After the Sikh holocaust in the first half of the 18th century, their depleted population was only replenished by mass adoption of the Sikhism by the Hindus. The adults of the 1914 era were born in late 19th century at a time, when the Sikh population was boosted by the eldest males, in Hindu families, baptized as Sikh. This practice still continues in many *KHATRI* families - like the Bhatias, Kapurs, Walias, and Malhotras of Punjab that have family members both Hindus and Sikhs. Certainly, the pre and post 1984 Operation Blue Star have damaged the Hindu - Sikh ties. That is one of the main reasons of the reported decline of the Sikh population in Punjab during the last five years.

Names and Headwears

The middle name, Singh is not exclusively used by the Sikhs even in Punjab. In the districts of Amritsar and Gurdaspur, some *Brahmins* use Singh after their first name. In Bathinda District, I have personally known some *Banias* using Singh too. There are many local legends behind such practices. *Pag/Pagari* was a common headwear of the males in north India and had numerous styles and designs. The Hindus, by and large, would stop wearing a *Pagari* after joining the service of the British Raj.

How Many Hindus?

The Hindus numbering 12 as mentioned in an article has no bases. In the list, the typical Hindu names in alphabetical order with their frequencies in parentheses are as follows: Arjan (7), Bhagwan (3), Bishan (5), Chanan (7), Indar (11), Kishan (6), Lal (4), Nand (5), Narayan (6), Partap (4), Ram (5), Sundar (11) From a large group picture of the passengers standing on the ship deck one can see out of 19 persons, there are only seven Sikhs. It is difficult to conclude that this sample statistically represents all 372 passengers. Nevertheless, putting the entire analysis together, I claim that at least 100 passengers were Hindus.

Let it be made clear that the passengers were not illiterate villagers. Some were city dwellers with no village connections. Clearly identified are one physician with his wife (Dr. and Mrs. Raghunath) and two other women Kishan Kaur and Prabha. The name Chanda is unisex.

Komagata Maru in Indian Waters

Instead of returning to the originating port of Hong Kong, the British colonial authorities forced Komagata Maru to sail towards **India.** In order to contain possible recurrence of violence, the ship was directed to Budge Budge situated at the mouth of Hoogly River. It was a few miles away from **Calcutta, the capital of British India till 1912.**

This conspiracy further aggravated the passengers already suffering from every physical deprivation for over three months. **Consequently, there was a second and more violent revolt at the sea.** The authorities, being better equipped and positioned, controlled the Punjabis this time. Nearly forty passengers died or reported missing. Some were arrested, a few hanged and most put behind the bars. The Komagata Maru was heavily damaged and went out of service for a while.

The two local Canadian leaders Bhag Singh and Balwant Singh were hanged for trumped up charges of treason, though Balwant Sigh had served the British Army with distinction. He was a Gurdwara priest in Vancouver. The trailblazer Gurdit Singh's life was transformed once he came in contact with Gandhi. He also served five years in prison, but lived long enough to see India free. He died on July 04, 1954, at the age of 94.

(May 30, 2005/ July, 2011)

NOTES AND COMMENTS

1. Hello Mr. Bhatnagar, Thank you so very much for a very insightful and educative article. I learnt that I know so little about a part of my people's history. I hope that we can collaborate to bring out some of these aspects of history to other people. I just called Mr. Sibia in Davis to thank him for introducing us. Thank you very much again. I am mailing the film "Neither Milk Nor Yogurt" out to you. You should get it in a few days. with warm regards, **Arti Jain**

2. My dear Bhatnagar Sahib I feel very much educated by this piece and would like to request you to communicate it to the ***ORGANISER*** so that wide readership may have the advantage of this historical event in our fight for freedom from the British and also the inner strength of Hindu/Indian society. With best wishes and personal warmth. Sincerely, (R.S. **Nigam**)

3. Life is truly a Komagata Maru. Rest is BS. In the event BS is not known to you I shall oblige Uncle Sam. **Subhash Sood**

FIRST INDIAN PIONEER IN LAS VEGAS

In any new settlement of a community there are two kinds of people. One is a small group of pioneers, who are driven by quest for new opportunities away from their present home and hearth. The rest are followers and settlers into newly discovered green pastures. I wanted to identify the first pioneers amongst the Indian immigrants in Las Vegas. Did I find one? Well, you be a judge.

It is almost a fact that no Indian (from India) moved to Las Vegas for employment or as a fortune seeker before 1960. I did my best research on it. However, it is always open for revision, if new facts are discovered. Then, I moved the search period to 1961-65. I don't know if a city or county maintains a record of its new residents. That may go against individual privacy privileges. I did not check with DMV about records based on national origin. I called friends and acquaintances in an old-fashioned way to identify individuals. Lo and behold, a pioneer turned out in my own backyard, UNLV's Math Dept!

Joginder Singh Ratti is an Indian pioneer who came to Las Vegas in 1963. He is a clean-shaven Sikh and lived true to the Sikh Gurus' edits to found new cities and explore new opportunities. The Sikhs are the most visible people even in remotest parts of the world. At the time of joining math faculty of UNLV, Joginder had completed all requirements for PhD, except dissertation from Wayne State University.

When Ratii came to Las Vegas, UNLV was known as Nevada Southern University. In 1969, it was renamed as University of Nevada Las Vegas. After two years, he went back to Wayne State to finish his dissertation. In 1967, he moved to a PhD granting Southern Florida University in Tampa. On finding his address from a Yahoo search, we had a long conversation. At SFU, he has served as a department chair for three years.

Before 1970, Las Vegas was considered quite an inhospitable place for its hot and harsh climate. Centrally air-conditioned homes and shopping malls were rarities. There being no agriculture and factories like in the Midwest region, Las Vegas was no attraction for Indians. Moreover, Indians are not known to have a gambler's instinct and itch.

The opportunities at Nevada Test Site were limited for Indians due to security reasons. Joginder was attracted to Las Vegas for a job - offered without any interview. His career trail, from Detroit to Las Vegas, may have been followed by Sadanand Verma joining UNLV in 1967, though he had done his PhD from Wayne State in 1955. Verma served as the Department Chair for 22 years (1968-1990).

(May 16, 2004)

NOTES AND COMMENTS

1. Professor M.C. Shukla, first Professor of Commerce at Delhi University (I am the third one) visited Las Vegas in 1957; I do not know in what connection. When I first went to Las Vegas and sent him greetings from there, he wrote in his own handwriting setting up DOs and DON'TS for me at Las Vegas (as sincere fatherly advice). I feel extremely happy when I hear of their achievements in India and abroad in various fields. **NIGAM**

2. Thanks for all of your stories...great.
    My suggestion, however, would be to call your people "East Indians"...here in this country, we think of "Indians" as the American Indians...a bit confusing to some. Clarification is always good so all are on the same page. **Renee'**

INDIAN COMMUNITY AT CROSSROADS

There is a clear image of each ethnic community in the USA, though debatable. An image may be local or global. For instance, the image of Indians in the USA is not the same as in the UK, or in neighboring Canada. Images change, but slowly. Nevertheless, a bottom line is a popular Cannon camera commercial: **Image is Everything!**

The professional image of Indians in the USA, as defined during 1960-80, has started changing. Primarily, it is due to the immigration of unskilled and retired dependents of the first generation of professionals coming from India. Also, the second generation is more entrepreneurial in every aspect in taking advantage of the variety of opportunities that the US offers.

Two recent news reports have shaken up the Indian community of Las Vegas (LV). One is of a 24-year old Indian woman arrested for prostitution in a casino. An undercover agent apprehended her for willing to perform an act for $500. The second is a 21-year old Indian - arrested for DUI and related auto accident that killed the other occupant.

My thoughts naturally went back to 30 years when there were hardly 20 Indian families in LV. Three of us were in education, 3-4 engineers, 4 nurses, 3 architects, 2 casino workers. In business, there were only a couple of Sindhis in custom tailoring - working out from Hong Kong. There was not even a single medical doctor or a motel owner when we moved here in 1974!

It was about 20 years ago when we heard of a young Hindu homeless pregnant girl. My wife and I were shocked. We drove around and located her walking dazed along a roadside. She was mentally imbalanced. Besides, immediate help, we even arranged money for her airfare to India, and contacted her relatives there.

The point is that we were no less concerned about Indians' image getting a bad rap. LV reminds me of my hometown, Bathinda (BTI), a big railway junction of seven railway lines. The mentally sick, thrown out of homes, due to poverty and social stigma, would board up the trains. Since trains would eventually pass through BTI and halt for an extended time, they would get down and live off the streets of BTI. LV, the fastest growing city in the US has also exploded with Indian population - now touching 15,000.

Since the 1980s, with ample economic opportunities, Indians of every shade of character, profession and trade have been moving to LV. In the skin business, call girls and prostitutes thrive in legal brothels of Pahrump, only 50 miles away, or in the casinos under the protection of some employees. Every weekend, youths are caught and killed in auto accidents while driving drunk. Thus, Indian kids can't stay unaffected. On the top, LV parents are busier in their jobs, earning more money, have less family time, and little to do with their teens.

Fifteen years ago in LV, it was unheard of an Indian youth living away in an apartment while parents owning a 4-bed room house. It is very trendy today. On the top, there is no conforming holistic influence of religion, particularly of Hinduism. Hindu temples seem to be out of bound for the Hindu youth, and conversely. Christian and Mormon churches have several youth programs on sex and drug education besides social gatherings. In contrast, the Hindu temples have yet to embrace community activities as integral part of Hindu religion.

The point of this **Reflection** is not just to bring a general awareness of the social problems of Indian youth and adults, but also to bring the community together in addressing the issues. The places of worships are ideal to assume new roles and provide supporting environment. The federal government has generous funds to support youth programs. The problems are never eliminated, but their effect can be minimized. A new challenge always opens a door for new opportunities.

(Feb 27, 2005)

NOTES AND COMMENTS

THE MOVING SPIRIT OF THE *GADAR*

Background

This is my third visit to the Gadar Memorial Center, San Francisco (SF). The first one was in Dec 2002, the second in July 2004 and this one in May 2006. Such places are like classic books, great personalities and historic monuments, as they evoke different feelings and ideas at each trip. The Center building is a simple double storey house with a basement. It is located in a residential neighborhood of a busy section of SF.

The visits are not deliberately spaced out on my part. Every year, before visiting my son living in Northern California, I contact the Indian Consulate office, as the Center operations are under its jurisdiction. There being no regular hours for its opening, a consulate staffer specifically comes to open the Center. In fact, a quarter of the Center is used for a make shift residential purpose.

I am not aware of any liaison committee of local Indian Americans and Indian Consulate. With active involvement of Indian community, some volunteers would gladly help the Consulate in keeping the Center open for at least two days a week. Fortunately, this year, the Consulate General, B. S. Prakash, being himself a writer, made sure that some one was there to open it when I arrived there.

From Davis, CA, the Amtrak train and bus combine brought me in two hours at the Union Square in Downtown SF. Since I had an hour before the appointed time, a leisure walked to the Center psyched me up. First time, my daughter-in-law drove me there and second time, my son. Having been raised in the US, they had no idea of the Center. But they are now beginning to understand what the Center means to me, and the pivotal role it has played in India's real fight for freedom.

Research Material

During the last two visits, I had only scanned the Center by looking at the titles of the books and Gadar publications, particularly, displayed in two small glass showcases. The moment I see them a fountain of energy douses me over. The previous articles captured these emotions mixed with the data gleaned. This time, I was able to page through **two** pamphlets for extracting eternal messages. In fact, it is equally significant how these manuscripts dig the ideas out of my core. These articles are essentially **a braid of three strands. One is the raw historical data, second - present context, and third - my incisive analysis and bold interpretation**.

1. ***Anka Di Gwahi*** (Evidence of the Data) # 4. It is a 16-page Punjabi pamphlet dated 1924, and in a very poor condition. 10,000 copies were published. It appears a hand written type setting and unclear read. It indicates that the *Gadar* Party members, working in printing press, came from rural Punjab with little education. Most likely, they wanted nothing to do with the Macaulay System of education imposed on India after quelling India's 1857 Rebellion. **The sole objective of pre-independence education was to train Indians for servicing the British in India and other colonies.** The *Gadaris* believed it was better to remain unlettered in the English sense than brainwashed.

    There are startling references as to how the post 1857 legislation made life very difficult for the Indians. One instance tells of Indians' inability to buy silver (forget gold!) for ornamental purposes also used for family emergencies. A concerning data was that according to the President of INC (Indian National Congress), the death rate had increased from 24/1000 to 34/1000. The taxation on Indians was making their life very unbearable. Little money was spent on education as compared with on army and police meant for controlling the Indians. **Taxation on poor Indians was more than twice than on the prosperous British living in India**.

During WW I, the British had banned or censored the postal entry of all material going in and out of India. Despite these restrictions, a distribution of 10,000 copies to the Punjabis in Indian Diaspora was a mark of *Gadar* network. Indian freedom fighters, particularly, in China, Japan, Canada, Germany, the Philippines and Hong Kong etc. were in communication with each other - mostly in small groups.

This networking is no different today - the way al-Qaeda and Tigers of Tamil Eelam (LTTE) are operating through their cells all over the world. The only difference is that the *Gadar* network was infiltrated by the US and British spy agencies. It is absolutely unthinkable that any one will ever betray Osama bin Ladin even for $50 million bounty on his head. It was an act of such a betrayal that Lala Hardayal, the founding leader of the *Gadar* Party was suddenly arrested and forced to leave the US in 1914. Despite the fact that he was a visiting lecture at Stanford University!

In contrast to the LTTE, the Hindus and Sikhs in Kashmir have not forged any alliance against the international Islamic fighters. Since 1989, they have been leaving their century old domiciles in Srinagar and living in refugee camps. The camp residents are not like the Palestinians, who have vowed to take back their homes. Unfortunately, neither the Indian Government, nor the Hindus and Sikhs Diaspora have stood by them. **They are all for their flight from Kashmir, and not fight for it!** It has lead to the largest ethnic cleansing (95%) in modern times. Once, I pointed it out to the US Senator Harry Reid, from Nevada.

2. ***India against Britain***: It is a reply to Austin Chamberlain, Secretary of State for Indian Affairs; Lord Harding, Former Viceroy of India; Lord Islington, Under Secretary of State for and others. It is a 62-page booklet written in English by Ram Chandra, Editor Hindustan Gadar Party and dated November 01, 1916.

Ram Chandra was also one of **three** founding members of the Gadar Party and became the editor of the ***Gadar*** (name of the publication too) after Lala Hardayal's forced departure from USA. Ram Chandra lived up to his name! **He was a lion when it came to fighting the propaganda spewed by the British in Canada and USA.** This booklet contains his letters and articles published in all the leading newspapers in the US. His command over the English language being thorough, he challenged the British bigwigs for discussion while educating the US public and intelligentsia.

It is obvious that while the US Government clandestinely cooperated with the British in monitoring the activities and membership of the *Gadar* Party, yet the US press was relatively free. Never once, Ram Chandra complained against it. Today, though the internet has crossed all the geographical boundaries yet, there are equally advanced technologies to block, censor, and trace or decipher any internet message. There is no substitute for human vigilance and loyalty - either based on a global ideology like Islamic for al-Qaeda or regional like political freedom for the LTTE!

It is also interesting to draw a comparison between the Gadar Party and Gandhi's contemporary political activities in South Africa during 1904-15. Gandhi also had his own printing press and a publication named ***Indian Opinion*** to unite Indians and keep them informed. But Gandhi was able to win the hearts of a few British thinkers towards his beliefs and approach.

For lack public relations and vision of the leadership, the Gadar Party did not make an impact on the US public. **I have seen isolated articles and letters of support, but no instance of any white American joining the Gadar Party.** In contrast, early officers of the INC were mostly British. After permanently returning to India from South Africa in 1915, Gandhi fully used the press to his advantage while winning the hearts of many British elite and activists.

It is interesting to discover that the theory, philosophy and practice of **Whiteman's Burden** were not limited to the USA, but extended to Western Europe and their colonies. Furthermore, it goes back to the middle of the 19th century! By the end of the 19th century, there was a well-orchestrated propaganda in the colonies that the British were god-sent to improve the lots of blacks in Africa, browns and yellows in Asia and aborigines in North and South America, Canada, Australia and New Zealand. Theories of Whiteman's Burden also stereotypes the incompetence and genetic inferiority of the natives. **However, it still goes on - every couple of decades only the labels change.**

It is similar to the doctrine of the **Divine Rights of Kings,** as practiced in India and medieval Europe. This propaganda was at a pitch during WW I. Under Gandhi's leadership, only the INC decided to cooperate with the British with a promise of self-rule after the War was over. But the British projected the INC stand for the entire India, as this booklet brings out the facts.

The WW I started in November 1914, but in Sept 1914, 300 Indians were killed in Budge Budge, two miles from Calcutta. They were mostly Punjabis who were forced to return to India, as their ship **KOMAGATA MARU** was not allowed to dock in Canada. At the same time, rebellions had started in Singapore and Ceylon. The states of Bengal and NW Frontier were most active in sabotaging the British plans. But the Reuter and other news agencies never reported it. India was placed under Martial Law on March 18, 1915.

Ram Chandra Bhardwaj was a great intellectual. In the very opening of the booklet, he blasted the British with his data. He often educated the American public how the British in the 1770's called the American freedom fighters as **"plotters and seditionists"**. His exhortation of the Indians and the denunciation of the majority of Indian princes went on parallel. What shocked me was to **read how the proud ruling prince of Udaipur touched the feet of King Edward at his Delhi Coronation Darbar in 1911!**

It was Gandhi's rising popularity amongst the emaciated masses of India and the lack of robust base in the *Gadar* Party that it did not gain ground in the US. **However, in India, Subhash Chandra Bose's (*Azad Hind Fauz*) Indian National Army was only a reincarnation of the *Gadar* Party in India.** Once, Bose and INA got recognition from Germany and Japan, the *Gadar* Parry naturally merged its identity and operation with the INA. That is why almost all the upper echelon officers in the INA were Punjabis.

The rank and file in the INA came largely from Bengal and Punjab, who believed in the armed overthrow of the British from India. They fought from the East, won some battles, marched up to Burma (Myanmar) where they unfortunately lost to their Indian brethren and Nepalese Gurkhas fighting for the British! The genius of Gandhi was to shift this unflinching loyalty of Indians from their British rulers to mother India. **It came to be known as Gandhi's Non-Cooperation Movement.**

Conclusion

For me, these visits are turning into historical and cultural pilgrimages! About the *Gadar* material, it is time to save it for the scholars and interested parties by having it digitally scanned. A young Indian documentary producer, Arti Jain has also shown interest in this project. Once an estimate is taken for turning this archive into CD's, I have assured of raising the necessary funds for it. The time is critical for some material, as it is almost decayed. Also, it is too much of a hassle to go to SF for serious research work.

PS: *Gadar* is an Urdu word adopted in Punjabi language also, which is equivalent to the word 'revolution' in English. A traitor in Urdu would be transliterated in English as *Gaddaar*, which is also popular in Punjabi and Hindi. An English reader must see the big difference in their meanings caused by this subtle difference in the Romanized spellings.

(June 02, 2006/ July, 2011)

NOTES AND COMMENTS

1. As you can see, I have received your Gadar paper and you have to believe me that I have read it with great interest. Good stuff. Better still, is your idea at the end to get all the materials that are there on CD. I will want to have a CD when it is done. Then may be we can collaborate on a "scholarly" historical account. Sincerely, **Harbans**

2. Dear Professor Bhatnagar, Good , very good, again. I was really moved. Such reflections serve so educating, particularly for a person like me who started breathing, I mean sensibly, only in independent India. Anything historical that took place as a part of the Freedom Movement, specially events like those you mention in your reflection and continue to be unknown, untold and unwept for, are bound to be not only highly interesting but of paramount importance. Regards, **B. S. Yadav**

3. Dear Satish Bhai; I have been a regular browser of your highly informative and interesting reflections on varied shades of life. However, as mentioned earlier, your frequency and pace of reflections of ideas generating in your fertile brain, allows me to respond only a few of them within my time frame. Well, I think I should try to do better.
   One which interested me the most was the – *Gadar Memorial Series*. I am pretty much impressed by your priority of visiting the museum over other routine ones, and then propagating this rare information to your mail group. I made it a point to propagate it further as I reckon, that frequent peeping in to these land mark historical events not only build up eroding nationalist feelings in us, but also align us with right perspectives.
   Yes, the German massacres were prominently highlighted due to victor's dominant position and superior media control where as those of much bigger proportions in history were passed off without a whimper. I appreciate your deep understanding of the devilish British designs of perpetrating human

carnage in India, thru that biological aggression importing dreaded diseases the likes of, Tb, Plague and Typhoid. **S C Gupta**

4. Rishi Dayanand also did a yeoman service to the society in instilling strength of standing firm against injustice and immoral practices. Well I am not placing you in this league, but people like you do make their contribution in their own small ways thru indirectly educating our countrymen this way. Well done. Keep it up. Regards, **Ravi**

KNOW THY BLOOD

'Blood is thicker than water' is a common phrase. However, there is a social grading in blood too. In college, I remember reading about blue blood signifying high social status in the 18th century England. I never cared to figure it out - why it was called blue, not green. May be, it was the color of a mantle or armor the knights wore. Lord Byron (1788-1824) boasted of the blue blood in his veins as a kid until he learnt its truth after a hard knock out by a school bully.

Last month, while researching in a library of the Gadar Memorial Center in San Francisco (SF), I came to a conclusion that **through the 20th century, kinship amongst the Whites was stronger than it was in the browns of Indian subcontinent**. One may observe its superiority over the 'black' blood of the Africans and the 'yellow' of the Orientals - including the Chinese and Japanese. Racial affinity is an undercurrent of life.

During the colonial occupation, the British created exclusive clubs for their segregated life styles in India. Initially, they were closed to Indians. Later on, they relaxed membership for Indian princes and landlords - the British stooges. The historic Gaiety Club on the Mall in Shimla remained mysterious even after independence. I never went inside during my three-year stay (1962-65). I also remember a small Civil Club in Bathinda near railway station that had the only tennis court in the region during the 1940s. The kids of the disadvantaged sections proudly worked as ball boys - one of them was my classmate.

The exclusive clubs and magnificence churches were situated in the prime locations of the cities that essentially bonded the Whites. Particularly, if any Indian group has to be penetrated, then a club provided a conduit too. This pseudo government network enabled the British officers to exchange information on freedom fighters in India, Canada, UK, USA, and other colonies. The British knew that there was a proverbial Jaichand (traitor) in any Indian community who could be bought off.

During a two-month standoff over *Komagata Maru* in 1914, two members of the Sea Shore Committee colluded. It ultimately brought a victory to the Canadian Government. The *Gadar* (Revolutionary) Party in SF met its worse fate. First, the founding leader of the Party, Lala Hardayal was suddenly arrested and quickly deported. Afterwards, when the Indians, recruited by the Gadar Party, sailed from SF back to India to fight the British on Indian soil, they were immediately arrested on landing and tried. It happened in 1918. Many were hanged and vast majority languished in the prisons of Andaman and Nicobar.

The bottom line is that an individual is always vulnerable before a group that is organized. Aristotle stressed upon individuals to join some organization more than 2000 years ago. Unfortunately, the Indians groups, particularly of the Hindus, are often very porous.

(June 10, 2006)

NOTES AND COMMENTS

1. *Dear Professor Satish, Thanks for the write up. Yes, I did like the punch line of the piece, '"...individuality is vulnerable before an organization". The reader may perhaps wonder why you didn't visit the historic Gaiety club in Shimla though you stayed there for 3 years. Was it closed for the visitors? If so why? Something mysterious!...Hope you have read E. M. Foster's "A Passage to India" where Foster describes the English club in Chandrapur where they have denied entry to the natives...The problem I think is India was never a united country and I wonder if we are even now...and we are still carrying that 'colonial hangover' especially when we see the white skin. "United we stand, divided we fall"... It is indeed rare that a Mathematician could write such literary pieces. Congratulations! How about starting a literary magazine in a small scale?! Regards* **Abraham**

2   ....and lend themselves into factions and sub-factions till they literally become a group of 1-2. Case in point: for every Punjabi group, there will be a Jatt group etc. I have issues with having a Punjabi group in the first place :-) as opposed to an Indian group. **Harpreet Singh**

KHALSAS IN THE USA

The ability of mind to see connections between remote entities is thrilling sometimes. A couple of months ago, a Sikh friend spoke high of Sikhism as practiced by the White Sikhs in the US. He is 74, retired university professor, and an eminent educationist. For most of his life, he had an irreligious outlook. I don't like to call it secular, as its practice has been convoluted everywhere, except in Muslim countries. After retiring in Punjab type climate of Tucson, Arizona, he has been re-discovering his Sikh faith in Sunday *SANGAT* (prayer congregation).

Being curious, last Sunday, I drove another 100 miles to Tucson from Phoenix, where I was on a short visit. The gathering of nearly 50 persons takes place in a hall of the Khalsa Montessori Academy - started ten years ago by the White Khalsas. The program was run by a White middle-aged lady fully attired in a white long gown and hair tied up in a White Khalsa headwear. The hymns were sung in an organized manner from a collection placed in various folders. She had a laptop to check various ceremonial details of the service. Her persona was relaxed, and so was it while speaking about Harbhajan Yogi and his wife. The *KARHA PRASAD* (sweet offering) and *LANGAR* (community meal) are not cooked in the premises, but brought by the families like in a potluck lunch.

Harbhajan Singh Khalsa Yogi (1929-2004), his legal name after the US citizenship, came to the US in 1968. I was 29, when I came in 1968 too. Recently, on reading the life of an Indian pioneer, Bhagat Singh Thind (1892-1967), it occurred to me that Harbhajan Yogi picked up where Thind had left off, as far as the Sikh spiritual traditions were concerned. Thind has a unique place in the US history for having his US citizenship revoked twice by the Immigration and Naturalization Service before getting it in 1936.

Thind was a scholar of western philosophy and Sikh ethos, and authored several books. Just as he traveled west to east to fight for his US citizenship, so did he in spreading the Sikh Dharma in the USA. He touched the lives of thousands of people without converting any one to Sikhism. At age 48, he married the daughter of his White female disciple.

Harbhajan Yogi had a charismatic personality and successfully blended the spiritual aspects of Sikhism with ancient Kundalini Yoga of India. Many Whites were converted to the Sikh Dharma. The post Vietnam era of the 1960s was a culture of drugs and affluence. Mahesh Yogi (1917-present) and Srila Prabhupad (1896-1977) also arrived in the USA during this period, and captured their share of spiritual market. Of course, they ventured into multimillion dollar businesses. The US public was fed up with militancy.

A good friend of 30 years, related with Harbhajan Yogi and close associate of Mahesh Yogi for 30 years, is amazed at one and disillusioned with the other. A person, too near, cannot get over human frailties and fallibilities of a life that becomes famous. I have witnessed them come to the USA and impact the lives of millions - but not mine!

(Oct 22, 2006)

NOTES AND COMMENTS

DANIEL DEFOE AND ROBINSON CRUSOE

Daniel Defoe's adventure novel '*Robinson Crusoe*' continues to inspire the public at large - the way stories and movies have been spun out in each time and place. I had heard about it during my college days in India of the 1950s. Primarily, I wanted to capture Defoe's writing style. I was quite amused to notice that Defoe, born in 1660, started writing at the age of 60, when I did it. In all, he wrote eight novels. **It is inspiring when most Indians, in my era, used to quit on life at 60.** Robinson Crusoe did not hold my interest though. However, its 60-70 pages churned around a lot of my thoughts.

The book, being 350 years old, does tell of an established British literary tradition at that time. My first thought was to identify such a tradition in any part of India. Literature was not in public domain in India and hence no comparable literary tradition is known. To the best of my knowledge, the oldest surviving book, during the last 500 years, is *Ramcharitmanas (Ramayana*) by Tulsi Das (1543-1623). The impact of *Ramcharitmanas* is very deep amongst the Hindus in north India. Incidentally, Shakespeare lived in that contemporary era (1564-1616).

The setting of the novel is the 17th century England, and is based on a true story of Alexander Selkirk, who was marooned in the island of Juan Fernandez for five years. The rough and tough men from every West European country were sailing out in quest of gold. Gold had become a metaphor for life. It meant a total control over environment including men and nature. Collectively, it also meant the colonization of Africa, Asia and America. India was at the peak of its splendor in wealth and prosperity. The monuments, built in Delhi and Agra, during the reigns of Akbar through Shah Jahan (1542-1666), attracted the attention of everyone in the world. Just as the twin towers of the World Trade Center symbolized the might and prosperity of the USA, so did the Taj Mahal for India - 400 years ago.

Today, everyone - from poor to rich, talented to untalented, wants to enter legally or illegally into the USA, so was the story about India during the 14th and 16th century. Even today, people in Turkish villages remember their forefathers talking of "*Dilli Chalo*" (**Go to Delhi** - for making in life). The destination of every talented Muslim from a Middle East country was the Emperor's Court in Delhi. The world remembers only the names of Columbus and Marco Polo, but there was a legion of such adventurers. Some died, some lost, and a few, who made their dream come true, continue to inspire the coming generations.

Daniel Defoe has effectively captured how the spirit of adventure got the better of the parental love and concern. Robinson had two brothers; one wanted to be a professional soldier. His parents let him follow his dream and they accepted his death in a Spanish war. They were not heart-broken and did not stop living. Mercenaries are unheard and unthinkable even in present India. Presently, Jihadi

Muslims are also mercenaries besides being fighters for Islam. From all over the world, they come to fight in Kashmir, Afghanistan and old Soviet republics for their liberation. All their expenses and support to their parents are generously met.

Growing up back in India of the 1950s, I only knew the dictionary meaning of mercenary, but could not visualize any one fighting for money for any paymaster. In the 17th century, European mercenaries were as sought after as the software engineers from India today. Soldiers of fortune are professional like any other. Robinson's other brother left home and no trace of him was ever known. His parents never brought it up either. It is not any lack of love that Indian parents may think of it, but their understanding of the greater realities of life and aspirations of their children.

The Hindus during 1000-1600 AD, gradually became punching bags and kick balls for any invaders - starting with bands of Arabs under Islam, the new religion of Arabian Peninsula, Afghanis, Mongols, Mughals from Samarkand and Tashkent of Central Asia, Iranians, Turkish, and others. They sapped the heart and muzzled the soul of the Hindus. Amongst the Hindus, there was a total absence of a spirit of adventure and discovery. The Hindu masses and intelligentsia retreated under various Bhakti movements - as the turtles go underneath their shells at the sight of danger. Even in 19th century when the British were in control of India, Gandhi described in his autobiography - how his family was opposed to his leaving the shores of India for fear of defiling his brand of Hindu religion!

Within a few pages of its reading, I wondered at Defoe's one-mile long sentences, at times, covering an entire paragraph. It is in contrast with today's easy-going style and simple vocabulary. Way back books were rare and considered status symbols, and there was a degree of elitism amongst intellectuals. Today, you visit any bookstore and there seems to be a publication explosion in every conceivable domain of life. I often discover that name and fame of a person or work is equally accidental and deserving.

This book reaffirms a few observations on human slavery. One can argue on slavery at different levels - physical, mental and intellectual. From this novel, it is imperative to see how slavery was indispensable to the life of European colonizers, when they would take hold of an uninhabited or even inhabited territory. Manual labor was needed to clear the land before cultivation. Slaves from West Africa provided a perfect solution. However, the slave brokers were native Africans. In fact, the Arabs had Africans, as domestic slaves since they conquered North Africa in the 8th century, much ahead of the Europeans. The Europeans used them on a larger scale - in farms and fields.

It was after the emancipation of slavery in the US in 1865 that invention in agriculture machinery exploded. Necessity is the mother of invention. Today, despite the latest machines, the exorbitant labor cost in the US, all manufacturing has been pushed out into China and other Asian countries, where the labor is 'cheap', or 'slaved' by despotic political systems and local bosses. What a marriage of convenience between capitalism and communism!

The other observation that stands out is that the West marched on the superiority of its firearms. They invented canons and gunpowder, and thus colonized the world. Robinson carried a lot of ammunition during his travels and used them for pleasure and defense. Today, the race for the superiority of arms continues. The possession of a firm arm is a fundamental right in the US Constitution. It reminds me of Punjab, where the Sikhs still carry long spears in one hand and sword and dagger hanging on the other side. A little provocation may turn into bloodshed. Nothing is good and nothing is bad, provided they become defining moments of life.

Through sixty some pages, no woman has entered Robinson's life! He left home at 18 and was enslaved by a Moore for 3 years. Some events and description are repetitive. However, Defoe is very successful in capturing rise and fall of life style due to bad decisions or natural calamities. **Fatalism does not rule, but the will to change the unpleasant present prevails.** That is what I feel it distinguishes the Hindus from the rest of the ethnic groups today.

(Nov 27, 2002/Oct, 2011)

NOTES AND COMMENTS

PETS, FOREST AND BUDDHA

A few days ago, while driving to work, I noticed a dog scampering on a major one-way and six-lane highway. The dog was very confused and had no idea what to do. But for the consideration and kindness of motorists, it would have been crushed to death. It happens all the time. Sometimes, people leave their old and sick pets out in the desert and drive back home. Unless picked up by kindly persons, such pets meet tragic ends.

The US pets cannot adjust to an independent life after leaving their secured environments in human homes. They simply cannot hunt for food. Their claws and teeth are not sharp enough to bite on raw things. It is amazing to see that how the natural animal instinct of attacking and fighting for food has been nearly blunted in 20-30 generations of pet industry in the US. This 'unnatural' life of pets used to amaze me initially, when we came to US 35 years ago, but now I understand it. **Sometimes, a man molds an environment and sometimes, an environment molds a person.**

Suddenly, I started wondering about the young prince, Siddhartha who later on became Buddha (563-483 BC), the Enlightened One. Being the only son of a powerful emperor of Eastern India, he was raised amidst luxuries of the palaces. A battery of attendants was always at his command. Without having to say a word, the best dishes were served to him and he wore the finest clothes. The best tutors were hired for his education in the premises of the palace. It must have raised his intellectual curiosity to a level that his tutors were not able to satisfy him. Siddhartha grew into a 6', 5" handsome man, and was married to the most beautiful princess of the region. A short time later, a son was born. He was still in his 20s, when his restless mind goes off the tangent. In the middle of a night, he walked out of the palace –leaving behind his family, luxury and power.

I have lived the following scenario many a times in my mind: When Siddhartha bids farewell to his charioteer on the edge of a forest, before dawn, how would he have really felt finding himself alone for the first time? How did he take care of his food? Even going to the 'toilet' must have been a traumatic experience for a prince. I actually observe this toilet trauma when my family members visit India. About food -Did Siddhartha know how to climb a tree to get the fruit, or save himself from various creatures of the forest? Surviving in a jungle is tough. Siddhartha did not first go to the hut of any other hermit in the forest for any orientation on jungle living. It is all beyond logic when one actually places oneself into such a predicament. In the US and India, certain parts of major cities are very dangerous even at daytime, yet no one moves out to a forest for safety!

The bottom line is - if the pets cannot survive in a forest, it is much less for the humans to do it, particularly, the one who has lived a highly protected life.

Buddha's first 24 hours in the forest is an open question for history and legends. I have read a lot on the life of Buddha from *JATAK KATHAEN* (Stories on the life of Buddha) and nowhere this question has been even raised. They portray forest life as a piece of cake!

(April 25, 2003/Oct, 2011)

NOTES AND COMMENTS

A LESSON FROM AJANTA AND ELLORA

It was after a month that I watched my videotaped lecture delivered on Sep 3. Being an inaugural lecture, it was quite an honor to kick off the 25th season of the **University Forum Series**. The title, ***The Monumental Caves of India - Ajanta and Ellora,*** attracted more than 100 people from the community.

My objective was to share the amazement felt while visiting these caves for the first time in Dec 2002. On seeing the tape, I felt that I did succeed in it. In public speaking, I am my worst critic. For years, I simply avoided any speaking opportunity – whenever, I was to stand up and say even a few words. It began to change when I joined a toastmasters club five years ago.

My passion and enthusiasm gushed out while describing the art and architecture, paintings and carvings, statues and sculptors of Ajanta and Ellora. They depicted every facet of life. Little is known about the economic and political conditions of the state that nurtured and commissioned these mammoth projects for over a century. With library research and extrapolation of the present artworks, I conveyed that **these caves are indeed the greatest monuments financed by some of the greatest Hindu kings of India - during 200 BC to 800 AD**.

Establishing a family genealogy of 10 generations, spanning 100 years, is an onerous task. It is awesome to descramble this long past. Some data on the construction of Mount Rushmore, a US National Monument can give a perspective on time and money that must have gone into carving out incredible number of various kinds of pillars and decorative halls - totally inside a mountain. Stressing that the word 'caves' is really inappropriate, I challenged my audience to coin a new word for them. For example, the word 'buildings' do not describe the size of the WTC towers.

It was in conclusion that I tried to carry my audience to a new height of thoughts by posing a question as to **what went wrong with India that was so advanced in the first millennium.** In fact, this question possessed my mind, when I was touring the interior chambers of Ajanta and Ellora. What really brought a decline of this nation? Confronting the audience with this question, I made its connection with **9/11 Attack on America**.

Just as the USA is the greatest nation in the world today, so was central India during 600-800 AD. The Hinduism, the most tolerant religion, had made the Hindus tolerant. When people become soft and weak, then they begin to tolerate people and ideologies that are known for intolerance towards outsiders. It is the beginning of the decline of that nation. What happened to the WTC on 9/11 - likewise, it happened to India. Gradually, India was run over and ruled by invaders - one after the other, in bits and pieces, pillaged and parceled, debased and destroyed. It went on century after century. I warned my audience of what is happening in the US in the name of diversity today.

PS -Response to a Reader
It is the vigilance that you and I exercise every day – persons whom we let in our houses for a few minutes to entertaining for a few days; whom we don't open the door when checked through a peephole, or at times, dial 911 without any delay. That is how we protect our loved ones, values and things - we treasure. This principle applies from the home of an individual to a nation. That is the context of my thesis.

(Oct 5, 2003/Oct, 2011)

NOTES AND COMMENTS

ALEXANDER THE GREAT: A PERISCOPE

[**Note**: This article is not an account of any segment of Alexander's life. There are many books, movies and videos on it. History is not a cookbook (Henry Kissinger), but those who don't understand it are condemned to repeat it (George Santayana). My effort is to highlight some events from Alexander's military, political and personal adventures, and link them with events in the present, as well as in ancient India. To the best of my knowledge, it is a unique braid of different strands. The article is not smooth, but is more like a ride on a Las Vegas high-speed roller coaster. The objective is to provoke and stimulate a new thinking on some current issues.]

Background

For the last one week, I have been totally absorbed in reading a history of Alexander's great march from Egypt to all the way to the western fringes of India of the 320s BC that is now western Pakistan. My study is incidental. But it may be subconsciously connected with some Greek thoughts generated after watching a newly released movie ***TROY*** twice during this month.

It was while browsing a table full of titles in the UNLV bookstore, that ***Alexander***, a 1998 award winning internationally bestseller trilogy by Vallerio Massimo Manfredi, Volume III, ***The End of the Earth***, caught my attention. Strangely, Volume I and II were neither there, nor were they of my interest. Initially, the reading was unfocussed, but soon it gripped me. For the last three days, I was so consumed that some historical incidents became the fabrics of my dreams. Perhaps, I am one of Alexander's reincarnated scholars who accompanied him during this campaign and stayed back in India!

All my life, I have been attracted by men who dramatically change the lives of their people. Gandhi and Hitler come in the same category for me. Alexander and Buddha are together, and so on. For instance, two months ago, I needed to check a reference in Gandhi's biography, ***My Experiments with Truth***. I just could not put it away before finishing it. That was my 4th reading in 40 years! It gives newer insights at different stages of life. **That is the mark of a great life, and also of a great book.** For ages, the religious scriptures have been known to inspire people all the time.

My Interest in Alexander

Manfredi is a well-known classical historian and archeologist at Luigi Bocconi University of Milan in Italy. My first thought was that here is a man who must have had a long fascination with Alexander's life that he wrote a novel on his life in three volumes! Actually, he has given objective historical accounts in a readable form. I was curious to know Alexander's leadership of holding his caravan of over 100,000 people together during a six-year long march of great setbacks and greater victories.

Also, I wanted to check Manfredi's description of Alexander's battle with Indian King, Porus (Greek name of Hindi *PAUROOSH*). Each historian has his own facts and interpretation of the past. If any two historians have identical views, then one is certainly a fake or free rider. All I have known about Indian history is through the eyes of British scholars, or by Indian writers spun out by the British education system.

Contemporary India and Greece

While reading it, my thoughts switched gears between India of contemporary era and back to Alexander's. Alexander lived only for 32 years between 356-323 BC. After surviving many conspiracies and assaults on his life, he suddenly died of a typhoid fever in Babylon. That is around the time of Ashoka's grandfather, Chandra Gupta Maurya. The Greeks had heard of the Hindu empires in north India stretching from present Myanmar (Burma) in east to present Afghanistan in west. Magasthenese was a Greek ambassador in the court of Chandra Gupta Maurya. Manfredi affirms the existence of great Hindu empires 700 years before Ashok (reigned 290-232 BC) who ruled over the largest territory for over forty years.

What a tryst of destiny that it is King Ashok whose extreme practice of non-violence doctrines of Buddhism eventually sapped away the fighting juices out of the Hindus. By renouncing wars and yet ruling over a greatest empire, he betrayed his kingly roles. Had he abdicated the throne first, and then denounced wars and preached Buddhism that would have done little damage to Indian political landscape. Unfortunately, he did not have a preceptor like Chanakya or Aristotle to counsel him. **Nor was there a Krishna to tell Arjun not to forsake his arms for being a king.**

Greek civilization at that time was at the acme in intellectual traditions and democratic in a limited way. Before Alexander, there was a long lineage of great scholars, heroes, and schools (of philosophy) perfected by Socrates, Plato, Pythagoras and Aristotle. Though Aristotle remained Alexander's tutor throughout his life, but it was his nephew and royal chronicler Calisthenes who accompanied Alexander in his 'conquest of the world'. The greatness of Alexander is also measured by the types of scholars who surrounded him. During his crusade of conquering the world, he kept his mental faculties sharp by engaging his mind with scholars, and by training with the strongest soldiers in his army, he maintained his physical prowess. The exercises and regimen of soldiers prepared them for the worst combat conditions. On several occasions, his soldiers chased the enemies with lightning speed and shocked them into surrender without further fighting.

Empire and Scholarship

I see a parallel between great intellectual traditions of the Greeks and the extent of their political empires. One feeds off the other. In contrast, India's borders started shrinking right after Ashok. Though a few centuries later, Buddhism and Jainism submerged back into the main stream Hinduism, but it was weakened. The Hinduism became abstract, obtuse and distant from the masses. Despite being elitist and *Brahamanical*, its intellectual traditions went into a nosedive. That is reflected in multiplicity of petty principalities in India. In the 10th century, Arabs were the first wave of foreign invaders to take advantage of the porous political conditions of India.

Empire Building and Crumbling

A remarkable similarity between Alexander and Chandra Gupta was their belief in total annihilation of the enemy. Chandra Gupta killed every scion of Nand dynasty. Several times, Alexander went on massacre spree of the populace to strike a terror in the hearts. **Never the same enemy fought Alexander twice!** In contrast, Prithvi Raj Chauhan of the 12th century never pursued Mohammed Gohri and finished him off. After 16 defeats, when Gohri finally won, it changed the map of India forever.

It can happen again, once Pakistan wins and occupies a part of India. **The Hindu majority lacks the will to fight back.** Its present intellectual traditions, far from being nationalist, are either pseudo-socialist or British colonialist. China has annexed over 100,000 square miles of Indian territory after routing India forces in 1962. Two generations of army generals and political leaders have let it go by. By and large, public is least concerned. New generations of Indians hardly know this fact.

Alexander knew when to be ruthless in taking revenge. On Persians for the mutilation of captive Greek soldiers, 20-30 years before him, he ransacked Persepolis, then the most beautiful city in the world. Being a symbol of 200-year old Persian Empire of Dairus kings, **he personally torched its beautiful palace after holding an orgiastic party of 20,000 people in it**. The ruins of the palace still stand near the present city of Shiraz in Iran. During this campaign Alexander planted his own symbols on vanquished lands. In addition, he founded scores of cities and named them various Alexaendrias.

Charisma of a Leader

Alexander, being young, handsome and victorious, married with princesses of Egypt, Persia and India besides keeping several concubines in his entourage. On reading this account, I felt pity for Bill Clinton for his sexual escapade with Monica Lewinsky. How a US President, the most powerful man on earth, could be limited to the pleasures of only one woman, and that too of a middle-aged one? Alexander must be mocking Clinton in his grave! Around any man of power and wealth are scores of Manekas and Monicas to pull the Vishwamitras and Clintons down to their ground zeros. I think such unions are good for a superior progenies. It applies to Kobes and Tysons, and any rich and famous.

One vanquished governor, Dravas of a region that is in present eastern Tashkent offered his 12-year old daughter to Alexander. Alexander declined, "Your daughter still needs the love and the care of her mother and I have no wish to take her away." **He won a lasting political pact with Dravas.** However, during his return sojourn in Susa, Alexander first slept with his newest bride Barsine, then with Stateira, step younger sister of Barsine he married four years earlier when he conquered Persepolis, and then with his Indian queen Roxane whom he married after defeating her father a few months earlier. According to Manfredi, he slept with all three in one night! **Alexander justified it to Roxane as his kingly duties.** Let us trim Manfredi's literary stretch, but not forget that Monica Lewinsky had given high score to Clinton for his virility.

Emperor Porus (Pouroosh)

Alexander did not cross all the tributaries of the Indus River. Porus was the ruler of the region presently identified with the present northwest part of Pakistan. In Indian history books, Porus is described as a tall person of 6' and 6" in height. **But Manfredi's description of Porus is of a very huge and powerful man over 7'.** Porus was defeated by superior weapons and Alexander's shrewd battle plans in the worst rainy conditions. Yes, the famous line of Porus that he should be treated as a king treats another king is exactly the same that has been known in Indian folklore.

Visions of a Leader

It may be added that Porus was not the first defeated king to have been reinstated. Alexander did it several times; sometimes to the anger, jealousy and protests of his commanders. Alexander was a great visionary and farsighted, though hardly 30 years old. Many a times, he was proved right against the judgment of his counselors and the War Council. It reminds me of Gandhi, an uncrowned king of India and his 'cabinet' of Nehru, Patel, Azad and Rajgopalachari. Abdul Kalam Azad wrote in his book that several times on certain issues Gandhi alone was on one side. Reluctantly, the rest would submit to his will, because Gandhi always proved right.

Alexander set up garrisons in new lands after disarming the enemies. Also, the goodwill of matrimonial alliances helped him in consolidating his empire. To Porus in particular, he left the authority over seven 'nations'(kingdoms) and 2000 cities, with the obligation of providing tribute and contingents of troops to Macedonian governor he had installed in Alexandria Nicaea, near the ancient city of present Taxila in Pakistan.

Traitors in Indian history

One amazing thing that I discovered that the King Taxiles of Taxila refused to join forces with Porus to defend the first line of kingdoms in India. When Alexander defeated small kingdoms over the Indus River, the king Taxiles welcomed Alexander and aligned against Porus! **The history of the Hindus is rife with all kinds of traitors, called Jaichands. Loyalty and friendship that Porus could not get from his neighboring king of Taxila against a foreign invader to India, Alexander got it from both of them!** Porus lost both of his sons in the battle and Alexander lost his legendary horse Bucephalus from the fatal wounds. He founded a city Alexandria Bucephala in the name of his horse! Though Alexander had won a battle with Porus, but his commanders finally prevailed upon him to start his return to Macedonia.

Symbols and Empires

Empires are built and nations are unified over great symbols. Many a time symbols of the enemy and infidels have to be razed to the ground. Four years ago, the Talibans in Afghanistan blasted away the 2000-year old Buddha statues. Babari Masjid and other mosques in the armpits of great Hindu temples are symbols of Mughal atrocities and reminders of perpetual insult to the Hindus in their own homeland. Though, the Muslims are no longer theocratic rulers of India, but the 80% Hindus, in the name of tolerance, continue to live in cowardice. **There is not even single block of 10 % Hindus in present political India!** Presently, the **Hindus** are divided amongst the two communist parties, several socialistic, Janta parties, Congress, and BJP.

On the contrary, Babri Masjid has further united the Muslim world. In retaliation, they have razed over a 100,000 Hindu temples all over the world. The British in India planted their own symbols of supremacy. Go to any hill station and a big city of India, 150-200 year old cathedrals are still standing in the most central locations. A majestic church in my hometown Bathinda is older than any Hindu temple.

Alexander's Intellectual Curiosity

Alexander's encounter with a Hindu yogi, Kalan, is significant, as it paved an exchange of ideas between the Greeks and Hindus for decades to come. After a massacre of 17,000 people of Sangala, Kalan is introduced to Alexander by his royal oracle. Kalan had similarities with Greek Sufi Diogenes that Alexander knew. Manfredi has recreated its detailed account. While going down the Indus River, Alexander's forces were challenged by warriors of a walled city near the present city of Multan in Pakistan. Alexander is almost mortally wounded. His dog Pertas died in trying to save Alexander. When all sacrifices and efforts of his personal physician, Philips fails to revive Alexander, he implores Kalan to use his 'divine' powers. By harnessing his yogic power through meditation for four days next to Alexander's sick bed, Kalan brings him back to life.

During this journey, Alexander and his commanders got regular 'lessons' in Indian philosophy. Kalan considered Alexander of a **Rajyogi** stature. Despite being impervious to any physical hardships, Kalan is suddenly tormented by pain when he envisions Alexander's imminent end. But he does not tell it to anyone. Kalan's last wish was to go into **SAMADHI** while seated on a burning pyre; a scene witnessed by thousands of people in Persepolis. After a few months Alexander succumbs to the unabated high temperatures of a typhoid fever in Babylon. The dialogues between Kalan and Alexander are masterpieces in Manfredi's writing.

Alexander and 9/11

I can't help interpolating Alexander's action in the context of 9/11 Attack on America, and 12/11 attack on the Indian Parliament, in 2001. Alexander was incredibly vindictive and unforgiving on unprovoked attacks even on his occupied cities. Being on a mission to conquer the world, he could not afford to entrench himself at any place with an enemy for a length of time. There are instances of the power and brutality of his shock brigades that the enemy forces would just run away! He was an embodiment of fearlessness, but always struck a terror deep in the heart of the adversaries. He was unmoved by sights of any Kalinga war aftermath that had moved Ashok in India.

Alexander would have nuked Afghanistan within a month of 9/11 and a total annihilation Osama Bin Ladin, Al Qaida and Taliban leadership. Iraq would not have been necessary. President Truman nuked Hiroshima and Nagasaki and history has proved him right. In a combat, or a sport like boxing, by holding back the powerful punches, one may not only end up losing a fight but a head forever. The principle of using the best weapons applies to a nation at war, particularly when provoked by unprincipled enemies.

(June 17, 2004/Revised: July, 2011)

NOTES AND COMMENTS

1. This write up is highly informative. You have admirably summarized the third volume and have linked it up with timidity of our people right from the days of Ashok. Even today, you are right; Hindus are meek and badly divided nationality and have no courage to defend themselves, their rights and traditions. 'Hindutva' is now a dirty nomenclature even among most of Hindus whose history perception is that of Marxists or colonialists. Babari structure was the most visible demonstration of continuing humiliation; most of the mosques in India have been built up by demolition of Hindu temples and places of worship and even building material used is that of the temples concerned. No Hindu has moral courage to say this. In the name of secularism, they go on giving up their basic rights even. Your reading and interpretation of our history culminating with slavery from the days of Ashok is highly appreciative; but our historians and other leaders of the society deliberately ignore it in a perfectly cowardice manner. In our country, Muslims, in the name of minority have got so many concessions, most of which are not even available to them in any Islamic country. And these have been accorded by Hindu leadership over a period of time. Hindus are in reality second-rate citizens in a country where their population if more than eighty percent. Unfortunate. Thanks for the e-mail. **NIGAM**

2. As for Alexander the Great, I've always wondered who gave him that title and why. His ability to lead massive armies and maintain control over such a vast empire is certainly 'great' feats themselves. Yet... "When Alexander saw the breadth of his domain, he wept for there were no more worlds to conquer." This suggests to me that in the final analysis, Alexander was a man no different than any other. Empire expansion pursued by the Alexander of yesterday is equivalent to wealth expansion pursued by the Bill Gates of today. It all boils down to the quest for power-- which is as timeless as history itself!

    The final reference to nuking Afghanistan is flawed, forced, and ultimately detracts from an otherwise interesting portrayal of Alexander. **Avnish**

3. I think the purpose of this article through Alexander is to justify and glorify individual chauvinism. Expansionism by a society and total annihilation of the vanquished. With this there is sprinkle of sexism. Using this criterion I think Genghis Khan was superior to Alexander. Mind you he was Buddhist. Personally I do not see much difference between Alexander, Hitler, Napoleon and likes to them. They were military genius but the bigger question is - were

they good human beings? That I don't think so. USA being also the moral leader of world cannot use Alexander's analogy of what he did in Iran. However it is well worked on article but I differ with the conclusion. Regards, **Rahul**

4. Your article'Alxdr..' deserves abundant accolade for its skill of neat compiling of historical facts, subtle analysis and inferences and selective vocabulary. **Ravi**

5. Hello Dr. Bhatnagar, Thank you very much for yet another very exciting article.
    Some day I would like to introduce you to a friend- Shafi Hakim, who is an ethno-musicologist by learning ..but a very avid student of history and interpreter, almost a sleuth of history. He has been living in the Bay Area for the last thirty odd years...so maybe you know him already! Thanks again for the article...Please keep sending more my way. Best regards, **Arti**

WHEN A SOCIETY SOFTENS UP

Suddenly, a couple of events and ideas converged in my mind. It started with exploding ethnic riots in France - at par with an uprising. They are spreading to neighboring regions in Belgium and Germany, where the Muslim population is huge. Today, while listening to a talk radio, I heard how Condoleezza Rice, the Secretary of State, has thrown an Eid Party and spoke of the benevolence of Islam. The White House has also hosted such parties and President Bush came under criticism for calling Islam a religion of peace. Never, on this scale, a Dewali Party has been thrown at the White House to celebrate the most auspicious Hindu festival.

It all started after **9/11 Attack on America**! For the last one week, I have been reading ***Bury My Heart At Wounded Knee*** (1970) by Dee Brown, an American Indian historian, an author of 15 books. It focuses on native Indian history of the American West with the most comprehensive chapter notes and bibliography. It is no exaggeration to call the years, 1865-1890, a period of genocide of the Native Americans and their life styles.

Where is the parallel I see? By every account, the Native American Indians welcomed the European Whites, wherever they landed on the east coast of the American Continent. It was exactly what the Hindus did when the English, French and Dutch landed on the western cost of India - from the Raan of Kuch to Malabar. The local Hindu kings granted them lands for their churches and small garrison to run their affairs. After a period of only a few decades, this hospitality towards the strangers proved fatal to the native Indians in America as well as to the natives in India. With the superior firepower, on the top of their organizational skills, the Whites took control of large tracts of new lands.

Let me keep my ideas within bounds by staying close to my first hand experiences. The first wave of Asian immigration in the US was started in the 1960s. Like many thousand Asians, I came to the US in 1968. At that time, Indian Government allowed $5 in foreign exchange! With sheer hard work in USA, we have made many dreams, unthinkable in India, come true. I could apply for a job anywhere in the US with fair chance of getting it. This is not possible in today's India - driven by caste, language, region and religion.

The immigration laws were very liberal and getting green cards was easy. My generation coming from big families lost no time in sponsoring brothers, sisters and parents. That was the second immigration wave of Asians peaking in the 1980s. I recall many Indian women, in particular, who would get a job, quit after a few weeks, and start getting unemployment benefits! The real suckers of the US system were the elderlies over 60 who got social security benefits after they would land in the US. They did not contribute even a dime in the system. I said to myself that the whites in the USA showed the same hospitality that they had received from the native Indians 3-4 centuries ago!

A natural question: Since the native Indian eventually lost their lands and freedom to the Whites, does it mean that the Whites are going to lose it to the new generation of immigrants to USA? Or, for that reason, will the west European colonizing powers of yester years will be weakened from within? I see the signs. The historic events never repeat in identical forms. That is why even the intelligentsia often misses it and the society pays heavy consequences.

The US is a perfect laboratory of human specimen - how tough and marauding group of people weaken after decades of affluence and property. Before the **Emancipation Act** of 1965, the Afro-Americans in the US, called blacks and Negro, were not considered human. Their rapes and murders by their White slave owners was not a crime! Those who cringe at lynching and burning of black churches, after 1865, cannot fathom at the living conditions of the blacks before 1865. Ironically, it was during this era that the foundations of this great nation were laid down. There are legions of blood and horror stories in the making of any great nation. The Mughals in India did worse than the Whites, and so did the British when they vanquished the Mughals.

In 1960, the number of Indians in the US was hardly 10, 000, and now it is close to 2 millions. Based on religion, the number of Hindus in the US may have grown from 5000 in 1960 to 1.5 million today. There was no Hindu temple in the US in 1968, when I came. The number Muslims, then and now, is a different story. Islam is the fastest growing religion in the USA today. It adherents come to the US from African countries, Middle East, Indian subcontinent and Far East.

The Hindus are as divided and scattered in the US, as they are in India, or anywhere else. The Buddhists are not better organized either. However, Islam is a powerful glue to unify its believers irrespective of their national origins.

I am bringing to focus, the softening of the European White race over a period of last one century. The White believers of a saying - a good Indian (native of the US) is a dead Indian, are now succumbing to its own moral and ethical pressures. The wheels of history always move forward. The rise and fall of civilizations is a lesson of history. It may be delayed, but never circumvented.

(Nov, 2005/Oct, 2011)

NOTES AND COMMENTS

THE HOLOCAUSTS IN INDIA

April is remembered as a Holocaust Month in the US. It was in April 1945 that the liberating Allied Forces brought the human killing factories to the attention of the world. More than 10 million people including 6.5 million Jews were systematically killed in scores of Nazi concentration camps in Germany and its occupied territories.

Every year, it transports me back to the holocausts of the worst proportions in India that even the Hindus know little about. **The world remembers only what you let the world not forget it.** The stories of Hindu holocausts are of such magnitude that over the centuries, **it reduced the Hindu lives of lesser significance**. These thoughts were triggered last month by a visit to the Gadar Memorial Center, San Francisco.

In 1398, Temur declared *KATAL-E-AAM* (means sparing no life) in Meerut, then a city of nearly 300,000. His anger was ignited when one of his soldiers was beaten to death for raping a Hindu woman. Temur had invaded India on the pretext that '**the Muslim Sultans of Delhi were showing excessive tolerance to their Hindu subjects**'.

Mind it - the Hindus were living in their own homeland! The trails of Hindu carnage in Panipat and Delhi, during three months (Sep to Dec) were so devastating that Delhi took 100 years to rebuild it. The Hindu mothers used to hush their crying babies to silence by Temur's name. The *Hindukush* (means the killing fields of the Hindus) in Afghanistan is a living testimony of Hindu genocide when that region was islamicized by the 9th century.

The atrocities over the Hindus reached new heights during 48+7 year reign of Mughal kings, Aurangzeb and his son. In essence, it was a religious genocide. *SAVAA MANN JANEU JALAANAA* (nearly 1000 Lbs. of sacred thread worn underneath by the 'baptized' Hindus were burnt everyday) is proverbially etched in the memories. **The Hindus paid two separate taxes for their lives spared and not converted to Islam!** Today, even an atrocious act linked with Quran is rationalized, and the world looks aside. It was during this period that the Muslim population in India grew from a few thousands to more than 50 millions. At the same time, a continuous stream of Muslims migrated to India from far west.

The British fully understood the psyche of the Indians drawn from three religions - Hinduism, Islam and Sikhism. Their major thrust was to cut the roots of Hindu culture by spreading nonsensical theories – like on the origin, Vedic interpretations, and imposing damaging systems on education, agriculture and cottage industry. After quelling the 1857 Revolt, they imposed extraordinary levies on land and special taxation that gradually broke the will of the people to live. A weakened nation can never stand up and fight.

This is the approach that the Germans took in working the inmates of the concentration camps to death while keeping them under nourished. The new diseases of plague, small pox, tuberculosis and typhoid, unheard in India before the advent of the British, started wiping the Indian populace in hundreds and thousands a day! It also happened to the native populations in many countries in North and South America when the European colonizers occupied them. It is the world's first biological warfare!

According to the British Gazetteer, 19 millions died of famine. 15 millions died of plague and malaria according to Sir William Dig by, during 1891-1900. Hundreds died in Bankura, Bengal and Rajputana in the famine 1915-16. 7,251,257 (Yes, more than 7 millions!) died from plague during 1897-1913.The actual numbers may be double. **These are the most recent holocaust of India, and the Hindus were the worst hit.**

The movie, *Gandhi,* captures this human condition when Gandhi, after his return from South Africa, tours India during 1915-18. During my 1987 tour of Rajasthan, I wondered on not noticing tall and strong men who could carry 100 Lbs. of battlefield armor of Maharana Pratap, as displayed in Agra Fort during the 1980s. What happened to the generations of such sturdy men? The same was observed in Gujarat and Bihar. Most men and women were hardly 5' tall and weighing 80 Lbs. Orissa, Bihar and Bengal are still worse. Imagine the lost generations from the 1880s through independence in 1947.

In his half autobiography, *My Experiments with Truth*, Gandhi has tangentially mentioned how in South Africa, the British treated the Muslims, as a race, superior to the Hindus. But the most glaring example of Hindu racial inequity is the crime punishment schedule in Saudi Arabia. It is like a fine of 100,000 for a crime against a Muslim, 50,000 against a European, but 500 against a Hindu! There are numerous instances that go on to prove that the Hindu life was deemed cheap and dispensable.

When a member of Nazi death squad was asked, "How could you shoot at the innocent Jews?" The answer was," Because they don't resist!" A similar question was posed to Gandhi, "Do you believe that your non-resistance policy would work against the Germans?" Men have been killing the sheep for ages, as the sheep meekly follow their leader and place their necks on the chopping block.

The Sikhs faced the gruesome genocide after Banda Bahadur. It is incredible that his torture-to-death moved Nobel Laureate Tagore 200 years so much that he composed a poem. According to reliable sources, 43% of the Sikh population in Punjab was literally hunted down like animals by the Mughals, during 1716-1738.

This holocaust is called *GHALUGHAARAA* in Sikh History. However, the Sikhs remember it in gurdwara museums, and during the *Ardaas* (prayer) performed at every congregation!

I owe it to my name, my scholarship, and my lofty Hindu heritage for bringing these forgotten holocausts out so that the present generations can stand up to political events in India and overseas. **The awareness of these historical monstrosities shall awaken the racial self-esteem of the Hindus**. Only then, the Hindus in India will emerge strong - like the Jews did in Israel. The time is ripe for a documentary on the *Holocausts of India*. I have broached this subject to the documentary producers; Arti Jain and Mira Nair.

(June 03, 2006/ Oct, 2011)

NOTES AND COMMENTS

1. Dear Shri Satish ji, Saprem Namaste! I sincerely thank you for bringing out this subject in the under noted article, which is a shame on us. I would say, you have written very well. Now, I have one more, perhaps a better suggestion: As in Washington DC, there is a Holocaust Museum. recreating the atrocities committed by Nazis during 2nd world war against Jews, so why can we not create something much better in various phases in a centralized place in north America, Canada, India etc, everywhere and in smaller way , in each & every Arya Samaj of the world. This will bring a new life to our sleeping Arya Samaj & will get our youths with us. Please think & think & bring this subject amongst the right thinking people of our Hindu Bandhus all over the world. Warmest regards, **Satish Gupta** (Retired Executive in Mumbai).

2. Dear Bhatnagar, your last reflection was a moving one. It brought tears. I felt how ignorant I am about my own country's past history! We are in far south untouched by any of these human butcheries. We study in history a little about it. Your global presentation with facts & figures could not but move anybody's heart. We have not learnt the historical lesson yet. Even today "holocaust" goes as a political game in African countries, (Somali). Your presentation of Indian holocaust scenario is a good remainder for Hindus like us. We never harmed anybody in the name of war, but we were wiped off like insects. "Holocaust" has taken a different nomenclature today as "terrorism". We don't know where will it lead to? Thank you for this thought provoking, balanced, educative & human value presentation ------friendly - **Soori** (Retired Physics Professor, Madurai)

3. Your historical information is mostly correct. Now regarding burning of 1000 lb of sacred thread every day for 55 years will mean 2,007,500 lb. or approx. 1,000,000 kg. If one sacred thread weighed 10 grams then it will mean one billion people were either converted or were killed. I think this is more of an urban legend coming from Sikh writings. Also it is controversial if Kush in Hindu Kush means killing fields or it is derived from koh which means mountain.

   Do you know of any culture or country which did not commit these atrocities or these atrocities were not committed against them. I think more important than what you are suggesting is to install pride. **Rahul** (MBBS)

4. It is a sin to be week. Week attracts the cruel. The cause of genocide is weakness of the population. Making a film can highlight and could be useful. The solution of this problem is STRENGTH. **Subhash** (MBBS)

5. Thanks Satish, Very informative article. Much of it is new to me. Love, **Gopal**

6. Dear Bhaisab, This is an excellent article. I think the world does not know this fact and bringing it out like a documentary or a movie will enlighten the ignorant. **Pramod** (MD)

7. Hi Satish: This is once again a historically-researched piece on Holocaust. We don't want history repeat itself. While we have Indian Diaspora, we don't have a Hindu Diaspora. There needs to be an aggressive campaign to promote and advance the cause of Hindus, not simply building temples, paying the pujaris for the various rituals, and fighting for recognition. There is no collective vigilance on the part of the Hindus. **Moorty**

GHALIB PERISCOPE AT SIXTY-SEVEN

The mark of a great book or person is that they evoke different thoughts when re-visited at different points in time. Watching the 1988 serial videos on Mirza Ghalib's life is such an experience. It was ten years ago when I first saw it at the instance of my nephew. Ghalib's name is synonymous with poetry, and familiar in every household in North India and Pakistan. The **9/11 Attack on America** has changed some of my contemporary perspectives on persons, places and faiths.

Ghalib (1792-1869) lived at a time when a few smoldering embers of Mughal Empire around *Dilly* (now **Delhi**) were completely smothered by the British in 1857. A few years later, the British capital of India moved from Calcutta to *Dilly*. Subsequently, new extensions of *Dilly* were named, New Delhi - like 'New' York, 'New' Zealand and 'New' England etc. That is the stamping of a new regime. The current names of metro cities, Mumbai, Chennai and Kolkata are signs of renaissance of de-colonized India.

Mine was the first generation in Punjab that had no formal schooling in Urdu language in which Ghalib wrote his poetry. Urdu, by and large, is Hindi written in Arabic/Persian script. It was considered a mark of culture and scholarliness amongst students and teachers to quote and recite Urdu poetry in normal conversations and functions! For BA/BS, Urdu was one of the optional languages, but I chose Hindi. A close friend studied Urdu for which I nicknamed him Ghalib, and it has stuck on him. The funny thing is that Urdu was taught by Karam Singh, a Sikh lecturer of Punjabi, who had a flair for Urdu!

Ghalib's poetry rubbed on me in the 1970s when his works were published in Urdu-Hindi format. Ghalib lived during the reign of the last Mughal ruler, Bahadur Shah Zafar, who was also a poet of acclaim. **No wonder when such a poet king sits on a throne, then sooner or later, he has to be toppled by any gun totters**. While watching this movie, I sensed, as if I was witnessing the decline of the present great American Civilization. The nation born, as the USA 200 years ago, seem to have reached its zenith during three decades after the WW II.

My familiarity with Ghalib that began at age 17 has undergone a total phase shift at 67. The independence of India in 1947 had a special significance for the 85% Hindus, who as a society, actually saw this freedom after one thousand years! The Sikhs had tasted the freedom 100 years earlier, when Maharaja Ranjit Singh established a great Sikh Empire covering most of the present Pakistan. The Muslims, having ruled India, aspired to do it again. Looking back at my college days and gratification with Ghalib's poetry seems so incongruous today. **A free mind is a long shot from a free body!**

Whether you examine the last decades of Roman Empire, or Mughal, the signs of the decadence and debauchery are not very different. The indulgence in entertainment, sports and gambling had eaten the vitals of the masses, elite and rulers alike. Currently, the Americans are obsessed with every kind of sport and sexual gratification in the name of entertainment. The associated gambling and adult business is turning over billions of dollars. A paradox is that whereas competitive sports build individuals and collective character, its indulgence, at extreme ends, destroys the nursery of the nation, when the youth is consumed in watching, playing and gambling on it.

It reminds me of the historic line: **(Emperor) Nero was fiddling when Rome was burning**. His fiddling was both literal and metaphorical during of his era of Roman decline. It also happened exactly during the fall of Mughal Empire. The passionate pastimes of the 19th century Mughals were pigeon flying and kite flying. People were crazy about cock fights, chess and its variations called *CHOUSSAR*, *CHOUPAR*. They are sedentary games like the modern video games.

Umrao Jan, a Lucknow prostitute, was a great dancer, singer and poetess. She reminds me of Monica Lewinski and gay pride in the public life of the US today. Popular movies have been produced and novels written on Umrao's life - both in India and Pakistan.

Empires are always built on blood, sweat and tears. Invariably, there is an exploitation of some sections of human beings. Ironically, the exploitation of natural resources is called the development of science and engineering. Historically, the vanquished are slaved and subjugated. Ethical and moral questions are raised only by the subsequent generations. **The times of peace and prosperity soften the masses and intelligentsia alike**.

I am not against Ghalib's poetry. I only question its place and timing in Hindu society. **It is great to study and quote him at 60, but is wrong before 20**. It was all politically motivated to start Ghalib Academy in Delhi in 1969 on his 1st death centenary. Ghalib's understanding of human nature was divinely. Gulzar, the script writer and director of the serial, has portrayed Ghalib as an antagonistic of some Muslim social practices. With the world wide rise of Islamic fundamentalism since the 1980s, too much of footage has been wasted on Ghalib's addiction to gambling and drinking that are taboos in Islam.

On a personal note, Ghalib's famous couplet (*Sheur*), on the minds of every youth, is: *ISHAK NE GHALIB NIKAMMA KER DIYA, VARNA VHO BHI AADAMI THA KAM KA* (romance has disabled Ghalib, otherwise, he was a useful man). My college classmate, Roshan Singh, twisted this couplet into: *ISHAK NE GHALIB KA LAMBA KER DIYA, VARNA VHO TO AADAMI NAMARD THA*. For over

45 years, it has brought smiles and laughters whenever I recall it, or meet Roshan Singh in Bathinda, my home town in India.

The lives of Umrao Jan and Ghalib crossed over during the 1857 Indian rebellion against the British. The movies on their lives stir my mind over this piece of Indian history. Increasingly, I get disappointed at the role the Hindus played during these mutinous conditions in India. Some Sikh princes of Punjab sided with the British, and it ultimately turned the tide in favor of the British. But the Hindus joined the Muslims, and the incompetent King Zafar became a symbol of Hindu-Muslim unity! **It was awful as it meant that the Hindus had stopped aspiring to become the rulers of their own land.** However, I 'll be around to see the Hindus en mass turning a corner in near future!

(Dec 16, 2006)

NOTES AND COMMENTS

1. I have known it for long that AMERICAN CULTURE IS DEAD. It is possible (please you are permitted to laugh) that Scientology may save it. Morality is the basis of any culture. Sex will exterminate any society where it is rampant. Sexual perversion will kill more quickly. Stoics knew that one lived for simplicity and hard work. Sensual pleasure should not be more than spices in a meal. But when spices become the meal itself, end is not very far. **Subhash**

2. Bhai Sahib, It was great to read your interpretation of Mirza Ghalib's life and decline of India's prosperity. Your examples and comparison give convincing theory of cycles of rise and decline of different nations and how much it's related with human behavior/psychology. **Ranjana Kumar**.

3. I enjoyed the piece. I think the Sikh princes sided with the British as they were afraid of Ranjit Singh. They allowed recruitment of Sikhs in the British army from their princely states while the Sikhs from the area Ranjit Singh ruled were generally barred to join the British army. A few years after 1857, Sikh recruitment into the army started and then the time came when more than half of the army comprised of Punjabis (Hindus, Muslims and majority Sikhs). **Inder Singh**

5. Satish, I must say about your "Reflection" article that with your Math expertise, you are also an excellent student of History. I am particularly struck with your definition of Urdu language written as Hindi described in Arabic-Persian language. But, don't tell this to a Muslim. If you do, you

could be in trouble even from educated Muslims. I also liked your friend's description of Mirza Ghalib's Couplet, *ISHAK NE GHALIB **KA LAMBA** KER DIYA, VARNA VHO TO AADAMI **NAMARD THA"**. . Best Wishes,* **Rajinder Singal**

BENJAMIN FRANKLIN PERISCOPE (I)

For the last several years, I have increasingly found myself starting on a book, but seldom finishing it. Actually, it is the book that deserts me, primarily for its lack of substance beyond the opening pages. Thus, I am urged to bring out my own book and be publicly scrutinized. Two years ago, I did make it a New Year Resolution!

The Autobiography of Benjamin Franklin (1706-90) is an exception. No wonder, it is the most widely read autobiography (he called it memoirs) in the US. Once I laid my hands on it, it followed me into the bathroom, kitchen and bed, till I was soaked with Franklin. Now, it awaits my ***Reflections*** to come out in a serial. It is relatively a small book of only 220 pages - recommended by a chemistry professor known for 20 years.

At any age, it is essential to have clear objectives before reading a life. Try not to be overly awed that any sense of inferiority may creep into you. I constantly look out for holes in a persona. After all, no one is free from imperfections. Uniqueness of my own life and some edge over any august life remains a bottom line in its reading. Earlier, I knew Franklin like a tip of an iceberg; now I don't recall a person, as multi-dimensional as he was.

Naturally, Franklin is the best periscope to look at the present events. Problems of love and hate, crime and punishment, war and peace are perennial in every age and time. It is, how the leaders emerge to tackle these problems, is noteworthy. The focus should not be on technical aspects, as they are irrelevant today, but on the steadfast mindset.

There is a remarkable similarity between Gandhi and Franklin. Both came from humble beginnings, but they harnessed their physical, mental and moral powers. Gandhi summed up his life when he said ***God is Truth***. He sub-titled his autobiography, as ***My Experiments with Truth***! Franklin spent the last 50 years to achieve moral perfection. His twelve cultivated virtues are: ***Temperance, Silence, Order, Resolution, Frugality, Industry, Sincerity, Justice, Moderation, Cleanliness, Tranquility, and Chastity***. The Number 13, **Humility** was added later on. Eventually, he was humbler than ever before!

In the 18th century, when modern democracies were not even conceived, only despots and monarchs ruled the world. Franklin was presented before five kings and he dined with one. I envisioned Gandhi, in loincloth, walking up the steps of the Buckingham Palace. He was the uncrowned king of Indian masses and intelligentsia, and rose above all the symbols of power and prestige. However, whereas, Gandhi was a pacifist, Franklin fought in wars.

Franklin kept journals of his life, as he meticulously maintained the data on the science experiments he performed in his personal laboratory. He made many scientific inventions. But with equal diligence, he polished and chiseled his life with virtues. He also shined as a businessman and great communicator for which he was always sought after. He was a true Founding Father of the United States of America!

(Dec 23, 2006/Oct, 2011)

NOTES AND COMMENTS

I am glad you are finally looking at a model. Long ago I was toying up with the idea of working on Benjamin Franklin's works for my dissertation. Franklin was a multi-faceted individual--writer, scientist, diplomat, printer, inventor, satirist, et cetera. Good. **Moorty**

2. You should publish your Reflections in 2007, or send me your date of birth, a numerologist will announce when it is published. *Tathagat* said RIGHT THINKING AND SELF CONTROL can lead to ENLIGHTENMENT. I have enjoyed reading quite a few of your REFLECTIONS, but I am a religious person. **Subhash** (Died four months later in April 2007)

BENJAMIN FRANKLIN PERISCOPE (II)

A measure of a good book is the number of times it stops a reader to savor an idea. Franklin's autobiography could be finished by a 'speed' reader in two hours, but it took me two days! Also, mathematicians are slow readers. At some places, every sentence is profound and quotable. Like a good wine, social and political ideas mature with age. Scientific ideas are very different. I kept underlining and making margin notes. It is not a good habit, when the book isn't mine. But I make sure to erase them before returning it.

One thing has to be understood that Franklin started writing at a ripe age of 65, and did it in four parts - the last pages done before his death at 86, in 1790. His writing is in a distilled form. In the first part, he spent more time on his family history and his youth that laid a firm foundation of his life. Actually, he did not mention a single word on colonial war and independence in 1776! He stopped it at 1765, as the rest of his life was all public. Gandhi (1869-1948) did the same about his autobiography, when he stopped it at 1921.

All great public figures have contributed to the cause of education for the development of the youth. Gandhi experimented with it when he was in South Africa and later on in India. Franklin gave to the world the first subscription-based public library. His objective was to spread education by encouraging book reading. It is a topic of research whether he ever thought of public education as considered today. Historically, free public education was first conceived by Lord McCauley, and implemented in London around 1830.

Public school education in India, modeled after the British and started around 1950, has already proved wasteful of taxpayers' money. In the US, it has been delivering less each year. A child of Franklin's curiosity may be damaged by the present US school system. Franklin worked at his father's wax business till the age of 12. Under the present child labor laws, father would be prosecuted! The basic and moral education begins at home.

On a personal note, from Dec 73 - April 74, my kids traveled in India. I told their teachers of educational value of travels. It was done again during March - June 77. The kids did not miss even one education beat. Under the current school policies, a child is not permitted long leaves. Attendance in schools is like roll calls in prisons; no wonder schools in metro cities are like prisons with uniform guards patrolling inside. Children are bored in schools and assaults are frequently reported. The state role in education is to provide options rather than mandatory regulations. It is time to cut down on universal education after 16, and encourage alternate instruction before 8. Structured education is oversold in the US public schools. It is based on being in education all my life!

In the aftermath of **9/11 Attack on America**, it is worth examining religious freedom as enshrined in the US Constitution to which Franklin was a signatory. He believed in God and thanked **him** ('h' is lower case). He rarely went to a church and ruled out clergy as a profession after reading on divinity. However, he was active in the clubs he founded that influenced public opinions. Nevertheless, he always supported his church and preachers.

People today have forgotten why the early settlers fled England from the religious persecution the Protestants faced there. Here is a quote that Franklin wrote after reading one of the 8 volumes that his clergy uncle, Benjamin (he was named after) wrote before sailing to America: *"This obscure Family of ours was early in the Reformation, and continu'd Protestants thro' the Reign of Queen Mary, when they were sometimes in Danger of Trouble on Account of their Zeal against Popery. They had got an English Bible, & to conceal & secure it, it was fastened open with Tapes under & within the Frame of a Joint Stool. When my Great Great Grandfather read in it to his Family, he turn'd up the Joint Stool upon his knees, turning over the Leaves then under the Tapes. One of the Children stood at the Door to give Notice if he saw the Apparitor coming, who was an Officer of the Spiritual Court. In that Case the Stool was turn'd down again upon its feet, when the Bible remain'd conceal'd under it as before......"*

This is the kind of religious freedom that was denied in England during the 16th and 17th century. During this period, nearly 100 % settlers, coming to New England region, were from England. **After 200 years, religious freedom has taken new political overtones.** The religious freedom enshrined in the US Constitution was never envisioned for the practice of any other religion - be that Hinduism, Islam, Judaism, Buddhism, and Sikhism. But the interpretation of law has been turned around by the Americans themselves - living in unprecedented affluence and moral decadence.

This is a danger to the American way of life and its civilization. It happened to the Hindu civilization flourishing through the 10th century. The Hindu kings sheltered the Jesuits, Parsis and Arab traders in the coastal areas. Dissentions within India encouraged foreign invasions. Subsequently, the Hindus became second class citizens in India! History repeats itself. I often think, that had the native Indians of America not welcomed the early White settlers and allowed them to build their forts and churches, they would not have lost their nation. Hindus lost it, and now the Americans will. A famous line of great American historian, Will Durant, comes to mind: **No civilization is destroyed by attacks from outside unless it is first weakened from within.**" Civilizations also rise and fall.

The freedom of speech, a corollary to the religious freedom, is another weapon that the enemy within is exploiting while the US is at war. The Americans are not aware that religious freedom - like in the US, exists perhaps nowhere else, except in India. In most Muslim countries, no one can bring in even religious literature with baggage – forget any religious preaching. But the enemy within is using the US liberal laws against the US - like the hijackers who used its life style, training and planes to implode the WTC towers.

I have come to a conclusion that all religions are not same. All places of worship are not same. All modes of worship and prayers are not same. All scriptures are not same. All gods are not same, as gods are conceived in the images of their believers. Each religion has its unique agenda for the development of the individual, society and nation. Its understanding is the key to survival and progress. **That is a harsh lesson of history**.

(Dec 26, 2006)

NOTES AND COMMENTS

1. Dear Satish, There's so much in this that I'll have to think about an earnest answer. Wow,,,,,,,,,,,I'm overwhelmed with so much information and so many thoughts. Thanks, Pal. **Dutchie**

2. "Franklin Periscope "was good reading..thanks...I think except Saudi Arabia, all Muslim countries have religious freedom...there is no harm bringing deities or their holy books, except SA...in Yemen we have 3 churches in Aden.. We celebrate Christmas...and other religious festivals...there is a Hindu temple in Aden and Indians worship publicly...no problem..Yes, not like US or India... And I believe that though all religions have their own agenda, in essence they are all the same. it is Man who in his narrow way of thinking making it an instrument of hatred and violence...Swami Vivekananda once said" We have enough religions to hate man, we have no religions to love man"..I like to consider myself as "spiritual" rather than "religious"..which according to me is a very "narrow" terminology. **Raju Abraham**

3. One more thing which brings Civilizations down is misguided wars. Remember the downfall of Mughal Empire began with Aurangzeb's long time involvement in Deccan. So much resource was spent on that long war that it made Mughals bankrupt and weak. Similar things happened to Hitler who opened the second front in War with Russia and the same mistake was made by Napoleon. US 's involvement in Iraq is the mistake on similar lines. **Rahul**

BENJAMIN FRANKLIN PERISCOPE (III)

My granddaughter stopped by when I was reading Benjamin Franklin's *Autobiography*. Excitedly, I told her how was I enjoying it, but could not believe that she had no clue of him! Last year, she graduated from high school amongst the top 7 students in a class of 700. It often alarms me how extreme liberalization and diversification of education is damaging the intellect of the youth. **Great minds transcend any ethnic agenda**.

Franklin (1706-90) founded a university, advocated women's education and even suggested a course of studies. In a fast paced modern society, when single mothers and grandmothers have to raise the kids alone, special courses for women in schools and colleges are called for. Under the diversity flag, most colleges do have Women Studies Programs, but their focus is mainly on feminism rather than on femininity.

The British ruled over India with the 'consent' of the Indians in the army, colleges and offices. The secret was the McCauley system of education developed by England for their colonies. It turned out generations of Indians completely ignorant of their heritage and pride-less. Personally, I studied the history of India under the British and history of England! I questioned it, when I was in the 7th class (grade).

While reading it, my one curiosity was about Franklin's views and dealings with the African slaves. He mentioned a bit about the native Indians, but did not use the word slave in the entire book! Twice, he used the word 'servant' which has a different connotation. However, from his early life on, I got an insight into the genesis of slavery as practiced by the British. Slaves from West Africa were unique to North America. To the best of my knowledge, there was no import of African slaves in any other British colony including Canada, Australia, and New Zealand. **In African colonies, Apartheid was a rule of law**. England did not have any slaves. However, 'modern' slavery had long existed in several contemporary African countries and most Arab countries.

Once the British Empire was established in far flung regions of the world, the man power was badly needed in plantation and settlement. An indentured labor system was introduced under which a person was literally a slave for a certain number of years. During the 19th century, Indians from different parts of India were lured into this system with the connivance of Indian princes! However, after five years, they were absolutely free to go back to India, or settle in the colonies.

Here is a paradox of human condition. Indians who were physically lethargic became hard working under the 5-year bond. Consequently, they prospered in the colonies after their contracts were over, and never returned to India, particularly, when it was famishing at the end of the 19th century.

It was eye opening to read how the father "persuaded" his son, Franklin to sign a 9-year Indenture bond with his elder brother running a printing business. **Franklin was then hardly 12-year old**. Today, such a bond is void and illegal! The young Franklin worked for long hours, beaten at times, despite being on the right side. Teen Franklin indulged as younger brother, but the older brother acted like his master. After 5 years, due to a strange turn of events in their business, "the old Indentures were returned with Full Discharge written at its back... signed new Indenture for the Remainder of the Term, and kept secret". After the very next dispute, Franklin "asserted his Freedom". The bother was "legally helpless" to stop him. Nevertheless, he went around making sure that 17-year old Franklin was not hired by any other printer in Boston. The big difference is that the slaves were never free!

My analysis is that in a building phase - whether a brother needing help in business, or a nation needing help in farms, fields and plantations, the logical mind set is to keep the labor tied up till the project is done! In a blunt way, **what qualms the early settlers had in importing sturdy men and women from Africa, if they treated their own people and white Europeans 'unkindly' through indentured labor?** It was happening at a time when the settlers were constantly fighting battles with the native Indians.

It is interesting to look back at a long stretch of nearly two centuries (1680-1860) of African slave traffic in USA. Just like the indentured Indians have fared far better than their kith and kin left behind in India, so have the African slaves in the USA. Their brethren in West Africa are still living in dark ages! Chinese too brought, as indentured labor from mainland to the mines of Malaysia peninsula, have prospered far beyond their ancestors in China known for opium addiction. **It is wrong to assess slavery or indentured labor with moral values and legalities of the 21st century.**

In all probability, African slaves were uncommon during Franklin's period while growing up in Boston and Philadelphia. During his active public life and travels, he may have encountered and observed slavery in homes and plantations. However, he may not have considered it significant enough, as despite vivid memories of his own indenture labor, he had a forgiving attitude towards his brother.

A corollary of human cargo from one continent to the other is the movement of British officers from one colony to the other. This is most fascinating. I have read stories of many British officers who failed in one colony, or plain good for nothing in England, but made fortunes in India-China. For instance, Clive who was a flop in Canada, but he laid the foundations of British Empire in India by winning crucial battles in the 1750s. Franklin mentioned several persons who went back and forth between Philadelphia, Barbados, and West Indies; one even to India.

I know several stories of financial success of Indians in the US. Some came illegally, but within a few years they became millionaires in various businesses. Adventures in travels and youthful risks ultimately lead to name and fame far more quickly than living **out quietly at one place**. Franklin combining it with his ever increasing knowledge from reading and writing skills became extraordinary. He came from very humble roots in Boston and England.

(Dec 28, 2006)

NOTES AND COMMENTS

1. Hi Dr. Bhatnagar, Wish you and your family a Very Happy New Year. Your Reflections are very nice reading. They help the reader remain in touch with his/her mooring and always bring a sparkle of light. I always meant to write to you, but somehow my other preoccupations kept me tied. **Bhaskar Goswami**

2. It is interesting to note that Franklin did have slaves, as house servants, I think. This is commented on by Walter Isaacson, author of a recent and excellent biography of Franklin. Jefferson was also a slave owner and fathered a good many children by Sally Hemings who accompanied him to Paris where he and Franklin were promoting the 13 Colonies' interests. Some white members of the Jefferson family have finally acknowledged the existence of Jefferson's and Hemings's descendents. George Washington had slaves too and he is said to have bequeathed some of his estate to set them free. **Dave Emerson**

BABUR'S WILL, BABRI MASJID & 9/11

Sometimes, history is unbelievable. In ancient lores, the facts and myths become indistinguishable. It boils down to what is oft quoted, where, when, and by whom. That was my first reaction on reading some lines from Babur's **will** (real name, Zahiruddin Mohammed) written to his eldest son, Humayun (real name, Nasiruddin Mohammed). Babur was born in 1483 in Samarkand in present Uzbekistan. He marched into India with a strong army equipped with the latest gunpowder weaponry. With his military genius, during **four** years of his life spent in India (called Hindustan, means the land of Hindus), he won three decisive battles in 1526, 1527 and 1529 before his untimely death in 1530.

The **Wikipedia**: According to the document available in the State Library of Bhopal, India, Babur left the following **will** to his dear son, Humayun: "*My son, take note of the following: Do not harbour religious prejudice in your heart. You should dispense justice while taking note of the people's religious sensitivities, and rites. Avoid slaughtering cows in order that you could gain a place in the heart of natives. This will take you nearer to the people.*

"*Do not demolish or damage places of worship of any faith and dispense full justice to all to ensure peace in the country. Islam can better be preached by the sword of love and affection, rather than the sword of tyranny and persecution. ....*"

Yesterday, the existence of this **will** came to my attention - while reading a weekly report of a student in my graduate course, *History of Mathematics* (MAT 714). During the past week, the focus was on mathematics in India during its Islamic period.

First, the historic authenticity of this **will** needs to be understood from the concept of **Wikipedia**, the world's largest free online encyclopedia - launched in 2001. It remains under continuous scrutiny. Of course, any 'final' revisions on its 'good' and 'featured' articles are subject to the acceptance by its 'Board'. The **will** has been viewed online perhaps a 1000 times since posted in 2002. Babur died in Agra, but as per his last wishes, his body was re-buried, after nine years, in Kabul, Afghanistan - of which he always cherished the fondest memories. Humayun was born (1508) in Kabul and grew up there, as Babur ruled over it before invading India.

Babur being a seasoned general and visionary ruler knew that without the support of the Hindus, his easygoing son, Humayun, may not be able to control the region that he had secured in four short years. He had specifically cautioned Humayun against the ambitious Afghan General, Sher Shah Suri, who after defeating and exiling Humayun, ruled north India for 15 years. After Sher Shah Suri's death in 1555, Humayun regained his power in 1556, but died only **seven** months later.

It seems that Babur's words of tolerance towards the Hindus were not meant for practice, as it amounts to apostasy for Islamic fundamentalists. Any softness towards the *Kafirs* (infidels) goes against the very tenets of Islam. It is different for the **People of the Book**. As a matter of fact, the religious intolerance towards the Hindus increased with each successive Mughal ruler. It reached newer heights during the reign of Aurangzeb (real name, Mohiyuddin Mohammed) when double taxation was levied on the Hindus in their own homeland, their temples demolished, and their sizes scaled down. The religious conversion, started gently under Akbar (real name, Jalaluddin Mohammed), was forcefully implemented under Aurangzeb. It tremendously boosted the Muslim population in Hindustan.

No Muslim leader in India has ever advocated the non-slaughter of cows sacred to the Hindus. Babur occupies a unique distinction in this respect - at least in words. Historically, masses are easily united around a point of common hared than of love. For example, the Muslims are united in their hatred for pigs, as the Hindus are united in their reverence for cows. It has been so easy to inflame communal riots between the two communities.

In a global arena of love and hate, during French Revolution, the center of hatred was the French royal family; in Russian Revolution, the Czars; for Nazis, the Jews. On the love side, Gandhi, through truth and non-violence, brought changes in the minds of the British colonialists compelling them to leave India in 1947. In the US, Martin Luther King Jr. peacefully succeeded in his civil rights movement.

It was during Aurangzeb's rule of 49 years that the Hindu temples were torn down and small mosques were built - jutting out of the famous Hindu temples in all the holy cities of the Hindus. The annexed masjids symbolized a cultural indignation and constant reminder to the Hindus of their subjugation to the Muslims. Rarely, the Muslims went there to pray.

The controversial Babri Masjid was built next to the most ancient Raam Temple in Ayodhaya, Lord Raam's birthplace. The ancient magnificent Raam temple goes back to the 7th century, the golden age of Hinduism. Islam being against idolatry, their smashing of the idols and statues goes back to its birthplace, Saudi Arabia. In India, Muhammad Gori and Mehmood Ghazni targeted the Hindu temples, plundered and destroyed them during each invasion. Only the intensity varied with rulers.

Whether it was the destruction of famous Somenath Temple in 11th century, or the blasting away of the 2000-year old huge Buddha statues in Afghanistan, in Feb-2001, despite worldwide indignation, it is a continuing saga of Muslim iconoclasm. The re-construction and re-destruction of the Hindu temples, including

Raam temple, have also gone on for centuries. The fundamental question remains of the Hindus ever fighting for the protection their shrines.

Did Babur build this Babri Masjid? On the basis of his will alone, the answer is No. **Neither, he had no time, nor, resources to build any monument**. During his last year after three major battles, first his dear and eldest son, Humayun got gravely ill. Babur had the best Hindu and Muslim physicians treat him with no success. A popular legend is that Babur's prayers worked miracle at the price of his own life! While Humayun was on a path to recovery, Babur, who was already not in good health, became terminally ill, and died shortly. Under such a emotional trauma, Babur and Humayun would not have ordered the construction of anything like Babri Masjid next to Raam Temple in a place too far from Agra, and incur the wrath of the Hindus.

Above all, Babur's campaigns of three major battles in three years had emptied his already light treasury. He was forced to order his army to return one third of their income to the royal treasury! Wars are never cheap, particularly, when the land, people and resources of the vanquished are not occupied. The US fighting in Afghanistan and Iraq for the last five years has adversely affected the domestic social projects and services.

The collapse of Soviet Union was mainly caused by the economic drain due to its 10-year (1979-89) war with Afghanistan. On the top, the economic policies of Reagan, Thatcher and Gorbochev expedited the collapse of Soviet Union. However, communism may have gone out of the Russian government, but it is far from being a model of western democracy. Since Bush Administration is too late in using the nuclear weapons to cut the war short (as President Truman did in 1945) at this stage, the US economic hemorrhage is going to continue. It is pushing the US towards neo-socialism. Also, the classic US capitalism, based on individual(s) and corporations, is changing into multi-nationalism created by humongous corporations with loyalty and patriotism towards none.

A question that begs an answer is who built the Babri Masjid and when? It is ironic that the building of Babri Masjid and its demolition are the rallying points both for the Muslims and Hindu, though at different points in time. After the central authority of the last Mughal was gone in 1709, the regional rulers became independent. The persecution of the Hindus and genocide of the Sikhs in Punjab were worse than under Aurangzeb.

Babri Masjid is a refurbished structure completed off and on during the 19th century. By naming it Babri Masjid, the objective was to bring the Muslims of the Oudh region together and slow down the Mughal decline. Historically, the Mughal rulers prided in being identified as **Timurids**, related with Timur, the 14th century empire builder of Central Asia.

Furthermore, the name Babri Masjid does not imply that it was built by Babur! It is a common practice amongst the Hindus, Muslims and Sikhs to name a place of worship after a saint, prophet, guru who may have lived decades ago. During the 1980s, thousands of 'historic' gurdwaras and madrassas sprang up in north India in cites and along the borders - common with Bangladesh, Pakistan, China and Nepal!

With the kind of **will,** purportedly Babur wrote, he must be turning in his grave at the dispute over a masjid that he never built! It has now taken international stage. **However, the fundamental question is the 'liberation' of the Raam Temple, and not the demolition of Babri Masjid**. Unfortunately, the two are tied. In the last millennium, for a number of reasons, the Hindus have never destroyed places of worship of other religions. India, being the only living museum of religions, creeds and cults, speaks of the ultimate tolerance in Hinduism. Ironically, it is also the fatal weakness of the Hindus!

In retaliation to the 1992 'demolition' of one Babri Masjid, hundreds and thousands of Hindu temples have been demolished in many Muslim countries. The number of Hindu temples, desecrated in Kashmir alone, runs into thousands. After the Amarnath pilgrimage, I witnessed this fanatic havoc during my 1998 visit to Srinagar. The Muslims worldwide have challenged the Hindus to liberate the next Hindu temple/demolish another masjid, and face the dire consequences!

After the demolition of Babri Masjid, the Hindu exodus from Kashmir and Bangladesh has accelerated. The Hindu-Sikh population in Kashmir that was nearly 25% before 1989 is hardly 1% now! In a historic perspective, the demolition of Babri Masjid is a tiny awakening of the Hindus after a thousand year of foreign subjugation. A paradox of Indian politics is that though the Hindus still make 80 % of the population, they do not constitute even one solid block of 10 % Hindus.

In the present democratic set-up of India, the Hindus continue to remain out of political power. The Muslim League takes care of the Muslims and the Akali Dal for the Sikhs. But there is no political party that openly stands for the Hindus. The Hindu Mahasabha was formed in the 1930s when the Muslim League and Akali Dal were also formed. The Hindu Mahasabha changed into Jan Sangh after 1947, and then into Bharatiya Janta Party after 1977. **The word Hindu is taken out, as it supposedly connotes Hindu fundamentalism!**

There is a global dimension to be factored into the rise of religious fundamentalism. After the successful over-throw of powerful Shah of Iran in 1978, the Islamic fundamentalism of Iran took off. It found a fertile soil in neighboring Afghanistan and Pakistan that gave birth to the Al Qaeda movement in the 1980s. Its seismic effect was felt in India. During the 1970s, Sant Jarnail Singh Bhinderwala led a movement of Sikh fundamentalism in Punjab. Eventually, Islamic fundamentalism swept Bangladesh, Malaysia, the Philippines, Indonesia, and has even penetrated into Australia - in Far East.

It seems that the Muslim fundamentalism has completed a cycle with its tryst of destiny with the US. The religious fundamentalism is sweeping the US and western countries. During the 2004 US presidential elections, the Christian rightist organizations played a key role. There has never been a tumultuous change in life styles of the civilized people all over the world, as it has happened after the **9/11 Attack on America**.

The ideology behind the attacks on two WTC towers by Al Qaeda is somewhat similar to the one behind the liberation of the Raam Temple/demolition of Babri Masjid. Call it a Hindu resurgence or renaissance. The difference is that one is global, the other is local.

(Feb 09, 2007/Oct, 2011)

NOTES AND COMMENTS

1. Very interesting, Satish. I didn't know about Babar's will. **Hemendra**

2. This is one of the best pieces of your reflection. I will definitely save it. My only **curiosity** is about Babur's will. As you know Wikipedia is far from authoritative. Last semester, one of my students in his mandatory presentation in "Foundations of Geometry" course, quoted Wikipedia when questioned about a statement on Elliptic geometry. I did not get a chance to rebut him, a couple of A students trashed Wikipedia. That's it for now. **Subhash Saxena**
   I may have missed in your original version, but are you suggesting the use of nuclear weapons in Iraq? If so, we are poles apart on this subject. **Subhash I wrote:** My thesis is that in any fight, including solving a math problem, one must first use the most powerful weapon/tool from the arsenal. Right after 9/11, Bush should have ordered nuclear bombs on Afghanistan, and India should have joined this war after the Parliament escaped massacre on Dec 2001. For the world, it would have cleaned up Afghanistan and Kashmir of the Islamic terrorists converging from all over the world.
   There would have been then no Iraq in 2003, or Iran today! That is where I stand. But now it is too late for Bush, and Kashmir does not belong to the Hindus or is a part of India! He is lame duck on this war.

3. Hi Satish: This piece is well written and thoughtful. I loved reading it. Best wishes, **Alok Kumar**

4. Satish, Reagan did not effect the collapse of the Soviet Union. It was the collapse of the price of oil. The SU was the second largest producer of oil. With the revenues from the oil they could keep communism afloat. Reagan did nothing but bankrupt us. Best, **Bob**

5. You are in your elements when writing about history. Great article. Please consider starting a blog for your history articles. **Harpreet Singh,** Life Seeker

6. Dear Dr. Bhatnagar, Thanks, this has shed a lot of light on the subject. **Hasmukh Joshi**

7. Your wonderful summary of the age-old facts that have still been affecting the life of every peace-loving people of the world identifies those who want to rule the world by the infamous weapon called "religion.' It enhanced my knowledge a lot. **Saha**

8. Dear Satish Ji: I read this article with interest. I have some comments in regard to the principal premise for the article. I believe you are aware of a tiny (175 pages) book titled "The Ayodhya Dispute" by Prof. Harsh Narain.

In case you are not, this book summarizes all the arguments on behalf of the Hindu side on the origins of the masjid. The book came just a few months before the demolition, when talks were going on between the Hindu side and AIBMC (the Muslim side). This will is alleged to be a forgery. In his book Narain has reproduced the photocopies of both the authentic and the "no cow-slaughter" will, as well as given their translation from Persian. The author cites several authors who point out discrepancies regarding the dates and style, which are explained in Narain's book. I also found a website on this will: http://www.answering-islam.de/Main/////Index/B/babars_will.html

Narain, points out that that the Babur-Nama "contain(s) not a word tolerance towards the Hindus" and that he "exhorts Humayun to emulate Timur." Babur also rewarded himself with the title of "Ghazi" and "Mujahid ". I do not recall where I read that he erected a pyramid of the unbelievers' skulls. If I can find it I will send that reference to you. In this regard I might mention that Muslim scholars have been surreptitiously sanitizing their documents, including the Koran to present Islam as a benign religion. Just to cite one example, in a translation of Koran from an Islamic society the "72 virgins" have been replaced with "72 Raisins" or they are not mentioned at all.

Narain presents a facsimile of the inscription on a wall of the masjid, and establishes by decoding a cryptic phrase thereon, as 935 AH (1528 AD). I do not clear about this process, but other sources in the book agree. The inscription clearly mentions "Babar Qualandar" and the author names a nobleman, Mir Baqi, as the builder of the mosque. I too agree that Babur in all likelihood did not directly participate in the razing of an existing temple and building of the said mosque. You state that the controversial Masjid was built 'next' to the most ancient Ram Temple.

In other words, there was no demolition of that temple. So where is that temple? Historical records point out that temples were demolished and a masjid was erected on that very site. Oh yes, Aurangzeb razed the Vishwanath temple in Kashi, and built a mosque on the site, but left a wall standing. That wall can still be seen today. It was not generosity, but to remind Hindus of the supremacy of Islam. I happened to visit Ayodhya post-demolition, in 1997. The masjid was located on the highest site in the city, so that Hindus could see it as soon as they entered Ayodhya. Regards- **Satya**

9. I have really liked your Babur Reflection; it has logical, historical, and contemporary strands interwoven dexterously. Evidently you have done considerable research. Keep up the fine work. **Moorty**

A DEAR HISTORIC TRILOGY

My roots being equally deep in Bathinda (BTI) and in Las Vegas (LV), I am really thrilled at the upcoming 50th anniversary of the Teachers Home (T'Home). In 1957, at this time of the year, I was 17, and taking the FSc. Exams (non-existent now!). Whereas, a few close relatives were confident of my promising future, but only one man, Jagmohan Kaushal had a vision on the future of the T'Home! He conceived it, midwifed it, fought several battles to protect and nurture it into a place of learning beyond the school walls. He symbolizes the heart and soul of the T'Home. It is my pleasure to reflect on this man, the T'Home, and BTI, the ancient city - like **three beautiful strands of a braid**.

My thoughts are transported to the eons of time when I observe that BTI being older than Amritsar, Patiala, Jalandhar, Ludhiana…means, it is the oldest city not only in Punjab, but in the entire region. The history of BTI goes back to nearly two thousand years! **But where are the signs of its age and wisdom?** Amongst its surviving monuments, BTI Fort, built by Raja Ram Dev, is the only living proof of its legends, and folklores associated with Razia Sultana (1240) and Guru Gobind Singh (1705).

A stately church and a deserted cemetery in Railway Colony remind of the Christians who either came from England, or the Hindus lured into Christianity. Also, a masjid in Sirki Bazar abandoned after India's religion based partition, recently furbished, heralds the global resurgence of Islam. The tales of holy men like Googa Peer and Peer Haji Ratan still permeate the air of BTI.

However, neither BTI, nor any other town in Punjab claims even a single 100-year old Hindu temple. Magnificent Hindu temples, particularly in Punjab, were repeatedly plundered and razed to the ground by the Muslim marauders ever since the 11th century. The Hindus spirit was so much pummeled that their temples shrank in sizes and dispersed in wilderness. Their tiny models found haven in the closets of their innermost dwellings.

Nevertheless, BTI does boast of olden gurdwaras including 300-year old 5th **Takhat** (Sikh temporal seat), **Damdama Sahib** in Talwandi Sabo (also called Guru Kashi) - 18 miles south. BTI did not belong to the great Sikh Empire of Maharaja Ranjit Singh. By signing the Sutlej Treaty with the British, the Maharaja was prevented from extending his territory east of the Sutlej River.

It was in such a historic city that Kaushal, the architect of the T'Home has spent his life, from birth till *YAM RAJ himself* **Plucks** his soul away! Though he was only 1-2 years ahead of me in MHR High School, BTI, he always moved around with teachers, principals and community leaders. Neither he had any aptitude for sports, nor was any time left for it. Early on, he was mentored by Principal H L

Joshi, an eminent educator for taking on leadership roles - like publishing a Hindi weekly at the age of 16 or 17. Kaushal was already popular as a singer and actor in school plays. His latest brainchild, the *Sahi Buniyad* is in the natural order of his literary achievements.

The publication of the *Sahi Buniyad* is one of the educational missions of the T'Home. Every year, top students, teachers and retired principals are honored for their academic achievements. The participation in the T'Home functions is open to all the teachers - government and private. Visiting T'Home, during my BTI stay, makes great memories. Go there any times of the day, one finds various educational groups either meeting in the open amphitheater, or in two large halls. This learning scenario in BTI is so unbelieving to my eyes and ears.

BTI, before India's independence, in 1947, was ridiculed in the nation for its every natural and man-made hostility. It deterred new comers for its harsh hot climate, acute water shortage, and its unique brand of lawlessness. BTI was nationally ranked in relational homicides, liquor consumption and illicit distillation. I have seen more post mortems in the Civil Hospital, dead bodies floating in BTI canal and *DIGGIS* (water reservoirs) than a person may see in the movies today!

As soon as Kaushal became a primary school teacher after the Junior Basic Training, he plunged himself for the welfare of the teachers through its union. It is all a public record. But the public does not know the story of his early hardships and personal sacrifices including that of his family. Someone must research as to how in the 1950s when nothing was organized in Punjab, Kaushal succeeded in arranging funds for the purchase of this huge plot. In 1957, the present site of the T'Home was way out of the residential and commercial limits of the city. The original structure of the foundation stone was either dismantled by the vandals for their bricks, or swept away by the powerful red and yellow sandstorms for which BTI was feared before the 1950s.

On a positive note, BTI has been a cash cow for the British before independence and now for the national governments. Again, let me turn to another chapter on history. BTI, not being in any princely state, was fully exploited by the British by collecting handsome revenues from the farmers after the construction of (Bathinda) Sirhind Canal. They neglected education in the region. Mahindra College, Patiala, started in 1875, was a reward to the Patiala Prince for sending its forces to quell the 1857 national rebellion. It was affiliated with Calcutta University! After BTI becoming the second largest railway junction in the country, revenues poured into the government coffers. Few know the fact that BTI Telephone and Telegraphs Dept lead the nation in the earnings due to its Number Two *SATTA* market (an 'unregulated' Hindu stock market) in the country.

In 1957, Government Rajindra College was the only 4-year college within a radius of 30 miles. The 2-year science classes were added in 1955 due to the efforts of

HM Dhillon, the first woman principal of a co-educational college in the united Punjab. Incidentally, I was in the very first science batch! BTI is a perfect example in the nation where people finally woke up to their potential. They invested in private schools and colleges on the one hand and entrepreneurial business on the other. Private capital that hardly existed and little invested in ventures before independence, was ploughed in plenty. It started bearing fruits by the 1990s.

Today, BTI is famous for the most successful training centers for the competitive exams in the country! It is a thriving hub of business, education, industry, and the northwest military frontier of the country. Kaushal is an intellectual icon of Punjab, though due to family reasons and public engagements, he never pursued formal education beyond high school. For most people, the modern rote education stops at school or college, but for social activists like Kaushal, the life-long education begins afterwards. I have arrived at this conclusion after being in the business of education for 45+ years.

There is a saying that it is very easy to open a shop, but very difficult to keep it open. Societies are formed, but they quickly fade away for lack of purpose, commitment and leadership. The T'Home has defied its survival odds. It has grown in size and accomplishments into a cultural landmark of BTI. A serious question is of its future since, so far, it has been tied with Jagmohan Kaushal. In India, often an institution gets identified with one individual, and that is generally inimical to its long-term health.

BTI cannot look back! From a population of 60,000, 50 years ago, it has now reached 240,000. Kaushal's health was never good, and now he is running it on reserve 'gasoline'. Unless, he gets a new lease of life with full medical treatment of his diabetes and related ailments, it is time to seek his guidance in finding his own successor. The T'Home needs to look forward with a renewed spirit and newer vision during the next 50 years into the 21st century.

Some financial stability of the T'Home is provided by its rental income from a number of commercial shops on the ground floor. Also, it gets non-recurring government awards and grants from the visiting ministers and government officials. However, philanthropic private donations and grants need to be pursued by its permanent staff.

For making contacts with the NRIs, the T'Home must maintain a website of its activities and link it with other websites of the city and state. It requires renovation of the T'Home building for internet connections and high-tech meeting facilities. In order to optimize the use of space, adult evening classes, senior training and recreation in the morning, short courses and hobby classes may be looked into. All these semi and full-fledged academic activities must be run by a fulltime educator and financial manager.

The best living tribute to Kaushal would be the naming of the T'Home after him. Also, in gratitude, it is time for the T'Home to honor him with a monthly honorarium. Long live the legacy of Kaushal enshrined in the T'Home! Together, they have rewritten the history of BTI by making the ridicule phrase, **'Via Bathinda'** obsolete for the posterity!

(Mar 23, 2007/Oct, 2011)

NOTES AND COMMENTS

OUR FORGOTTEN HOLOCAUSTS

Hello, Artist Mira Nair!

A couple of things converged recently that it prompted me to write you. Last week, my wife and I enjoyed watching your latest movie, *Namesake*. Around the same time, I decided to re-circulate my 2006 *Reflection*, *Holocausts in India*, amongst friends and relatives on my mailing list. I don't post them on a web site.

For the last one year, comments and responses on this *Reflection* have been overwhelmingly in favor of a documentary or short film on this theme. Like any artist, or writer, you may have several small and big projects for production. Include this one too, or at least, place it on back burner.

On Googling your name, I learnt a little more about your Indian background and a list of your productions; documentaries and movies. Moreover, I do sense an India instinct in you for right projection of Indian culture and history. You may be aware of an hour-long documentary, *Continuous Journey* (2005) based on the true story of *Komagata Maru* by Ali Kazmi. Perhaps, he may be known to you - being in a small circle of Indian producers and directors.

Both my *Holocaust Reflection* and *Komagata Maru* articles are enclosed. On surfing the internet, I did not find your e-mail ID. The other information - like phone number and address, are out of question these days. However, I noted your name in the list of faculty of Film Division of Columbia University. Hopefully, it would be rightly delivered to you.

In due course, I would appreciate hearing some communication on this subject. Thanks.

Sincerely,

Satish C. Bhatnagar

(April 22, 2007)

PS: Oct, 2011: Nothing has been heard from her.

NOTES AND COMMENTS

1. Dear Satish Ji: I have been forwarding your emails to my very dear relative, Mr. Punsheel Kumar. He has become your fan. Could you do me a favor? Kindly include his name in you mailing list so that he receives direct mails from you. Have a fruitful day. **Shyam Narula**

2. Do you know Mira Nair is married to a Muslim (from India) but settled in Kenya?   I am not sure how receptive she will be to your idea on Hindu Holocaust. **Rahul**

3. Satish, Let me suggest to you few more names who may also show some interest in your project. They are in the Bollywood film Industry. People like Mahesh Bhatt, Anupam Kher, Bhandarkar (Who made the Traffic Signal Movie) may also show interest. Mr. Bal Thackeray, Shiv Sena Leader, will surely love to see your idea fly and he has no shortage of money or you can also contact some Banks in Bombay to fund your project. Try to do more extensive research from History Books on your project, and try to write a detailed script assigning the character roles etc. This way, you can have a better luck. Good Luck. **Rajinder Singal**

PERU (INCA CIVILIZATION): A PERISCOPE

I left Las Vegas for Peru (means the Land of Gold), South of Equator, on June 15 and returned on the 24th. It was my first excursion into the Southern Hemisphere. The journey time of nearly 22 hours was the same as for going to Peru or India. Historically, like the US today, India used to be the world destination - till the 18th century. Various Muslim nationals like the Arabs, Afghans, Mongols, Mughals and Turks invaded India since the 11th century. European explorers also thought of India in the 16th century. But their navigational science and political power were not developed enough to sail all the way to India. So, when the Europeans ships landed on the Atlantic coasts of America, they thought they had landed on the soil of India! **That is why, all the natives of the Americas continue to be called Indians till today.**

First, talking of the naval powers, I often wonder how the Hindus lost it. The Indian states of Bengal, Orissa, Andhra Pradesh, Tamilnad, Kerala, Maharashtra and Gujarat have coastline length comparable to that of the European nations. The Indians ships sailed to Africa, Far East and Middle East through the 4th and 5th centuries, the golden period of India. Enigmatically, by the 19th century, crossing the ocean meant social ostracization. Gandhi described this predicament when he was to sail for England in 1886. The misplaced emphasis on vegetables deprived the coastal people of their staple protein diet from sea food. Above all, the loss of adventurous spirit for ocean made India vulnerable from its porous coastline too.

The decision to leave the laptop was good one, as I could be worry-free while out of the hotel. However, I took plenty of notes for my *Reflections*. But it has been more than ten days, and I have not yet cranked out even single one; uncharacteristic of me! In Peru, I was bubbling with ideas. At times, I missed speaking into a tape recorder for its transcription later on. Even notes were time consuming. This *Reflection* is a smorgasbord of Peru *Reflections*; very condensed that a single sentence may be expanded into a nice article. But I don't think I would go back to individual *Reflections* as the tides of new *Reflections* continue to knock my consciousness.

The course was directed by two professional archaeologists with PhDs from University of Texas, known for their seminal archeological work on Mayan Civilization. I also had attended a similar course in 2005, namely, *Ancient Mayan Mathematics in the Ruins of Quintana Roo, Yucatan Peninsula, Mexico*. The lectures, discussions, and site tours were very stimulating. My thoughts were bouncing all the time from one pole to the other.

Archaeological work is very expensive. It requires millions of dollars in excavation, involvement of various experts for deciphering and dissemination. Any ruins, about 1000 years old, may still look ordinary mounds - often covered with trees and dense foliage. Only good research projects can get research grants and permits from foreign nations. What benefits do the universities get in return? Hiram Bingham brought back 70 boxes of material to Yale University after he unearthed the ruins of Machu Picchu (means **big mountain**) in 1911. The national park entrance has his name plate. Also, a tourist train, running between Cuzco and Machu Picchu, is named after him.

Whereas, most research is driven by long and short term goals of applications, the West also values knowledge for the sake of knowledge. It enhances the prestige of the universities to attract bright kids, and also kids of the rich and famous from all over the world. Later on, they support their alma maters. Rich universities get richer and more prestigious with new researches and service to the nation through distinguished faculty and administrators. For example, President Bush tapped Robert Gates, President of Texas A&M University as Secretary of Defense. Henry Kissinger of Harvard has counseled many US presidents. The poor and developing nations are years behind, and perhaps will stay back! **Yet, all great civilizations fall, and new rise up!**

Another ricocheting thought was that the countries of Asia, Africa, and America were colonized by half a dozen European nations; England, France, Spain, Dutch, Italy, and Portuguese. Germany always aspired to be a supreme power in Europe. During the last 100 years, all the major archaeological projects in the world have been undertaken by only a dozen universities: Oxford, Cambridge and Paris in Europe, Harvard, Columbia, Cornell, Yale, Chicago, Berkeley and Stanford lead in the US. The deep pockets of these universities allow the faculty to re-discover the lost lands and empires that their forefathers had decimated a few centuries ago!

I found this thought really awakening! **Is it now a reverse intellectual colonization?** The well connected young men and women from the poor and developing countries get elite education from great western universities. After completion of studies, they go back to their home countries and occupy positions of power and influence. They implement foreign management and planning models that come out of the thinking that had conquered their forefathers!

Let me put the lost civilizations in perspective. For instance, the Inca civilization (1200-1600) comprises a land mass of the size of a typical European country, or a state of India. The study of all the lost empires and civilizations are divided between great universities as their region of influence. Despite collaboration, there is a stamp of being the first. Indus civilization and Harappa Civilization in a region common to present India and Pakistan was accidentally uncovered by a British surveyor while laying out new railroad tracks in the 1860s. Once the British left the Indian subcontinent in 1947, this archaeological work made little headway. For the Pakistanis, there is no Islamic connection with Harappa and for Indians - no passion. **Archeological work measures the total development of a nation.**

The Inca civilization was decimated by the Spaniards in a brief period of 36 years (1536-72)! It boggles the mind. Nearly 50% of the populace died of small pox carried by the Spaniards into South America. The natives, having no immunity against the European diseases, died like flies. Though unintended, perhaps it was the first biological warfare waged in South America more than once. The surviving native population was emaciated, ill equipped, unprepared and divided, that they were quickly run over by the Spaniards!

It is troubling! If an individual or nation does not fight to protect its honor, valuables and treasures, then they are snatched away sooner or later by the barbarians or powerful. It happened to the peaceful Tibet in 1950 when the Chinese Red Army of annexed it. Due to divisive caste system and misplaced notion of non-violence, on the top of general weakness, the Hindus lost their will to fight, and hence lost their country. Either, Incas did not have any intelligence report on the Spaniards' victory over the Aztecs, 200 miles north, or they ignored it. The Inca kings did not spend resources on weapons and defense. Consequently, they lost all their gold, treasures and lives. **I see these ominous shadows casting spell on the US today that has come under attack from within and without**. The US public, at large, is impervious to the dangers.

Francisco Pizaro conqueror of the Incas was a pig farmer in Spain. His cousin, Herman Cortez who conquered Aztecs 10 years earlier, was perhaps a chicken farmer. I am amazed, as similar stories come from India too. Robert Clive, who in 1757, established English foothold in Bengal, was a clerk, who sailed to Canada to seek fortunes. After meeting no success, he was transferred to the East India Company, in Calcutta. Spaniards also remind me of the Turks who used to carve out the southern India among themselves before invading those regions. It is disgusting to understand how one nation wins and the other loses everything. History awakens everyone.

There are legends that Spaniards took lot of gold from the Incas. However, I was curious to know how did the Incas extract the gold in the first place? How and where they mined the Andes Mountains or panned the rivers, are unclear? Having lived in Nevada and India, I know the engineering skills required in the mining gold and silver. The genius of the Incas shines out in the construction of various walls and ramparts with rocks cut and polished - weighing from 100 lbs to 20 tons. No cement or mortar was used to bind the stones. It is a mystery how the Incas built roofs, as there are no signs of any woodwork despite thick forests surrounding the ruins.

Since the 18th century, an isomorphic thinking is noticed in the Western intellectual traditions. I label it Darwinian, in general. It cuts across all disciplines - like, geology, geography, biology, anthropology, psychology, and archaeology. There is an underlying assumption that every aspect of life and living was primitive in eons of time. It is so funny to see the timelines shift by a few hundred to a few millions of years. **The existence of pre-Inca culture justifies Spanish colonization of the region.** The British dis-enfranchised Indians by creating myths about Aryan invasion of India, the most preposterous theory! This intellectual mafia has spread over two centuries. However, its repudiation and refutation are not reported in mainstream media!

Finally, I must add some remarks on Inca mathematics. The fundamental nature of mathematics is as intuitive as of a dialect in speech, musical notes, or etchings in geoglyphs. As a society organizes into an empire, the role of mathematics gets sophisticated. Incas, having advanced knowledge of mathematics, is evidenced by their surviving monuments. Inventory and record keeping are the basic needs of any big organization. Incas developed *Kipus (Khipus)* using decimal system for tracking vast inventories. At the conclusion of the course, I made a *Kipu* of grade distribution of students in a course. While explaining its logic, I deduced that the Incas had a written language too. **It may be lost, but any claim of its non-existence is absurd!**

(July 05, 2007/Feb 2010)

NOTES AND COMMENTS

1. Dear Satish, Bravo for a very informative and sophisticated report. Yes, it's a *Reflection* and a report. It's full of so many interesting observations and facts. Thank you for your profound thoughts and experiences. Fondly, **Dutchi**

2. Dear Satish: I liked reading your new reflection. I only wish that you should start writing popular articles for magazines. You are good. However, you run away from the hassles of dealing with editors. It is a paradox from a rough and tough person like you. ..... Best wishes, **Alok Kumar**

3. Thanks Satish, very informative. **Gopal**

4. Hi Satish, Your comments are interesting. The Aztec had a written language. The Incas, even though a very advanced civilization, did not seem to go past a method of keeping records of things in their store houses. It seems written language was only invented 5 times and then the idea spread. Once a Cherokee observed the method of writing from the invading Europeans he quickly devised an alphabet and wrote down the Cherokee history. (I forget the Cherokee's name.) Of course, small pox killed off the Aztecs too or Cortez would have lost his battle as they had him boxed in. It did not help either. They were pressuring the neighboring tribes continually for sacrifice victims, and extorting goods from them. Small pox played a big pole in

decimating the American natives living in the Mississippi valley way before they saw a European. It presumably came from natives from Florida that became infected. The purposeful distribution of blankets taken from British small pox victims was an additional factor. Moreover, some USA presidents practiced a policy of genocide quite similar to Hitler's but on a grander scale. (The History of the American People from 1492, Howard Zinn). I can add more details to all of this but it is all very depressing.

With regard to cultures, I am now reading ancient history. It seems that once a group of people stop being hunter gathers, and develop agriculture, social organization etc. they start to enjoy a more luxurious life and to amass wealth they become not so warlike. A neighboring group of more warlike people then invades them and either destroys everything or become the overlords while the others become slaves. This process repeats itself from the time of the Sumerians and Egyptians. There are countless examples of this. It is a question of whether the Muslims will just destroy us or make all all convert. Best, **Bob Gilbert**

5. I was in Peru 10 years ago...62...climbed to the top of Machu Picchu went with the Edgar Cayce Foundation and at each city we had a different "spiritual guide" exposing us to varied beliefs...interesting and exciting. It was a mystical experience! Spent one whole a.n. under the single tree on the flat area. You didn't mention the Nasca lines...did you fly over them? Blessings, **Renee**

6. Dear Bhai Shri Satish Ji, Saprem Namaste! I was wonder-struck, how you could manage to study in a brief period so deeply about all the Peruvian History, its culture its Heritage, its Archeological ruins & their history which actually gets enshrined in the archeological monuments as was the case in Harappan & Mohan Jodro excavations (which you so rightly compared, totally Hindu Culture, entirely different than Islamic/ Muslim culture of today's Pakistan) , the brightness of Peruvians in Mathematics with its wonderful Geometrical usages in constructions of Heavy Stone Monuments & bldgs without Mortar or anything, its various Mining & wealth of Gold & Silver & amazing way of how they were recovering these precious metals , their & Spanish Naval powers with comparative studies for each with those of India & Spain in particular and so on.

I was amazed to observe your fantastic grasping power by just a glance of those Peruvian Sites during your brief visit. Your tremendous knowledge, intelligence & everything is so far remaining UNUTILIZED by our Arya Samaj, which should be used as early as possible for its own benefit, if not otherwise. Arya Samaj should also remember that when the GREAT MAMAJI (SWAMI DEEKSHANAND JI SARASWATI) was so intelligent & highly learned Scholar, then why his own nephew is being side-tracked, who requires to be recognized & utilized for the good & benefit of Arya Samaj only.

Possibly, the problem is, your talks or writings are far above or beyond a common person's understanding, they are more Scholastic in nature than ordinary way of putting those things to lesser knowledgeable & of lesser intelligent people. All are NOT as intelligent as you yourself are. Warmest Regards, **Satish Gupta**

7. Dear Satish, I liked your reflection on your action: involving a visit to Peru. **Bhola**

8. Very interesting. I found that trips like these were generally stimulating and often in ways that I had not expected. Looking back, even if a trip was taken for little more than sightseeing or getting away, it usually had the merit of broadening or deepening our interests. As for war and the looting of treasures, I can understand on an economic and cultural level the gains sought by aggressors, but I've always thought it an essentially immoral act in any case. Even so, it seems to me that there is something fundamentally more than it; some kind of collective madness people engage in that even aggressive sports like American football fail to assuage. Ah, the mysteries of the human condition. **Robert W Moore**

SEXY SERMONS IN STONES

What a blessed day, it has been amidst the most beautiful and well-proportioned women in their best hairdos! Like the showgirls of Las Vegas, the jewelry is their only costume. It is not in a dream, not in the Islamic heaven of eternal virgins, not in Hindu **Indralok** of **Apsaras.** As a matter of fact, they are chiseled out of the stones - decking the ancient Hindu Temples of Khajuraho. They are truly immortals amongst the mortal humans.

Never before so many questions choked my mind, as I was absorbed watching them. These temples were built during the 200-year reign of 23 Chandel kings of central India from the 10ᵗʰ to 12ᵗʰ century. Out of a complex of 85 temples, only 25 have survived. The Archaeological Survey of India (ASI) may unearth more. The very first question in my mind was, how come the subsequent Muslims occupiers of the region did not raze them to the ground, as they did it to many Hindu temples in north India, or converted them into mosques. Reason: Being located in 20 square km area surrounded by dense forests and rolling hills, the entire region was eventually deserted and lost to the ravage of nature.

It was in 1818 when Franklin, a British explorer, accidentally discovered these temples. Subsequently, Alexander Cunningham and Ferguson made the world aware of them. Such cultural discoveries by the English in their colonies are very common. It must be understood that the villagers around the temples fully knew of the existence of these temples. Here is a **social paradox**. A thousand Hindus knowing the ancient temples amounted to nothing to the world. But once one European explorer takes notice of them, then it becomes a discovery! **It is the quality, not the quantity that often counts in life**

Watching the copulating and amorous scenes in three-band idols on the temple exteriors is like watching XXX adult movies. Funny thing is that you are in a crowd of people from all over the world. In the darkness of an adult theater, one is likely to resort to some masturbation to release the 12,000-volt of sexual tension. I was never so much juiced up!

Every Indian has heard, read and seen the raw pictures of Khajuraho nymphs. I waited for 70 years! Last June, a friend had strongly recommended them. After 60 years of independence and international fame of its temples, the place is still not easily accessible by trains, buses, or planes. No wonder, it remained hidden for nearly 700 years.

In search for sexual gratification, man is driven to extremes. Sex can become a paradigm of life. In the US, a sex jock, Howard K. Stern exemplifies a sexually pervasive and obsessive way of life. What happens to a nation, at large, when it is driven by sexual appetites? These temples combine **Yog**, a union of individual mind with the Supreme and the ***Bhog*** - a union of the soul with sensual pleasures. The synthesis is remarkable.

The present Hindu society is understandably prudish about open display of sexual behaviors. In the US, on the other hand, sex, in the name of education, is being introduced too early. The temple statues depict sexual activities of every kind - like one man engaged with 3 to 4 women, 4 lesbian women in an act, two couples, and in a few instances - men and women with animals too. They epitomize sexual culture of its time.

The women are full bodied in contrast with pencil thin fashion models and actresses of the last 25 years. The round breasts of the statues exude vibratory firmness of the flesh over the stones. It captures a culture when the ladies of the evenings prepared for romantics escapades in the palaces. Some jewelry was customized to the body parts not seen from the front. That accentuates parts of the backs, sides of the thighs, buns, and ankles. These subtle depictions blow the mind away. The only contemporary sensual atmosphere that I could extrapolate is the Playboy clubs in the US and abroad.

A small Khajuraho museum of the ASI houses an amazing statue of an 'exposed' Lord Ganesh. I was confused whether it was His penis or a dangling ornament. But a museum curator explained that the huge penis was also decorated with jewelry! The holy penis head was studded too. It reminded me of a US body artist who had his penis tattooed and pierced with studs making it look like a cobra. He splashed it on a website! It is like seeking ***Nirvana*** though sexual ecstasy, a Tantric way of Hindu life. After the fall of Chandel Empire, Khajuraho also served a kind capital of sexually liberated cults.

The temple architecture defies every modern benchmark. The four US presidents carved out of Mount Rushmore stands nowhere, as compared with Khajuraho, where every square inch of outside and inside of tall temples are chiseled. The mining and carting of stones to the sites, generations of top artists, architects, engineers and masons boggle the researchers. Lot of scholarly work is needed. Where are those art schools? For financing these mammoth constructions, the Chandels must have a revenue base over a vast empire. The artistic legacy of the US Presidents of the last 30 years is relatively empty.

During the light and sound show, it was noted that in commemoration of thwarting one of the attacks of the Afghan chieftain, Mohammed Gazani, a new Vishnu temple was built up. It shocked me. **The money should have been spent in mobilizing armed resources, developing newer weapons, military training and attacking Muhammad in his home of Gazani.** Ironically, the Chandel king knew that Gazani was going to attack again.

That is where I supported George W. Bush in flying the US forces in Afghanistan, the home of Islamic terrorists and their Iraqi supporters. No second attack has taken place on the US soil since 9/11 Attack on the World Trade Center. **But not using the nuclear weapons in Afghanistan, like Truman did on Japan, is Bush's gravest blunder**.

Presently, the Hindus continue to follow the mindset of Chandel kings, as they are being attacked and run out in their own home country in the states of Kashmir, Gujarat, Maharashtra, and in eastern states of India. Due to the perennial lack of unity amongst the Hindus, their 80% figure, in the population, is ineffective in the government affairs.

Thanks Khajuraho for the memories! There was a plenty of food for thought, and lot of thoughts on the ultimate sensual food.

(Oct 28, 2007/India/Aug, 2011)

NOTES AND COMMENTS

THE HOLIEST, BATHINDA

Once in a while, one is shocked by one's ignorance of incredible, but hidden characteristics of an individual, or place – supposedly known. Just being close to someone or something does not always mean that you know it all of the other. My hometown, Bathinda (BTI) threw such a surprise on me. A few days ago, I got hold of a book, ***Bathinda*** by (Late) Professor Karam Singh, a BTI icon (1922-2007). For its academic value, it is published (1996) by the Punjab Language Department. It is so masterly written that I could not put it away.

Yesterday, I spent a few hours in an area of roughly one square KM on BTI's south side. A Sikh gurdwara and mausoleum of a Muslim saint are next to each other. The 10th Guru Gobind Singh visited this region around 1706. Right next to the Gurdwara stands a tree supported by five pillars (Number five is sacred in Sikh ethos). According to a legend, Guru's horse was tied to this tree while he was camping there. A bunch of simple rooms are marked as the resting place of the Guru and his entourage. Damdama Sahib, one of the five holy Takhats of the Sikhs, is only 40 KM away from BTI.

I went back in time while strolling the surrounding area. Walking through the by lanes of the neighborhood, I came out at the burial grounds including the tomb of Muslim saint, Haji Ratan. One of the many legends is that Ratan Lal or Das, a Hindu courtier of a BTI king, heard Prophet Muhammad's prophecy. He set out for Mecca and met Prophet Muhammad who gifted him a camel! Ratan, converted into Islam, spread it on his return to BTI. The legend adds that Haji Ratan, his camel and dog are buried near each other! The burial ground also includes a smaller tomb of Ratan's successor, Sufi Chandu Shah.

The Eastern culture markedly differs from the West in many respects - including a sense of history. The west, being relatively young as compared with say, Hindu Civilization, is crazy about its history. The east has lost count of time, the essence of history. It is best illustrated by a real story. A friend asked his mother about the birth date of his younger brother. It was a time in BTI when no official birth/death records were kept. His mother could only give him clues like when a neighbor's son or daughter was born etc. When my friend connected all the dots, his younger brother turned to be five years older than him! No wonders, some legends trace Haji Ratan to the 12th century AD - not the 7th.

BTI boasts at least two 300-year old gurdwaras. The site of Haji Ratan, subsequently known as ***Bathinda Sharrif***, is one of the four Muslim Holy places including Khwaja's Ajmer Sharrif. To my dismay, there is not even a single Hindu temple of comparable stature. I also discovered that the community and religious properties of the Muslims who migrated to Pakistan are protected and managed by Waqf Board in India. But there was/is no such Board in Pakistan that protected the religious and community property of the Hindus, who were forced leave Pakistan. It all boils down to unity amongst the Muslims and its absence amongst the Hindus. Thanks BTI for new memories!

(Nov 23, 2007/India)

NOTES AND COMMENTS

MAHARANA PRATAP: A PERISCOPE

During my 3-day stay in Udaipur, I was involuntarily soaked up with Maharana Pratap (1540-1572-1597)/(birth-throne-death). His brave and defiant spirit, pervading the air, is still seen in his statues, roads, businesses, and institutions named after him and his legendary horse, Chetak. Chetak and Natak were two thoroughbred Arabian horses presented before Pratap for sale; but Natak accidentally died during the test trials.

Had Pratap, like his personal horses, upgraded his army's artillery weapons and hired European mercenaries in contemporary warfare, history of India would have been different. Bhama Shah's wealth, as offered to Pratap, was enough to support 25,000 soldiers for 12 years! The weapons imitate the fighting character of an individual or a nation. Conversely, the heart of an individual or a nation is mirrored by the weapons in the arsenal. A war is fought with heart first, weapons come second, and army's size third. All the Muslim invaders had the edge over the Hindus in the first two categories.

In the present context, Al Qaeda, a global Islamic militant organization, goes after the latest in strategies and weaponry. In stark contrast, a few days ago, it was funny to watch the members of the RSS (*Rashtrya Swanmsevak Sangh*, a 75-year old national Hindu volunteer organization) marching the streets with *LATHIS* (sticks)! Historically, the Hindus disarmed themselves before the Muslims and English rulers without any resistance. Consequently, they have been robbed, plundered and massacred for centuries.

The 1962 debacle of Indian army was due to its gross unpreparedness - from soldiers' uniforms to military hardware, as compared with the marauding Chinese Red Army. However, Pratap's successful resistance to the Mughal rule in Rajasthan and his chivalry was the first example of guerilla warfare waged by a Hindu king. Fifty years later, it inspired Maratha king, Shivaji to fight against Aurangzeb, a great grandson of Akbar.

A visit to a newly built Museum and Hall of Heroism was worth it. Also, I went through *Maharana Pratap and his Times*, a publication of **Maharana Pratap Smaarak Samiti**, Udaipur. It is a collection of 26 research papers presented in a 1989 seminar. The papers, being short and interesting, were quickly read through. That deeply stirred my mind for making connections between the Pratap era and present times. **The history of a family or nation is burdensome, no matter how glorious its past has been, unless it inspires the present for a greater future.**

Objectively speaking, the leadership of young Jalaluddin Muhammad (Akbar only means great) (1542-1556-1605) stands out in comparison with that of Pratap. With the support of his fiercely loyal generals - like Bairam Khan and sterling advisors like Abul Afzl, Akbar successfully convinced many Hindu kings of his vision of *sulh-i-kul*, for a unified Hindustan under the Muslims.

Neither in any research paper, nor in my researches, had Pratap tried to unify the Rajputs under the banner of Hindutva for routing the Muslims. The Muslim population in India of the 16th century had hardly reached 400,000. Yet, the Hindus seem to have reconciled that the Muslims rulers are there to stay in India forever. This despondency enveloped them due to nearly 500 years of Muslim subjugations of different parts of India. Today, after 1000 years, the demographic map of India has changed beyond recognition.

Akbar fought battles with Pratap of Mewar and Chandra Sen of Marwar (1541-1581), the two rajputs coming from two proud dynasties. Together, Pratap and Chandra Sen could have vanquished unstable Akbar - the way Sher Shah Suri defeated his father Humanyu in 1540! **This scenario has a bearing on present Gujarat**. The Hindu BJP leaders - like Keshav Patel, fighting against the BJP leader, Narendra Modi, are repeating the Rajput history. What matters not Modi winning this election, but how he crushes the opponents. His victory will have ripple effects in adjoining states, and then all the way up to Delhi.

From the research papers, it is evident that Pratap fought out only being a Kshatriya. It is no match for fighting for Islam; its math is simple. Kshatriyas, comprise only 10 % of the Hindus, whereas, the call, *Islam-in-Danger* arouses 100% of the Muslims! Galvanization of present Hindu society needs generations of new leaders and first-rate institutions.

The Hindutva (essentially means reverence for the Vedic heritage - including its epics, language and culture**) alone can bring a Hindu renaissance in India**. Moreover, it is under the Hindutva alone that India was and can be truly secular. The secularism, practiced during the last 60 years of independence, is reduced to anti-Hinduism.

It is amazing to observe how in a short period of 20 discontinuous years of Mughal rule under Babar and Humanyu, Akbar won over key Hindus leaders. His diplomacy, along with stick and carrot approach, was very effective. By encouraging matrimonial alliances with brave Rajputs only, he broke a Mughal tradition of not marrying into the Hindus.

Akbar's matrimonial policy was so successful that the Rajputs vied with each other in sending 'dolas' (means daughters and dowries) to fill the harems and coffers of the Mughal rulers. It became honorable. On the other hand, it encouraged the Rajput kings to have their own stables of queens and mistresses. Udai Singh had 18 queens and 24 children - Pratap being the eldest!

In contrast with the Mughals, the Rajputs miserably failed in maintaining peace in their forts. Pratap's three brothers fought against him in several battles including the historic battle of Haldighati! Isn't it a travesty of Hindu culture of that era that a Muslim won the loyalty of a Hindu - to an extent, that he would willingly kill a brother for his Muslim ruler? The British exploited this Hindu mindset to an extreme. They had the entire Hindu police and army fighting for them at home and abroad. In order to break this yoke of Hindu loyalty to the British, Gandhi had launched a non-cooperation movement in 1920.

For the first time, I realized some merits in fratricidal wars for a crown. Whether it is modern democracy or monarchy, the political power comes from the blade of a sword or barrel of a gun, as Mao-Tse Tung put it. The Hindu succession of the eldest has not brought out the best rulers. The ruler of a nation must embody skills in administration, warfare and public welfare - besides vision and leadership.

Udai Singh, becoming ruler due to Hindu succession tradition, was incompetent. He nominated ill-prepared Jabal Singh, the son of his favorite queen, Bhatiyani, to the throne. In retrospection, it was tragic that the nurse Panna Dhai lost her son to save Udai Singh when Ranbir Singh came after to kill baby Udai Singh! Rajputs would have been better off without Udai Singh, as Pratap observed it too, later on. However, the court nobles removed Jabal and installed Pratap on the throne the same day Udai Singh died.

This succession of the eldest is a derivative of the weakened Hindus avoiding any fights. Its corollaries are seen in Hindu families at the deaths of fathers. The eldest son going through a *PAGARI* ceremony symbolically signifies a transfer of authority in the family. On a personal note, I was in the US when my father died in India. My younger brother went through this ceremony instead. Its funny sidebar is that this ceremony took place at the death of my mother too!

It is scheming deception that India was not a nation before Akbar. The British perpetuated this myth too! Since the time immemorial, India is precisely defined by its ancient culture, Sanskrit language, the mother of all Indian languages, reverence for the Vedas, great epics of Ramayana and Mahabharata. Akbar's mission of political and cultural unification of India was only to establish a lasting Muslim empire.

Akbar made sure that the history of another Afghan - like Sher Shah Suri, was not repeated in his lifetime. Sher Shah Suri had finished the Mughal rule in India only a few years earlier, in 1540. Unfortunately, most Rajputs, in their myopic visions, submitted and surrendered to Akbar's camouflaged doctrine. Its sole opponent was Pratap. But he had no doctrine of running Akbar out of India and reclaiming the Hindu rule. It reminds me of 500+ Indian princes towing the British rule in early 20th century.

The locust like Muslim invasions and their sporadic rules during the previous 500 years had taken the fighting juices out of the non-fighting and ritualistic Hindus. They only fended amongst themselves. In every chronicle from the 11th to 20th century, the Muslims and, later on, the English branded the Hindus as ethnically inferior, not worthy of equal status. It is an irony that the Hindu subjects, out of their bizarre caste superiority, considered the Muslims and English as **Asurs and Maleeches** (lower beings)!

A hallmark of Pratap's leadership was to get the non-Rajput Bhils to fight for him. For Bhil bravery, he broke the caste barriers by letting the Rajputs marry with Bhil women. It is difficult to pass judgment whether it was Pratap's failure to win Rajput kings including his own brothers, kith and kins, like Ami Saha, or was it the greater political acumen of Akbar. Incidentally, Akbar was only two years younger than Pratap!

Pratap's military alliance with Hakim Khan Sur, an Afghan, materialized out of the cliché that the enemy of an enemy is a friend. Hakim Sur, in his heart of hearts, had a vision of regaining the lost Delhi throne, when the Afghan ruler Ibrahim Lodhi was defeated by Akbar's grandfather, Babar in 1526, in the first Battle of Panipat.

Historically, the caste system made Hindus very vulnerable. Tragically, it has not changed in the present. It was easy for any foreign invader - since Alexander to crack the codes of Hindu war strategies, particularly in collusion with the Brahmin astrologers, who seldom fought. It was the genius of Guru Gobind Singh (1666-1708) to harness the fighting powers of the Hindus by eliminating their castes amongst the Khalsas. Any caste Hindu, converted to Sikhism, was declared a sardar, provided that he returned victorious in a battle with the Muslims. That has made the Sikhs 100% fighters and builders of nations. It fully shines out in the Sikh character today.

The Haldighati Battle, the most famous battle in the annals of Hindus, was fought on the 18th June 1576, just for one half day. Only 500 combatants died on both sides. At the end, neither Pratap lost this battle, nor did Akbar win it, despite his superiority in soldiers and resources. Its importance lies in the fact that Akbar found it too expensive and difficult to engage in gorilla fights. Eventually, Pratap re-conquered all the lost territories except Chittor. His sudden death was probably caused by tetanus infection in his leg while carrying out the guerilla warfare from his jungle hideouts.

Glorification of defeat and not turning it around into a victory is a weird feature of Hindu life of the last millennium. One can trace it from historic battles - Porus lost to Alexander (326 BC), Sanga lost to Babar (1527), or the 1857 Mutiny. Alexander never fought the same enemy twice; Muslims had the same strategy.

Incidentally, the ***Chanakya Doctrine***, espoused 2500 years ago, advocated for the total annihilation of enemy.

Typically, one reads of defeatist Hindu mindset in sport pages; 'how hard they played, but lost' etc.! There is an inherent contradiction in losing and staying hard to win. Losing reflects lack of physical and mental toughness. Kashmir Kargil exposed the army. The Indian army, comprising nearly 80% Hindus, believes in fighting on their own soil. That is not the history of the Christians and Muslims. President Bush sent American forces, wherever, America's enemies allegedly operate. Al Qaeda fights for Islam over the globe.

Pratap did not leave a flame of Hindu legacy burning for his successors to go beyond. His son, Amar Singh resisted Akbar for a few years, but succumbed to his hegemony in 1615, twenty years after Pratap's death. There is no evidence that Pratap created any academic or political institutions for nationalism to sprout. Though Shivaji took the gorilla fighting with Aurangzeb to greater heights, but he too missed Hindu nationalism by a mile.

Maharana Pratap is a benchmark of Hindu nationalism, but not the highest! Modi, in Gujarat, has already achieved no less in this direction. However, it will take several Modis to create a leader for the entire India. Had the BJP dominated governments of Vajpayee moved for the scrapping of the Article 370 of the Constitution on special status of Kashmir, and joined the US in fight against Al Qaeda in Kashmir that would have set high standards of political actions. The BJP losing the 2004 parliamentary elections over such actions would have been historical than losing it on the hypes of Shining India.

(Dec 04, 2007 (India)/Oct, 2011)

NOTES AND COMMENTS

1. An article written with real passion. This article is a true reflection of your thoughts about Hinduism. Well written article. Enjoyed reading it. If you read history of all civilizations, then you will find parallels among them. All civilizations had rise and fall. Fall was a result of lack of vision, arrogance, lack of unity and recklessness (Unfortunately Bush is taking US on that route). Even mighty Mughals fell because of similar reasons. Guru Gobind Singh although took ***Panj Pyaras*** from all the four castes could not create a winning combination and never won any decisive battle against Muslims. Look now Sikh community is as divided on caste lines as ever. As for Modi, he is no Rana Pratap. If he could fight with Akbar for 20 years he had a strong support base. Those people were highly motivated. As for all Hindus supporting him there was no internet, TV, radio during that time. Even Modi

is not supported by majority of Hindus. Raising Modi to the same level as Rana Pratap is an insult to Rana. **Rahul** (MD)

I wrote: I am talking about his role in the 16th century Hindustan!

Rahul: I think you are totally off the mark on this issue. Since my school years, Rana Pratap, Shiva Ji, Rana Sanga, Prithviraj Chauhan, all were considered Hindu heroes. We all looked up towards them. There were movies made about them and songs written. Shiva Ji has a status of a demi god amongst the Mahrashtrians. What more arousal do you want?

I wrote: Pratap never aroused and appealed to Hindu nationalism!!

Rahul: You cannot compare the obstacles Rana Pratap had to that of Modi. Rana Pratap fought with all odds against him and Modi has all odds in his favor.

I wrote: When it comes to reviving Hindu nationalism. If he wins the third term despite global Islamic opposition and internal BJP strives, then he will make history. **Thanks.**

FRACTALS IN STONES

A brief description in a telephone directory was enough for me to visit yesterday archaeological sites in Champaner, 40 KM from Vadodara. There was no information about transportation and public conveniences. The only way to go and come back the same day is to rent a chauffeur driven car, and take your own food and drinks.

Recently, the place has gotten a special status by its inclusion in the list of UNESCO monuments of World Heritage. What it really means is that for small grants and publicity, the external forces, inimical to Indian national interest, can dictate their terms and conditions. The 2000-year old Buddhist monuments in Bayamon, Afghanistan had this UN status too, but the Taliban Government blew them away in March, 2001, since they looked at them as the vestige of a religion foreign to the present Islam.

Some monuments in Champaner have been dated back to an 8th century king, Vanraj Chowda. There are nearly 120 monuments listed for preservation, but besides a dozen, no one knows about the rest. There are no signs, maps, or brochures anywhere - including travel agencies. The local Archeological Society of India (ASI) office is least helpful, as dealing with the tourists, is not a part of their job. There is no museum, though excavation and shoddy preservation work provide jobs to local people.

My interest in ancient places is generally two fold. Number 1, I look at the monuments from a mathematical angle, and Number 2, for its historicity. The intricate carvings on every square inch of 20'-25' high stone pillars with 24" in diameter, are still breathtaking. In Jama Masjid, the largest of the monuments, the hall had nearly 150 stone pillars. Besides, the entrance, windowsills and niches have carvings of incredible precision and detail. Some of them are nothing short than man-made fractals in stones!

About its construction, one has to pause here, and think about geological knowledge, mining sites, ancient technology for the excavation of marble and durable stones, labor and transportation, engineering training in stone work, where one wrong chisel hit can waste a one-ton slab. The stone cutting instruments must be of high precision. Lifting and setting 1-2 ton beams to a height of 30'-50' is beyond present imagination. Either they had cranes comparable to the modern ones, or some methodology, that is lost to us.

Unquestionably, the ancients had knowledge of material mixing, and weight distribution of stone beams, as it has stood the test of 1000 years. Some kinds of 'schools and colleges' must have existed to train the young aspirants. It was a trailing period of the golden age of Hinduism. Inside the halls, the pillars formed several octagonal 'concavishly' layered ceilings - corresponding to the domes on the exterior of the roofs.

Apart from Jama Masjid, there were only three other noticeable smaller structures - Kewada Masjid, one un-named tomb, and one wrongly named **Kabutarkhana**. All the four are strategically located. From the stonework, they appear to have been built around the same time. Next time, I will carry a compass and tape for precise measurements of directions, angles and lengths. Mathematical facts are hidden in stones.

The monuments, described as 'masjids' - dating the middle of the 15th century, do not tell a correct story. If a dozen Mughal monuments in Agra region took nearly 100 years of prosperous Mughal rule, then 120 monuments in Chamapner must have been spread over a couple of centuries. It is a Hindu dynastic tradition of clustering monuments to celebrate royal and public events during each reign. Maundu and Khajuraho in Madhya Pradesh provide similar architectural clusters, or gardens of monuments in small areas!

From a variety of lotus designs on the trims, walls, and underneath the windows, it is clear that these structures were Hindu temples and annexes built in the 8th century. There is unmistaken evidence of emptied out niches where the idols of various Hindu deities must have stood. Immediately behind the niches, on the external walls, there are pouts for the fluids to come out after abulition (bathing) of the deities. The insides of mostly bare stone niches have lotus carvings at the top and right above the crowns of the idols removed.

The ground, plinth of the monument, and the first storey of the temples are kept original. In a few frontal places, the carvings of Hindu deities are scooped out. Nearby, there is a huge octagonal tank with two levels of steps on either side for ceremonial bathing. The two smaller monuments are erected near a huge natural lake nearby.

There is a clear distinction between the stonework of the Islamic minarets built after dismantling or modifying the tops of these Hindu temples. The minarets have different stones and have no carvings at all, and are obviously of recent periods of the 15th century. How do I take such conversions of grand Hindu temples into mosques - done all over India? From the Islamic perspective, I have no problem with it, if they demolished smaller temples or modified the grand ones into mosques. That is a part of historic Islamization. If you have something good, then publicize it and 'convert' the disbelievers.

My problem is that the Hindus have repeatedly failed to defend their temples. The situation of Hindu temples is no different from that of thousands of Hindu girls slaved after plundering India. They were sold in the square of Ghazani. Recently, it happened at the 1947-partition of India. The Hindus parents never accepted their daughters after they were rescued from Muslim homes. Most girls were forced to go into prostitution. These social problems are the offshoots of Hindu beliefs in imaginary pure and impure states of 'mind', and the curse of untouchability. Consequently, Hindu society remains totally divided and vulnerable to any external forces. **It is so easy to divide the divided!**

A pertinent question is: Do protection and preservation of Muslim and Christian monuments rub salt on the wounds of Hindu psyche? It is time to make a distinction between the 'foreign' monuments in India built before and after 1947. The ASI should be decentralized and attached to work with history departments of colleges, and urban and rural developments. **Everything old is not gold, or has an antique value**.

(Jan 11, 2009/India)

NOTES AND COMMENTS

AN HISTORIC IF 'N BUT

A certain question-cum-insight bolts out of the blue, when the mind and the locale are synchronized. In other contexts, it may be called the right chemistry or perfect alignment of the planets. This seems to have happened today, when I asked Ahmed Yagi, "Do you think that the world's greatest library in Alexandria would have been spared from its destruction in 641 AD, if Prophet Mohammed were alive?" He died in 632 AD - only nine years earlier.

Ahmed, a native of Sudan, microbiology PhD from Norway, taught in Saudi Arabia before moving to Oman two years ago – is an assistant dean at the University of Nizwa (UN). As I gave him a copy of my *Reflective* article, submitted for publication, he shared a horrific story of his library visit in a Saudi Arabian university. One thing leading to the other, and I said, the students, graduating from the UN, after 5-6 years, may not have even single textbook in their homes. The instructors issue the textbooks at the beginning of a semester and collect them back, at the end. They are not sold on or off campus. It does tell of some disregard towards the books, in general. Also, apart from 3-4 tiny stationery shops, I have not encountered even single bookstore, or a public library in Nizwa, the third largest city of Oman.

A couple of hours prior to our meeting, I was preparing for my class lecture. In the textbook, a passage read, ***"For nearly a thousand years, until its destruction by the Arabs in 641 AD, Alexandria stood at the cultural and commercial center of the Hellenistic world. After the fall of Alexandria, most of its scholars migrated to Constantinople. According to one estimate, the library's entire collection of nearly 700,000 rare manuscripts was burnt to ashes."*** The clarion call of that time was: if the library books contain what is already in the Quran, then these books are useless - burn them away. On the other hand, if they contain any thing contrary to the Quranic teachings, then they must be burnt away. Over the centuries, hundreds of libraries and scholars have met the Alexandrian fate.

In any course of history, the victorious rulers always try to transplant their culture, and further disconnect the vanquished from their past and heritage. The reason is simple; it becomes easier to govern the defeated. The Spaniards burnt away thousands of records belonging to the Mayan and Inca civilizations of South America. Though the British, in their colonies, did not make huge bonfires, but they effectively used the scholars, missionaries, professional organizations, and native opportunists to distort local histories and heritage. It happened in India, and continues in all ages and places - only methodologies change.

However, there are other considerations too. In a broader analysis, if a large population of a society becomes scholarly, philosophical, theoretical, and abstractionist, then the will to defend values and beliefs at every level, much less, the fire to fight, is eventually extinguished from the hearts. **Men, not willing to die for anything, are eventually overrun by foreign invaders**. They live for their short-term survival and gains. The collective obligations and responsibilities are lost. Tibet is a perfect example in recent times. That is why, in history, the barbarians have also ruled and established some of the great empires. In present times, the Taliban and Al Qaeda provide new settings.

I recalled to Ahmed the annihilation of the educated and professionals in China under MaoTse-Tung. Mao used the youth in the Chinese Red Army to round up the dissidents and elitists and sent them to re-education camps. In China, it was called the Cultural Revolution of the 1960s. But it was also a holocaust of Chinese intellect. Subsequently, the neighboring Cambodia butchered thousands of its educated citizenry.

Needless to say, the emphasis on Quranic studies balances the secular education, particularly, of sciences and mathematics. The growing number of madrassas (Islamic religious schools) in India and Pakistan, and the young men voluntarily coming from all over the world to study in Pakistani and Afghani madrassas, until recently, indicates their popularity, and meanings they provide in life.

The question being typical if-and-but type, historians thrive on researching these hypothetical questions. However, it has bearing on the present and thus in the shaping of a future. I am not an Islamic scholar, but it is worth knowing, if there was a sudden shift in policies soon after the Prophet's death. Certainly, the men, holding the reins of a new faith after the Prophet, were of lesser caliber. It is possible that there may have been a natural shift in the interpretation of his teaching and execution of the policies.

Locally, in Oman, one sees the power of the sword all over. The *Khanjars* (daggers) are prominently carried in waistbands and partly revealed. It is also Omani national emblem, seen all over as insignia. In the folk dances, I have seen men, standing in files, and dancing with *Khanjars*, swords, guns and pistols - symbolizing an ancient martial society and free nation that Oman has been throughout its history. Here, the pen is subservient to the sword. Incidentally, as a nation, Oman was one of the first regions to embrace Islam during the lifetime of the Prophet.

(March 30, 2009/Oman)

NOTES AND COMMENTS

RE-DISCOVERING CHIVALRY IN ARYA SAMAJ

The September issue of the ***Navrang Times***, a bilingual monthly publication from Detroit, Michigan, has two readable articles. One is on a very close connection between ***Shaheed*** (martyr) Bhagat Singh (1907-31) and the historic branch of Arya Samaj in Kolkata. The other lists great Arya Samajis who laid their lives either for the tenets of Hinduism, or for India's freedom.

It raises two important questions of historic significance. Number One: How did Bhagat Singh, an ardent Sikh, get involved with Arya Samaj, a 19th century reformist movement of Hinduism? Number Two: What and where lies the magic of Arya Samaj which transformed a great number of Hindus into eminent scholars, orators, public servants, and fierce freedom fighters in a short span of its founding in 1875? They are important questions for the new generations of Hindus to be aware of, so that the mission of Arya Samaj is rightly served in the 21st century.

These questions first stirred my mind six years ago, while researching in the Gadar Memorial Center, San Francisco. The Gadar Movement was a brainchild of a few Indian revolutionaries in the US including an activist intellectual, Lala Hardayal Mathur (1884-1939), who, in his youth, was influenced by Arya Samaj. The Gadar Movement was headquartered in San Francisco, with a sole mission of armed liberation of India.

In 1930s, a British CID (Central Investigation Department) report clearly established that nearly 100% of the Hindu freedom fighters were influenced by Arya Samaj. The British Government was puzzled, as to how the Arya Samaj teachings were instilling courage and unity amongst the Hindus, known for centuries as the most divided and timid people in India. They recognized Sikhs as a martial race, so the Sikh militancy never surprised them. In fact, the Sikhs wanted to regain the Sikh Empire, stretching beyond present Pakistan, that the British had illegally and forcefully annexed ten years after the death of Maharaja Ranjit Singh in 1839. A lesson of history is that the masses, at large, are quickly transformed by voluntary adoption of a new religion, ideology, or an inspiring leadership.

For finding answers to these questions, I went back to the basics. While teaching a mathematical topic, I often tell my students, 'that whenever you have absolutely no ideas about solving a problem, then go to the definitions involved in that problem'. On my part, I studied the **Ten Principles of Arya Samaj** (Just Google/ Yahoo Arya Samaj) carefully and early crusades of its founder, Swami Dayanand Saraswati (1824-1883). At times, I felt like writing a ***Reflection*** on each principle both from their historical context and present relevance.

The first five principles of Arya Samaj are focused upon the **individual development**, but the last five are on the **community development**. That is a fundamental departure from the self-centric traditional practice of Hinduism. Arya Samaj temples are designated places for Sunday morning prayers. There are regular dues for the members, like in a club. The funds are used for community welfare. The genius of Swami Dayanand understood that the Muslims worshipped together every Friday, and Sikhs and Christians on Sundays. **Collective prayers bring unity at the deepest levels**. No research is known to have been undertaken into any organized aspect of Hindu religion before 1000 AD, but certainly, it had been completely absent till the advent of Swami Dayanand. That explains why the Hindus of Arya Samaj leanings became courageous and patriotic. **Chivalry attracts chivalrous people**.

Giving a personal touch to this scenario, Lahore, now in Pakistan, was one of the strongholds of freedom fighters in North India, as Kolkuta was in the East. My father-in-law (1912-1990) grew up in the narrow alleys of Guru Dutt or Bhatti *mohallah* (neighborhood), one of Lahore's many *mohallahs* perfect for organizing, conspiring and hiding, when chased by the police. Once, I probed him, as to how come he did not join a gang of rebels that he personally knew since his boyhood. He could not answer. But I knew in his heart of heart, he had missed an historic moment in his life. It was partly because, he never came into contact with Lahore Arya Samaj. That association would have unlocked his individual courage into greater collective courage and national pride. I told my wife that she missed being known as the daughter of a freedom fighter!

Though, the Hindu community was relatively poor and most divided of all other communities, yet even the modest buildings of Arya Samaj - temples, schools and colleges - played crucial roles in supporting the freedom fighters in all respects, besides providing the nationalistic education. **With India's independence as their only purpose in life, the freedom fighters had neither caste nor religion**. That is how and why Bhagat Singh was twice secretly sheltered and supported by Arya Samaj in Kolkata – once before and once after the assassination of the British officer, Sanders, in 1928. Incidentally, the most popular picture of clean-shaven Bhagat Singh wearing an English felt hat was taken during his brief stay in Kolkata.

With emphasis on the formlessness of The Supreme, there are no idols for worship in Arya Samaj temples. However, the Sunday prayer gatherings in the temples are usually followed by broad updates on community affairs. It keeps the community into the mainstream of life and helps in the development of histrionic and leadership skills. Again, Swami Dayanand seems to have borrowed this practice from the Christians, Muslims, and the Sikhs. Historically, Arya Samaj is characterized by public debates in the backdrop of the Vedas (*Shastrartha*) for settling and sorting out any differences - religious, political, or social.

The unity of minds comes only when people assemble at one place on a regular basis. It never takes place by only wishing for it, or working alone. However, willingness to sacrifice a bit of personal interest for the larger welfare of the community, sits at the heart of Hindu unity today. It is clearly enshrined in one of the ten principles of Arya Samaj.

(Sep 24, 2009)

NOTES AND COMMENTS

1. Good to be reminded. When I was in primary school I remember going on Sunday mornings to the DAV high school where havans were performed and all the mantras were recited. **Hemendra**

2. Namaste Satish, Thank you very much. Bhai Parmanand, a colleague of Bhagat Singh and another Sikh, started Arya Samaj in Guyana around 1910. I prepared a History of Arya Samaj in Guyana, My father did all the research and I prepared it on my computer. It will be printed shortly in Canada. Kind Regards, **Vijay**

3. Bhatnagar Sahib: You have a good exposition of the second question. Regarding the first question: what is the evidence that Bhagat Singh was close to Arya Samaj, and what is the explanation? By the way the more I learn about real Sikh teachings, the more I feel Arya Samaj is closer to Sikhism than to the ritual laden "Hinduism" both past and present. **Ved P. Sharma**

4. Hi Satish: Greetings! Yes, this 'reflection' is both informative and enlightening laced with historical connections. A good piece for everybody. **Moorty**

COMMENTATORS AND ANALYSTS EXTRAORDINAIRE

Ten years ago, I started writing Reflections, a reincarnation of my lifelong passion of writing letters. The big difference was that that my writings went public – from one to many. I started sharing them with friends and relatives, and from there it went to their friends and relatives. Four years ago, a student of mine created a blog, but, I seldom posted anything. I don't have a website either. It is all emails in a bcc mode.

I have several mailing lists and I am used to this inefficient mode of communication. I have Facebook and Twitter accounts too, but they too have remained unused. That is my approach to communication. Naturally, some readers write back and give comments, and at time, a small dialog takes place. It has added clarity in my thoughts.

Not all the comments and commentators have been included – only those which are concise and strong. In reflective style of writings, inclusion of some comments adds a new flavor. Initially, I never saved any comments; sometimes, no comments were received. That is why the space following NOTES AND COMMENTS is blank in many cases.

It is not merely a time to thank them, but also share a piece of immortality that this book may bring! When I look at the credentials of these persons I am myself awed and wowed. There comments come out of their incredible rich backgrounds. I don't think this list can be easily matched. Here are the names in the alphabetical order:

Raju **Abraham**: Known for five years. English professor –has taught in Baroda/ India, Sana/Yemen, and presently in Oman with University of Nizwa, where I was a visiting professor for a semester, Spring 2009.

Matt Azikhaketh: Physicist by training and became expert in nuclear reactor technology in Nevada Test site. After retirement, he studied Greek for the Bible studies. He and his late wife Connie were our first family friends when we moved to Las Vegas in Aug 1974.

Avnish Bhatnagar: My son, age 43, works at Google. His comments are few, but deep.

Rahul Bhatnagar: Distantly related - physician by training in India. He has an interesting job of medical director of drug safety with a pharmaceutical company. Very astute commentator and analyst of nearly all my Reflections - and can refine an issue to a state undistinguishable from the one started with.

Ravi Bhatnagar: My first cousin, served in Indian Army as a physician - retired as Colonel.

H S **Bhola**: Emeritus IU professor of education - known since 1971 – remains witty and sharp at 80. He often tells me, how exceptional I am, as all math professors that he has known, can hardly write a sentence in English - far from being a literary writer. He continues to write papers and give invited talks.

Ved Bhushan: An 80-year old businessman in Ambala Cantt, India– known since 1980. He still enjoys the pleasures of skin.

Cyriac Chemplavil: Well known lung specialist of Las Vegas, acquainted since 1982.

Ram Chaudhary: Emeritus professor of physics of NYU dedicated to spreading Hindi in the US and Sciences in India – remains active at 85.

Gopal Dass: Retired cardiologist, settled in Las Vegas- has interesting hobbies – known for five years.

Irma **Dutchie**: Our 81- year old neighbor, who lives life with and zing and zest – extremely generous. She is now a friend of our extended family.

Mahesh Gautam: Researcher in Desert Research Institute in Las Vegas. Native of Nepal and has also studied/worked in India, Thailand.

Robert P. Gilbert: My Math PhD thesis supervisor at IU – now Unidel Chair Professor at University of Delaware, retiring in Jan, 2012, at age 80. Many hobbies – including reading histories, keep him fit and sharp.

S. C. **Gupta**: is a businessman and Arya Samaj leader in Mumbai, India – known for five years.

Aarti Jain: Director producer of documentaries on the life of Indians settled in the US. Met her in San Francisco in 2003.

Vijay Kapur: First generation immigrants from India, educator and scion of a Kapur family of rare industrialists of pre-independence India – known for five years

Mohan Khare: known since 1982, owns an environment related company in Maryland.

Alok Kumar: Physics professor in NY , PhD IIT, Kanpur - Known for 25 years.

Ranjana Kumar: Director of an Adult Day Care Center in Charlotte, NC –known since 1977.

Satyam **Moorty**: Emeritus English professor, Southern Utah University – known since 1978.

Sham Narula: An octogenarian retired engineer – active in senior activities in Washington DC area.

Anjali Nigam: My daughter's daughter who has been reading, commenting, editing and proofing most of my Reflections ever since. Currently, she is doing a master's in occupational therapy from Washington University, St. Louis.

R S **Nigam**: Retired Professor of Commerce and Director of Delhi School of Economics – known for 25 years.

TV Rao: A coal-mining geologist and small business entrepreneur – known for 25 years.

Rene Riendero: Life explorer and realtor. Wrote a book on her experiences of visiting India. It inspired her to become a writer.

Gurdev Singh: 70+ year old Gandhian and a long-time associate of Subbarao – retired professor of Punjabi.

Harpreet Singh: A rare combination of computer science, finance, active spirituality, and creative writing – always exploring and stretching his limits. He is 36 years old and known for 13 years through his parents first.

Inder Singh: Age 74, a pioneer amongst the first generation of Indians in the US, community leader and social activist in several organizations. Currently, president of GOPIO (Global Organization of Persons of India Origin). Lives in LA and known for 15 years.

Rajinder Singal: Retired chemist – a family friend for over 25 years.

Subhash Sood: Physician by training in India, UK and USA. He never practiced for profit, though studied other systems of medicine too - eccentric to a certain degree. However, he was deeply drawn into by Scientology – established the first center in India and translated several scientology books from English into Hindi. He died in 2007 at age 74 - in a 100- year old, now dilapidated, mansion in which he was born, as the only son of a physician, in Ambala Cant. He was my most avid reader and friend for over 25 years.

E. **Sooriamurthy**: Retired physics professor Madurai University, India – known since 1968 – our common days at IU. His son, Raja, computer science professor at Carnegie Mellon is an avid reader of my Reflections too.

Surjeet Verma: Age 72, Retired CPA - settled in Minneapolis – though known for two years, but we frequently chat on the phone.

S R **Wadhwa**: Retired Income Tax Commissioner of India and author of books on Indian taxation. Known for 30 years - age 75.